# Targeting the Powerful: International Prospect Research

# Targeting the Powerful: International Prospect Research

## by Vanessa Hack

FITZROY DEARBORN PUBLISHERS
CHICAGO • LONDON

Published in the UK 1997 by
Aslib, The Association for Information Management

ISBN 1-57958-272-9 Fitzroy Dearborn

Published in the USA 2000 by
Fitzroy Dearborn Publishers
919 North Michigan Avenue
Chicago, Illinois 60611

A Cataloguing-in-Publications record is available from the Library of Congress.

# Acknowledgement

The author would like to thank friends and colleagues at Oxford University Development Office for their support and advice. In particular, fellow researchers: Pat Flavin (for advice on US sources), Samantha Tilling (for help with Australia), Chris Jeffrey, Judith Diggory, Frankie Airey, Conor Cradden, Amy O'Brien and Hana Lester. Also my husband, Karl Hack, for his patience and assistance.

# Contents

# 1. What is Prospect Research?

At its best prospect research is a method of one-to-one marketing. It demands high input, justified by the hope of a high return. The first stage involves in-depth investigation, whether into a person, company, charitable foundation, or other body (the 'prospect'). The second is the analysis of this material in order to recommend a line of approach most likely to succeed. It means you never go into a meeting unsure who the prospect is. Rather than simply listing what you want, you can address the needs and preferences of the prospect and show how you can meet them.

Whether you are fund-raising or making business deals, the better prepared you are the less time you waste in unsuccessful approaches. Prospect research gives you an edge over your competitors: through understanding the prospects' motivations you can draw up proposals which meet their requirements and your own. In an ever more competitive world, where even fund-raising is a professional business, you cannot afford to overlook any potential advantage, especially if the competition is already employing it.

## Prospect research focuses on one individual at a time

As prospect research has evolved out of the fund-raising world it is sometimes confused with other methods employed by charities. It is important to understand that prospect research is neither market research nor mass research. It is a new and quite distinct technique.

Market research involves asking how the market as a whole will respond to an approach. It views individuals as part of a wider pattern. Mass research techniques involve acquiring an information source (such as a database of lifestyle characteristics) and cross-referencing it wholesale with your own database of prospects. Again, the individual is lost in the mass. Both produce useful results, but neither is prospect research.

Prospect research involves looking very closely at one prospect as an individual. It is used with prospects who are so important that they merit more than a standard letter or an unplanned approach. For most prospects it would be too costly to be worthwhile, but for the top tier the personal touch is invaluable.

For many this is a new concept. However, it is becoming increasingly clear that having a powerful case and being skilled at presenting it is not sufficient. There are plenty of other organisations with good arguments, so why choose yours?

1

Organisations are increasingly aware of the need to market themselves to particular audiences, for example, by segmenting their database so that young people receive a different letter from the elderly, supporters from non-supporters, etc. This has been proven to produce better results than sending the same standard letter to everyone.

Prospect research takes this process one step further. For those few whose response can make a huge difference it is worth preparing an individually-tailored approach. That personal touch could be the difference between success and failure. What is more, as it is more widely employed, the prospects are coming to expect it.

## Prospect research is a skilled job

In some organisations prospect research is an undemanding task. Researchers do no more than present raw data, perhaps in the form of a database print-out with appended photocopies from directories and newspapers. There is a vicious circle of low expectations, poor resources, inadequate training and poor results. Everyone loses in this situation as research can perform a much more valuable role and provide a great deal of job satisfaction. Like many new professions it is held back by the limited supply of well-trained and experienced personnel and poor understanding of its capabilities.

A good research team should be capable of the following:

Firstly, and most obviously, they should be experts at finding information. They should have not only a thorough understanding of a wide range of sources, but also the initiative to find new ones as the need arises.

Secondly, they can present the information in an easily digestible form. They can read through the pile of photocopies, extract relevant information, and present it as a report. This saves requesters from ploughing through mounds of irrelevant and repetitious information, possibly missing what they set out to find. A well-structured report should enable them to go straight to the key points.

Thirdly, they can match the information to the needs of requesters. What do they want to know? And, equally important to people working under pressure, what do they not want to know? If requesters must meet numerous people at a party they are unlikely to have the time to read detailed reports on each. Absorbing so much information would be difficult. They might well prefer a summary of key points that can be memorised quickly just beforehand. This is a different proposition from preparing a well-planned approach to an important prospect, which requires in-depth knowledge.

Finally, the researcher can analyse the facts and suggest a way forward. The researcher should by then have a sound knowledge of the prospect and be able to provide well reasoned arguments. Whether or not the requester agrees with the researcher's recommendations they will at least help a decision to be reached. It is also a good discipline for the researcher, who might otherwise be tempted to view the collection of information as an end in itself. If the researcher always has in mind the goal of selling his organisation, it should be easier to select and present the information in the most useful manner.

The product is a detailed report which explains who or what the 'prospect' is, how much money or influence is available, and what the prospect's interests and attitudes are. On the basis of these facts the researcher can suggest the best ways of approaching the prospect: who can supply an introduction, what subjects might be discussed to break the ice, which topics are best avoided, what motivates the prospect, etc., and, most important, which aspects of your organisation's needs would most appeal to the prospect. The more information that is known about the prospect the more successful any dealings are likely to be. Later chapters will show how to compile reports and provide an indication of how they might look.

## Why is prospect research so valuable?

Firstly, prospect research narrows down the field. Building up a personal relationship is a time-consuming task, and it makes sense to ensure that you target your efforts on those prospects where the chance of success is greatest. Perhaps a prospect does not have as much ready cash as you thought, or perhaps firm commitments already exist to someone else. If this is the case then it is better to find out before you spend a great deal of time and money cultivating this prospect.

Fund-raisers and salesmen both know that the mere sight of a letterhead can result in an instant 'no'. So how do you ever get the opportunity to present your case? Ideally you should find someone to introduce you. Wealthy or influential people are usually well guarded by secretaries who ensure that the boss does not receive unnecessary distractions. It is therefore important that the introduction is made by someone who knows your prospect well enough to guarantee that the prospect will listen or read a letter. It is also important that the prospect respects the introducer sufficiently not only to listen but also to agree to the introduction. In some (rare) cases prospects will admire your advocate so much that they will be ready to say yes even before you have told them what you want. Prospect research can help identify such people.

So how do you persuade the advocate to introduce you? The advocate's own standing with the prospect can be damaged if someone inappropriate is recommended. Equally, if an introduction results in a successful deal the advocate's kudos will increase. This is where the public relations aspect of prospect research can come in useful. Good research shows that you are committed and highly professional in your approach. You can use it to demonstrate that the prospect would be likely to find your programme interesting. You might even wish to give the advocate a copy of the research report (having first removed any sensitive areas). Most people have little idea just how much information is available in the public domain, so it is likely to impress.

Research can also ensure that your approach is targeted as precisely as possible. It is counter-productive to use every single argument: why should a prospect read a five-page letter or maintain concentration through a fifteen-minute monologue? Instead, you should work out beforehand which arguments will hit home and which aspects of your programme are likely to appeal most to this particular prospect. Even if you have only one goal in mind, a little thought will probably reveal various facets, each with their own individual appeal. Then you can approach the prospect with a clear message and a simple goal, or a limited number of alternatives. You might still receive a 'no', but your chances of success will be higher than if you went in blind.

Another consideration is that prospects are coming to expect a more personal touch. As prospect research becomes more widespread and organisations realise that they can gain an advantage by building up a personal relationship, anyone who does not use these techniques looks increasingly unprofessional. Prospects are not necessarily aware how much work has gone into marketing a proposal specifically to them; they may simply think it is better than the competition.

Finally, it is important to know that your 'ask' is pitched at the right level. If you want money you must ask for no more and no less than can be afforded. If you want the prospect's influence, again it must be no more and no less than can be managed. If you are asking for more than has been done for other organisations you must be ready to show that you know you are asking a lot and have a series of strong reasons to support your case. It is very tempting to pitch your ask on the low side as this seems easier and more likely to be successful. In fact, so long as you are prepared for a moment's shock, a high ask might be a better tactic. Prospects rarely negotiate upwards, but moving downwards is less of a problem so long as you do not frighten them off altogether with something totally impossible.

Prospect research is thus an immensely useful tool for directing approaches which involve a substantial commitment of time or resources. If you cannot afford to get it wrong then it makes sense to stand back and study the situation rather than rushing straight in.

## Who might use prospect research?

The techniques of prospect research can be applied to any situation where a key player is involved. Whether you are engaged in a business deal, political lobbying or fund-raising, knowing more about the other participants can only improve your chances of success.

This technique has already been used with great success in fund-raising. The wealthiest prospects are given individual attention as their potential for giving is so large. It has been said that 80% of the money raised comes from 20% of the donors, or more recently even 90% from 10%. A standard letter would be inappropriate when there is so much at stake. In these cases it is only after a research report has been prepared and the approach carefully worked out that anyone actually meets the prospect. A single mistake could totally wreck the whole solicitation as it is so much more tempting to say 'no' than to listen to a sales pitch.

Just as a banker would not invest in a company without researching it first, anyone who is willing to invest a great deal of time and effort in a relationship which might be very profitable or totally unsuccessful would be well advised to know as much as possible beforehand. Whether you want a donation, a sales agreement, a competitive advantage, political influence, or simply information, the techniques of prospect research can be of use.

### Further applications of prospect research techniques

- You wish to lobby politicians over family issues. Do they have families? Are they divorced? What public statements have they made on this subject?
- A potential client has agreed to a meeting. He or she will not be very impressed if you know little about their business interests. What companies does the client own and what do they do?
- You are organising a conference and must invite appropriate speakers. Who are the potential candidates, what are their backgrounds, and what are their opinions likely to be?

- In the first few weeks of your new job you must represent your company at a trade fair. You need briefings about the key companies and the people you are likely to encounter.

- Your daughter's school would like to acquire new computer facilities. Are there any foundations which might provide funding?

- You are arranging a dinner for a group of important people. Some of them are known for their strong views. How should you arrange the seating plan so that they enjoy the company of their neighbours rather than being offended by them?

- You are trying to sell your product to a large multinational. Does that company have other interests in the area? If so are they an important part of the business or are they performing poorly and in danger of being sold off?

- You are writing a profile of a well known tycoon for a newspaper. How do you get further than press releases from the public relations adviser?

- You have acquired a new supplier and would like to ensure that you are on good terms in case you ever need to extend your credit or place an urgent order. You are to meet the Chief Executive at a social gathering. What sort of person can you expect and how do you establish a rapport? Should you discuss opera, your grandchildren, or the state of the economy?

Prospect research can thus make a valuable contribution in many fields. It is the personal touch provided by careful preparation that wins results. It therefore makes sense to take research seriously.

# 2. Setting up a Prospect Research Department

Prospect research departments come in all shapes and sizes, and their potential is often poorly understood. The worst scenario is where the manager considers that the job involves little more than checking *Who's Who* and scanning the press. It is therefore decided that anyone who seems to have a little spare time can take on this extra responsibility. The researcher might also end up doing a great deal of photocopying and data entry, leaving little time to do more than struggle at the margins of this new role. As the researcher has no training and would not know what training or tools to ask for there is limited scope for impact.

As is often the case, the more you put in the more you get out. The more training, resources and manpower you have the more effective the department should be. If one-to-one relationships are important to you then prospect research can be genuinely useful, and its expense should be set against the likelihood of high returns.

This chapter describes the optimum requirements for a prospect research department operating in a large organisation. Those researchers who work alone and with few resources should not be intimidated by the scale described here. Gaining an overview of what is possible should enable them to pick out those books or methods which best suit their needs.

The key requirements are as follows: researchers, clerical assistance, and facilities such as information resources, computer equipment and office space. The cost implications must also be considered.

## 1. Researchers

At its best, prospect research requires a high degree of skill and experience in widely varying fields. Ideally you should recruit someone who already understands the work involved, but this can be difficult. The demand for prospect researchers is expanding rapidly as fund-raising becomes more competitive. The supply is not very great as it is a relatively new career and there are few specifically designed training courses. Fortunately there are other types of experience which can be very useful. The skills and attributes which would be useful when recruiting a prospect researcher are as follows:

- *Experience of online databases*. (i.e. databases full of company information, newspapers, etc., e.g. *Dialog*/Knight-Ridder, *FT-Profile*, *Textline*). It is possible to acquire this skill on the job, but preferable to employ someone who already has it.

There are two elements to being skilled in the use of these databases. The first is dealing with something akin to a computer programming language. This is rapidly becoming less important as databases grow more user-friendly. Old-style hosts each have their own language and rules, and moving between them can be very confusing. To attract more customers they are now introducing menu systems and help facilities which mean you no longer have to remember the commands unprompted. Even so, a well-trained researcher would still be better able to cope with the more complicated manoeuvres, such as displaying information in tabular format. She would also be more likely to search effectively, for example, she should not make a search so restrictive that it produced no results, nor so broad that it swamped her with information.

The second element is knowing where to look. Some hosts contain literally hundreds of different databases, and a large research department is likely to have access to more than one host. This means the researcher needs a knowledge of the contents and relative merits of the various databases rather than always going straight to the one he knows best. Similar databases will have different coverage and different costs. It is pointless paying a great deal for a lot of unnecessary information when a cheaper database would have provided the few facts needed. This is particularly important with company information, though press databases also vary in the number and type of articles they take and whether they reproduce them in full text. Simply going into the wrong company database can be disastrous as some are shockingly expensive, but stopping to think itself costs money as online time ticks away. However, you can often minimise the risks of going into expensive databases by setting up your system so that it only has access to cheaper databases or so that it tells you in advance how much each search will cost. The host will advise on whether and how this can be done.

Online providers offer training courses which are often relatively cheap or even free, though travel and possibly accommodation should be added to the cost. However, the cost in time lost can be substantial, and it can take a year or more to become fully proficient.

Job candidates will often attempt to meet this criterion by saying they have searched online library catalogues. The type of database which contains one type of information and prompts for one word searches is nowhere near as complex as some of the commercial online hosts. Try to work out whether what they have used requires so little skill and background knowledge that anyone could do it with minimal instructions; this would not give them any advantage over a candidate who had not used databases at all. If a candidate has no experience then it would be useful to see an aptitude for online searching shown by, for example, a background in information, computers or logic.

- *Computer programming.* If you have a reasonably sophisticated in-house database it is helpful for the prospect researcher to be able to interrogate it. Maintaining a database can be an all-consuming task, best carried out by someone other than the researcher; however researchers might not know what sort of information is available if they do not understand it too. This means the ability to manipulate the data rather than simply using standard enquiry screens. A query such as finding all the employees of IBM, all the contacts in France, all contacts who work in the law, or finding someone under her maiden name when she is indexed only by married name, might usefully be carried out by a researcher.

- *Foreign languages.* The choice or necessity of these must be determined by the type of prospects that must be researched. Fortunately many international reference books are written in English, and online database providers often translate newspaper articles into English. Many sources are in a standard format so that you need only acquire a limited vocabulary with the aid of a dictionary (e.g. born, married, profit, number of employees). Even someone who has the wrong languages is often better able to look up and make sense of foreign words than a person who speaks only his mother-tongue, especially as languages often share common roots. The most useful languages depend on your own particular requirements, but suggestions would be German, Spanish, French and Japanese. The speakers of these languages have both a great deal of economic power and a relatively low likelihood of using English in their publications. The Chinese are economically dominant in many Far Eastern countries, but be sure you know which of the many dialects you are likely to encounter.

- *Ability to assimilate large quantities of information and draw out the key points*: You might wish to test this by asking each candidate to produce a précis of a long and rambling piece of prose within a time limit.

- *Meticulous attention to detail*: Some people find this type of work very boring which inevitably leads to mistakes. One indication that a person can cope with this type of task is tolerance of a repetitive duty such as filing. (This does not mean that a filing clerk is the best person for the job!) Another is asking them to reproduce something unexciting such as the office telephone list. They would have to be warned that the key factor was precision rather than speed and that it was not a test of typing speed. It is surprising how often people make endless mistakes even when they know they are supposed to be ensuring 100% accuracy.

- *Initiative*: Although it is possible to produce basic check-lists, one source leads to another in an unpredictable way. A good researcher has to be able to spot the clue and be willing to pursue any lead rather than merely doing what they are told.

- *Keyboard skills*: Touch typing is the ideal. A research report is not the sort of document that can be dictated or written out longhand for a secretary. It inevitably goes through various drafts as new sources are suggested and information is added.

- *Ability to write clear, concise, grammatical prose*: Researchers should be capable not only of finding the information but also of presenting it in the form of a report. The volume of information which can be obtained is often too vast and too repetitive to pass on in raw form. It needs to be sifted for the little nuggets of extra information which might otherwise be missed and which suggest new avenues of enquiry. The result must be written up in a comprehensible, concise and well-organised form. In some institutions it will be essential that spelling, grammar and lay-out are of a very high standard, for example if reports are intended to impress key outside contacts. The organisation's own senior management might be intolerant of errors. Errors in spelling or grammar tend to reduce the reader's faith in the accuracy of the facts and analysis. Again, if you ask the candidates to do a written test you could either insist that they pay particular attention to spelling and grammar within a précis or provide them with a separate piece of prose to correct.

- *Knowledge of the business environment*: Elements of accountancy, business studies, law, etc. are useful. Researchers must know their way round a company's annual report, understand how shares work, be able to interpret balance sheets and the notes to them, and possibly understand the difference between companies in different countries. Again there are courses on the basics of accounts, though they are often quite expensive. A trip to a good bookshop should produce a paperback dictionary of financial terms or explanation of the workings of the stock market. As accounts tend to follow a similar format an intelligent person should be capable of working out the basics.

- *Knowledge of your own organisation*: Researchers will need some understanding of your programme if they are to help in marketing it to prospects. Whether or not this can be acquired on the job depends on the complexity of the programme.

- *Tact and diplomacy*: Some types of information can only be obtained by asking. Some contacts might be important prospects in their own right. It is therefore vital that the researcher follows the corporate line and does not alienate these people. Even better, they might be able to leave the contacts feeling pleased they could be useful and confident in the competence of the people they are dealing with.

Although the ideal is a candidate who satisfies all of the above, in reality you will probably find it difficult to find someone who meets all these criteria. Candidates with a background in librarianship or information often display many of these skills and attributes, though do not be so impressed by their experience that you let it outweigh their writing and analytical abilities. An intelligent person can acquire the relevant experience and knowledge, but a poor style of writing or thinking is harder to amend. You might also receive applicants from the research departments of organisations such as merchant banks. Since they come from a large department they are likely to be very specialised in one particular area, for example, they might have experience of online databases but not of analysing the output and producing reports. They are also likely to be much more used to finding information on companies or industries rather than people.

If you work in a small organisation and the choice of candidates is limited then at the least look for someone who has a good general standard of education and a willingness to learn. They must have the necessary intelligence and initiative to work independently, solve unexpected problems, and pick up any skills they lack. It might or might not be important to you that they should write well. You should also make a realistic decision, particularly in a small office, about the amount of routine work that will be involved (filing, checking directories, etc.), and judge whether the candidate is capable of tolerating this without being driven mad by it.

# 2. Clerical assistance

As well as the researchers themselves there should be clerical support. There are many routine jobs which should be carried out by the research department but which are not cost-effective for skilled researchers to perform (not to mention being demotivating). The sort of person who is content to spend a large proportion of their day doing this type of work is less likely to show the initiative to perform the more skilled aspects well. Asking a skilled researcher to do them is likely to result in that person becoming bored and looking for a more rewarding job elsewhere.

A rough guide is one clerical assistant to three researchers, though it does depend on the degree of emphasis on press cuttings and filing. It is assumed that the researchers will be able to type up their own reports, but clerical help will be needed for tasks such as the following:

- *Dealing with routine photocopying and filing* (largely stemming from press scanning).
- *Checking long lists*, e.g. checking names of directors, partners, trustees, etc., against a database for contacts.
- *Compiling indexes and lists* so that information can be found again. The researchers might scan a society magazine, mark the interesting names, and ask the clerical assistant to produce an index. This is easily done by listing the names and source in a word-processing document. The word-processor should be capable of scanning the document for a particular word. Accuracy is vital for this task, otherwise it is impossible to find the name again.
- *Doing the ground-work for reports*. It should be possible to compile a basic check-list of books and other sources for each type of report, with a space on the end for any other ideas. The clerical assistant should not be expected to start writing the report, but can create a file of useful information ready for the researchers. Provided they can be relied upon to be thorough, clerical assistants are likely to view this task as a welcome opportunity to use their initiative. It gives a sense of responsibility and achievement in what is otherwise a fairly routine job.

The above is totally distinct from the task of maintaining a database which is used for mass mailings. Dealing with a constant flow of donations, changes of address, etc., is a much larger task than the one described here.

# 3. Facilities

• *A library* of some sort is essential. The size and range depends on which countries you intend to target and the accessibility of the books in public libraries. Ideally you should have your own books as it can be very time-consuming trekking backwards and forwards to the library and most frustrating if you cannot immediately check possibilities which are thrown up by your research. There can be many inconveniences to working in libraries, such as having to leave the building to find a cup of coffee or having to order photocopies rather than make them yourself. It is also possible that you might go all the way to the library only to find that someone else is using your book. Another problem is that the library is unlikely to have the complete range of who's whos, business directories and foundation guides for every country you require, and those there are will be kept in different parts of the building. It also means substantial time out of the office, which might cause problems if you are needed to answer queries or help others use the sources.

Ideally, you should try to obtain at least a *Who's Who* (and, if you are a fund-raiser, a foundation directory) for each country you are looking at. If you are covering many countries then business information might be better obtained by dipping into different online databases as and when required; however if you intend to focus very heavily on one country, such as your own, then a book or CD-ROM may be cheaper. See the next chapter for elaboration on whether to buy books, online or CD-ROM information.

• *Computer equipment.* Each person will need a reliable, modern computer complete with a good word-processing package. If you wish to use electronic information (and it is difficult to manage without it) each researcher will need a modem and/or CD-ROM reader. Again, the next chapter will help you decide on the value of online and CD-ROM sources. You will also require a printer, preferably a quiet, efficient one such as a laser printer, as there will be a lot of work for it. Access to standard office equipment such as a photocopier and fax is also necessary. You might wish to obtain a document scanner, though this is optional.

• *Space.* Research departments need to obtain and store large quantities of information. Major items are files of press cuttings and company financial statements, as well as the library of books. Information is likely to require as much, if not more, space than the people. It might also be necessary to provide a spare desk in case other members of staff wish to consult the information. If no provision is made for them to use the information within the research area they will take it back to their own desks which makes it much more likely that some of it will never return. It also makes it harder to maintain confidentiality if the information is being carried all over the building (and possibly to staff members' homes).

# 4. Cost

This will vary according to the size of department, the type and quantity of information required, and the ability of the organisation to pay.

*Staff*

• *The number* of staff depends on what they will be required to do. In a modern fund-raising office a reasonable ratio is one researcher to three solicitation staff (i.e. the people who actually make the approaches to prospects), and one clerical assistant to three researchers. Each full report might take one researcher two or three days to complete (bearing in mind that they will also be undertaking other duties such as press scanning and that not all reports need to be totally comprehensive).

• *The pay-scale* for clerical staff will be relatively easy to determine from the pay for similar jobs in the locality. Researchers' salaries are harder to set as this is a relatively new and small profession. Factors to consider are that these are likely to be graduates who are operating in a national (and occasionally international) market. The employers who are competing for qualified information staff are often city institutions such as merchant banks, so they can command quite a high salary.

Fund-raising bodies often believe they can offer lower salaries as some people appreciate their aims and environment to such an extent that they will accept this; however they also have disadvantages such as lack of career structure. Fund-raisers must be aware that for researchers they are competing with institutions that can pay highly, and if they do not offer sufficient money and training they will not attract and retain good staff. It is particularly important to find someone with initiative when setting up a new department. If you settle for someone with neither experience nor initiative then the results will speak for themselves. Unfortunately many institutions do just this as they do not understand what prospect research is capable of producing. This results in a vicious cycle of poor performance and poor pay.

In order to discover what level of pay is appropriate to the job speak to recruitment agencies that specialise in the field of information (not computer programming). In the UK these include Aslib and TFPL.

- *Training*. Information is a particularly fast-moving field. There is a constant stream of new products and new ways of using those products. This is particularly the case in electronic information, though many online hosts will provide courses either free or at a relatively cheap price. There is such a wide range of skills required of the prospect researcher that new recruits are not likely to incorporate all of them. It is also quite likely that researchers will be expected to keep pace with the changing priorities of the organisation, such as focusing on new countries. Training can be a way of motivating and rewarding staff. If they feel that their skills are falling behind those of their colleagues they might worry that if they stay in the job too long they will be unemployable elsewhere. The obvious answer is to find a new job as quickly as possible.

*Facilities*

- *The type of information* required for a prospect research library is unfortunately very expensive. A single *Who's Who* can cost £100-£300. Publishers find that biographical information is costly to collate and does not necessarily provide a very high return, hence the fact that the publication of who's whos is often unpredictable. Company directories are even more expensive, some of them in the range £200-£500, depending on the degree of coverage. CD-ROMs are generally even worse, possibly costing thousands of pounds each. These prices are for basic factual information rather than analysts' reports, which are more expensive still. The high cost of company information is partly due to the fact that buyers are often wealthy institutions such as banks. Foundation directories are generally very cheap (being designed for the charitable sector and often not providing a great deal of detail). The major exception to this is the US where fund-raising is big business, though in compensation the range of products is extensive and well designed.

  If you have a very limited budget then you should probably arrange to work in a major library. You might like to buy basic foundation directories and a *Who's Who* if these will be used most often. Alternatively you might have to buy whatever you cannot find in the library. It is not ideal to work in a public library, but it is possible if that is the only option.

  At the other end of the spectrum is the full research library. Inevitably if the department must cover many different countries the cost will be much higher than if it is restricted to one. Maintaining a good international resource centre could cost anything from £20,000 per year upwards (preferably closer to £30,000), divided 60:40 between books and electronic information. This assumes an existing stock of books and a rotational system of purchasing, i.e. not replacing every book each year. Who's whos and foundation directories generally have to be bought as books, but unless you do a lot of work on one country company information is probably cheaper to acquire online. This enables you to dip into any country file without committing you to purchasing a costly book or CD-ROM which only covers a very limited area and dates rapidly. For a more specific idea of costs look at the information sources listed in the later chapters of this book and decide which would be necessary for your own needs.

- *Computer equipment.* Prices fluctuate too rapidly to give a precise figure for this. See above for a description of what is needed.

- *Other overheads.* Fax, telephone and/or postage costs will not be negligible as books and company annual reports must be acquired from different sources, some of them international. Telephone research involving expensive overseas calls should also be taken into account.

- *Space.* This is often an 'invisible' cost borne by the organisation rather than individual departments. Again it cannot be costed as it will vary widely depending on location, the state of the property market and the amount of space allocated. See above for a description of what is required.

# 5. Analysis of performance

Prospect research is one area that cannot easily be judged by returns. So much depends on the ability of the people who deal directly with the prospect and on the personality of prospects themselves that it is not fair to judge the researcher on the outcome.

Nor is it easy to test the outcomes of alternative methods. Prospect research would only be employed where a great deal of effort is to be put into a small number of prospects. This means that there are relatively few examples to test and the penalties for failure are so great that an organisation would be reluctant not to use what are believed to be the best methods.

Speed of through-put is not necessarily a good measure. It might only show that the reports are less detailed or that routine work such as keeping up to date with new resources is being neglected. A backlog of work can actually be a good sign as it means requesters are relying heavily on the researchers.

One possibility is to judge the researchers on the number of new prospects that they come up with. This is a relatively small but sometimes important aspect of their job. Before using this measure make sure that the suggestions are actually being acted upon. If the other staff prefer to find new prospects through their own contacts then the researchers probably realise that they are wasting their time and will focus their activities elsewhere.

It is not recommended to ask the prospects themselves for their opinions of the reports. A great deal of their content would have to be extracted leaving rather a bland product. Even then reading a report about yourself can be a very threatening experience. People often don't realise just how much information is publicly available and they would not normally see it pulled together into one report. There is also the inevitable problem that even the best reports can contain inaccuracies. Sources can never be guaranteed 100%, and there is the possibility that the researcher might have misinterpreted a fact. There is much more scope for problems (even a libel suit) than for goodwill through showing a prospect his report.

In the end, the best guide to performance might be the opinions of the people who use the reports. Do the requesters (voluntarily) make a great deal of use of the research facility and do they rely heavily on the reports? Do they find that the information is both accurate and useful? Would they like the content or layout changed or are they happy with it?

Even more telling is the opinion of the contact who will be used to approach the prospect. This should be a person who knows the prospect, possibly very well. It might be a close friend if the prospect is a person or a director if it is a company. If anyone can judge the accuracy of the report it is the contacts, and to impress them is quite an achievement. Thorough prospect research is quite capable of doing this. However there is always the problem of whether you should show the entire report to someone so closely linked with the prospect.

If prospect research was not considered to be a valuable function there would probably be evidence that organisations had tried it out and abandoned it. In fact, those organisations which have discovered prospect researchers consider them worth keeping, even though budgets are tight. Although virtually un-known a few years ago, the profession has expanded dramatically in the US and is now taking off in the UK. As understanding of its possibilities and the professionalism of its members increase it seems likely to become still more popular.

# 3. Online, CD-ROM, the Internet or Paper?

Over the past decade the quantity and range of electronic information has expanded beyond all recognition. The end of the library of books has been predicted. This leaves many people feeling intimidated by incomprehensible jargon and unfamiliar new products. However there is less cause for concern than you might think.

In fact there is still a place for books in the modern research library. Many sources are not available in any other form, and books can be more accessible and sometimes more cost-effective than alternatives. Electronic sources have their part to play as well, but suppliers are waking up to the need for them to be as simple as possible (though with more complex features for those advanced users who feel brave enough to tackle them). If you have tried an online database before and been put off by its complexity, take another look. They are increasingly moving away from the unhelpful command format where you have a blank screen and no clue what to do next. The newer versions tell you, step by step, what to do next, and show you the various options in case you have forgotten. A little hands-on experience can often allay fears about these, so ring up and ask for a free demonstration. Alternatively, you could ask the suppliers for details of online exhibitions where you can tour competitors' stands viewing the various alternatives. In the UK Olympia hosts such an exhibition every December.

This chapter will look at alternative sources of information supply and storage: hard copy (paper), computer disks, CD-ROMs, online databases and the Internet.

## 1. Hard copy

This is the traditional range of books, card files, etc. This can be converted to a computer document by using a scanner, which is effectively a glorified photocopier with character recognition software. Scanners still struggle for 100% accuracy in recognising print and would not be any use with untidy handwriting, but they are improving rapidly. (NB – scanning information into your computer can put you in breach of the copyright laws.)

## 2. Floppy disks

Databases of information are often available on ordinary disks, like the ones you use in a standard PC. As the storage capacity of modern computers has increased it is normally possible to transfer the information straight onto your own PC as soon as you receive it. You then have a ready-made and normally quite easy to use database sitting on your own computer.

## 3. CD-ROMs

These look like the familiar music CDs, but contain information to be used by a computer. They are effectively floppy disks with a much greater storage capacity, except that you cannot save your own documents on them. 'ROM' stands for read only memory, in other words your computer can read what is on it, but cannot add to it. CDs which can be added to should become more widely available in the future. Because of their large capacity CDs are capable of storing pictures and producing colourful graphs.

In order to use a CD-ROM you will need to acquire a CD reader to attach to your computer (unless it comes complete with a CD drive). As CDs contain so much information it is still usual to read the information direct from the CD rather than transferring it onto your computer. Thus you have a library of CDs which must be swapped in and out of the reader as needed. Computer storage capacities are growing at such a rate that it should ultimately be possible to avoid this problem.

## 4. Online databases

Online information is obtained by accessing someone else's database via the telephone lines (or an alternative physical network). You might arrange to access a database direct from its creator. Alternatively, there are companies (known as 'hosts') which specialise in building up large collections of databases. These collections may come from hundreds of different suppliers and would be well beyond the purchasing power of most users. The host provides you with a password so that you can get into its databases and charges you for access. Once you have dialled into the host's computer it seems as if you are using a database which is actually stored on your own computer. The weak link is the telephone lines, which can occasionally throw up odd characters ('line noise') or drop your connection, but this is not normally too serious a problem.

A single host might provide access to hundreds of different databases. Some are simply electronic forms of books (e.g. business suppliers like Dun & Bradstreet), while others are only available as databases. They might contain information on companies, patents, science, or even the complete text of newspapers or professional journals. There are few who's whos available online, though Reed/Marquis and some of the Continental European publishers are exceptions. There is also little foundation information online, the major exception being the US Foundation Center.

The trend is for online databases to become increasingly user-friendly. At the most basic, you might be presented with a screen asking three questions:

- Which database do you want to search? (You might reply: *The Times* newspaper.)

- What word or words do you want to search for? (You can normally search for any word or collection of words that might appear in the database, except for the most basic ones like 'and'. Thus you might enter 'Clinton + forestry' to see whether any articles have been written about Bill Clinton's views on forestry.)

- What dates do you want to search? (Reply: June 1993 to the present.)

The host's computer will then spend a few seconds checking through *The Times* database and tell you how many articles meet your criteria. You can choose whether you want to look at the headlines, contexts (i.e. a few words either side of the word you searched for), or the full articles. As the information will then scroll past quite rapidly you may like to 'download' it into your computer's own storage space as it comes down the line. This means that once you have closed down the telephone connection you can retrieve the downloaded articles through your word-processing package, browse through them at your leisure and print out the more interesting bits. (Bear in mind that your contract with the host is likely to state that you may not store this information on your own computer; however, so long as you keep it just long enough to tidy it up a bit, put in headings, etc., and then print it out once, they are not likely to complain.)

On some hosts it is also possible (and occasionally essential) to use a language which is more akin to conventional computer programming. You might choose to focus on information from specified fields of a database, reorganise it, and display it in a different format, for example you might take a database which gives lots of information on individual companies, pull out UK-based retailers, select those with the highest turnover, organise them in order of size, and print out a table of names and addresses starting with the largest. It is not necessary to go to this level of complexity, but there are times when it is useful.

Alternatively you might choose to use codes to make your search more specific. A news database might employ coders to read each article and give it a few standard codes to describe its main points. Thus an article about the annual financial results of a company would have appended to it a code for that specific company plus the general code for annual results. Using codes should rule out 'false hits', e.g. if you wish to pull out articles on Boots plc's environmental policy your first thought might be to enter a basic search such as 'Boots + environment'. Unfortunately this is likely to pull out not only the articles you want, but also ones on the business environment's effect on Boots, or even the advantages of wearing waterproof boots in a muddy environment. If instead you use the codes for Boots plc and environmental issues then you can exclude unwanted articles and go straight to the ones which concentrate on the desired topic.

Online databases are increasingly becoming available over the Internet. You still have to pay, but if you already use the Internet you might prefer this route. Alternatively you can gain access to them via the telephone lines using the following equipment:

- *A computer.* Your ordinary PC will probably be adequate if it is reasonably modern. While the online facility is not in use you can still use it for word-processing etc.

- *A modem.* This is a box of electronics which enables the computer to interpret the telephone signals. The faster the modem can work (the baud rate), the more expensive it is; however it is best to choose one at least as fast as the speed of the database you want to access because this saves online charges. The faster the modem can transfer the information into your computer the shorter the time you need to spend in the online database, and many hosts charge by the minute. Check what speeds the host uses, and bear in mind that as with any form of computer technology they are regularly upgraded. If you are confused then it is in the host's interests to give you some advice.

- *A piece of communications software* that tells the computer how to handle the telephone signals. Some hosts offer their own software, which is very useful if you only want to use one source, but not so good if you want the flexibility to access others as well.

- *A telephone line (or other network).* You can plug your ordinary telephone into the modem, and while it is not engaged with the online facility it will continue to function as normal. This of course means that you have to pay telephone charges on top of the host's fees; however they might not be as substantial as you would imagine. Even if the host is in a different country it might be possible for you to ring a local number and tap into a network which carries the signals at minimal cost. This means you pay for a local call rather than an international one. Knight-Ridder's *Dialog* is a prime example of this: although the host computer is actually located in the US, British Telecom provides local access routes in many different countries. Despite the distance there is relatively little interference on the line. However make sure you ask the host where your nearest entry point is as some hosts are not set up for international users. Alternatively it might be possible to obtain access via the Internet or other networks. Your computer support team will probably be able to advise you on whether your office has access to anything appropriate.

- *A contract and password* from the host.

- *Training.* Most hosts are only too willing to help people use their services as this boosts their revenues. Some offer starter courses free of charge, though only at a limited number of locations. Once you have had your introductory course you can go back for further courses whenever you feel ready, or you can rely on the telephone help-desks. These are used to dealing with even the most basic queries (indeed they sometimes sound relieved that it's a straightforward problem they know how to solve) so there is no need to feel embarrassed to ask.

If you still feel that setting up an online database is beyond you, talk to the hosts. Some are better than others, but it is very much in their interests that you should be able to use their system, so they are likely to do everything they can to help.

## 5. The Internet

This is rapidly becoming the place to start your research, particularly if your prospect is involved with electronics or computers. Companies are increasingly developing their own web sites which might contain mini-biographies and even pictures of their executives. Some people even have their own web sites especially if they would like to be head-hunted. The Internet is also increasingly useful for ordering books, with large online shops like Amazon (US) and Blackwell's (UK).

The Internet is a network of linked computers all over the world. On these computers sit a vast assembly of odds and ends of information and misinformation which institutions and individuals all over the world have seen fit to make available on the network.

A detailed description of the various Internet tools can be off-putting to someone who is not confident in using it. In fact the system is quite easy once you have someone set it up for you. A full description of how to use the Internet is best left to books devoted to that subject, such as *The Internet for Library and Information Service Professionals,* by Andy Dawson (Aslib, 2nd edition, 1997). The following provides instead a layman's introduction to what you can actually do with it.

For more specific information on sites and discussion lists see the chapters on sources at the end of this book. Magazines are able to keep pace with new developments and often contain book reviews. The major UK newspapers also have weekly sections on electronic information.

*Major uses of the Internet*

- *A source of free information.* Suppliers include companies, institutions, government departments, universities, standard online suppliers, and ordinary people. Anyone, anywhere in the world can choose to set up their own information page. All they need is the appropriate equipment and an access point.

   The information is thus a peculiar assortment. A company might have a page explaining what its products are and detailing its financial performance. A government which wants to recruit expatriates might set up pages on living and working in the country. A university will advertise details of its courses and fees. A library might open its catalogue ('OPAC') to improve public access. A museum's list of exhibits might include memorabilia relating to an influential local family. A professional organisation might provide a directory of its members. You might find edited highlights or even the full text of a newspaper. Less commonly, an alumni association might provide an online directory or a university a list of donations and the names of its board of governors. Lists of university fellows can be quite useful, especially in business schools, as they might include visiting fellows who are prominent businessmen but who also happen to be graduates and donors to the school.

   There are no rules about what is or is not there: it is simply whatever somebody decided to share. Because universities have been on the Internet for so long they tend to have quite good information sites. More recently there has been an explosion of interest from companies, which are increasingly seeing it as a marketing tool.

   Because it is not a standard commercial product you will not find a salesman who can give a full and complete explanation of its content and uses. It is so huge and diverse that users tend to find out about one small corner of it by trial and error or word of mouth and know very little about the rest of it. Once you have found a page you like, unfortunately there is no guarantee that it will be updated or even that it will be there next time you look. As these are free services there is no commercial pressure to maintain them. However there is a constant stream of new information pages. People with similar interests will help guide you to them through bulletin boards and usegroups.

The Internet is not a substitute for other forms of information. At present it is slow, unreliable and inflexible in comparison with commercial online services. Its popularity is expanding at such a rate that it is in danger of becoming overwhelmed with electronic traffic. European users are often warned to use it in the morning as it will slow down in the afternoon when the Americans go online. Pictures can be particularly slow so it may be worth getting a fast modem or – if possible – switching off the graphical option so that you only receive text. As anyone can set themselves up as an information provider there is no guarantee that they know what they are doing: both the quality of the content and the technical performance of the sites can very considerably.

Many pages are disappointingly brief and uninformative. Before becoming too irritated by this, ask yourself why should anyone wish to make information available free of charge? It is in the interests of governments, companies and universities to sell themselves; however, why should a commercial publisher wish to do it? Some newspapers and magazines are only available in very abbreviated form, for example, they might place their recruitment section on the Internet because the sale of advertising space, which is a major source of income for them, is influenced by the number of people who will see the advert. Some services are in the process of being tested so that any problems can be dealt with before they are offered commercially. Once the supplier is satisfied with the test it will add in the full range of information and attach a password or scramble it so that only paying users can obtain access.

Even worse, some information is simply untrue. Policing is very poor and it is quite possible for someone to put up an information page which appears to come from a reputable company when in fact they have composed it themselves. It is also possible, despite attempts to prevent it, for saboteurs to infiltrate genuine information pages. It is therefore wise to check any information that comes from the Internet, even when it appears to be provided by an authoritative source.

Search tools are also crude in comparison with those of the commercial online databases. There is a wide range to choose from, and more are constantly being developed. They tend to offer relatively simple searches and may use relevance rankings rather than boolean logic. Instead of looking for a+b they might search for items which contain as many as possible of the words you want. Be sure you know whether you are searching titles, descriptions or the full text.

- *A route to paying services.* Standard online suppliers are beginning to make their services available through the Internet. This means that the Internet serves as an alternative to the telephone lines, in other words merely a connection. The services are totally ring-fenced and fee-paying: you still have to obtain a password and pay for what you use. Their range of information and search tools are quite distinct from those available free of charge on the Internet itself. Whether you prefer the Internet connection or the telephone lines might depend on factors such as speed (the Internet should be fast but can become congested) and cost. Although obtaining services via the Internet can be very convenient if you are already using it, there can be a problem with security. The Internet connection potentially enables outsiders to invade your privacy, steal your credit card number (if you use it) or infect your machine with a virus (if you download programmes).

One example of a hybrid Internet fee-paying service is Blackwell's *Uncover* database (email: *uncover@blackwell.co.uk*) which provides access to bibliographic information on journal articles but charges when it faxes you the full text of an article you select.

- *A means of communication.* Email (electronic mail) is rather like a fax: you type out your message then send it down the line and hope that it reaches its destination. This might be the next desk or another country. However mail frequently goes astray so if your package has a 'message received' facility it might be prudent to switch it on. When email works well it is cheaper than an international phone call or fax.

Discussion or distribution lists are like public emails. Instead of sending your message to one person you send it to everyone on the list. This may be a small one with controlled access such as a committee, or a huge international one that anyone can join. Lists can be rather like a multi-way conversation where everyone might be talking at once. This can be a nuisance because you end up being deluged with mail and there may be no-one to control the content. However read only lists can be an effective way of distributing press releases, news services, etc. You subscribe to a list by sending an email to the list's administration address (not the list itself). You will probably receive a message explaining how the list works. Of particular importance is the instruction for unsubscribing. Do not lose this as it might prove a relief after a few days of being swamped with mail. Although commands vary, 'help' might prove to be a useful one.

Rather than sending your message to individuals you can send it to a bulletin board or usenet newsgroup. All mail is posted in this one location. This means your mailbox is not cluttered with everybody else's messages and if you do not have time to read them for a few weeks they do not pile up waiting for you (though lists may well have commands to get round this problem). If you have a problem you can send a message to a relevant group and wait to see whether anyone replies with a solution. As these conversations are all visible to the group you can simply observe the discussions if you do not wish to participate. These groups may be moderated to exclude irrelevant or offensive material; however following the conversations can still be a time-consuming process if there are a great many contributors.

- *A source of software.* Anything from Internet tools to games might be made available free of charge or at a modest fee over the Internet. However beware that very occasionally viruses are incorporated in them.

- *Personal interest.* One of the reasons for the great popularity of the Internet is that you can follow up your own interests on it. You can join a usegroup devoted to your hobby, you can look up train timetables for your overseas holiday, or you can do your shopping. The range of services is constantly expanding. While this is great fun for the individual it is more of a problem for the employer who is paying for both the connection and the employee's time. If you consider buying goods over the Internet be aware that if you hand over your credit card details you cannot be entirely certain that they are secure.

*Gaining access to the Internet*

Academic users probably have free access through their institution, however other users have to find a commercial operator to supply an entry point. Service providers can be found through Internet magazines or through electronic information fairs. Rather than plugging in direct to the Internet you might prefer to let an online host or BBS service provide it for you. Companies like CompuServe and Delphi provide a gateway to it as part of a much larger package and are not necessarily more expensive. Such services are easier to set up and use and might provide better customer support; however they might not give you access to the whole of the Internet and their connections might be slower.

Factors to take into account when choosing a supplier include the following:

- *Provider's charges.* Whether you prefer a flat monthly fee or a price per hour depends on your level of usage.
- *Telephone charges.* You must pay standard telephone charges to dial up the access point. How far away is the supplier's nearest access point and which telephone charge band does it fall into? If you intend to be online for several hours a day at peak time you might find your next telephone bill is rather a shock. In some places local or off-peak calls might be free.
- *Number of access points.* How many are there in relation to the number of users? If the access points are all busy then you might have a long wait before you can use them.
- *Quality of customer support.* Ask other users for their opinion. Online hosts which provide gateways to the Internet are particularly likely to make life easy for their customers.

A useful guide to UK Internet access providers can be found in *Email for Library and Information Service Professionals*, by Simon Pride (Aslib, 2nd edition, 1996).

## Which format should you choose?

Many types of information are available in virtually identical form as books, online databases and CD-ROMs. The business information specialist Dun & Bradstreet is one example of a publisher which makes its information available in all three formats. The Internet is left out of this discussion as sources there tend to be less complete and less reliable (unless they are standard online databases which just happen to be using it as a connection route). Even when a source is not available in different formats there are often good alternatives from other suppliers. Which medium should you choose?

### Flexibility

Although the information is the same, the way that you can use it is different. A book is relatively inflexible, especially if it is not well indexed; but online databases and CD-ROMs have very powerful searching and rearranging capabilities. Thus, in a book you might have to be certain of a company's full name before you can find it, whereas an online database can find it using the latter part of the name or even clues such as directors' names. Electronic databases enable you to do more complex searches, such as the ten largest US companies which operate in the oil industry, or those news articles which refer to both a specific person and a specific topic. You can also rearrange the information, taking only those fields that interest you and making a table out of them. CD-ROMs even allow you to make colourful charts out of the data. In a book you are limited to whatever indexes the publisher sees fit to include: finding and presenting other data must be done manually.

## Timeliness

Many types of book and CD-ROM are inevitably out of date by the time they are published. It takes a while to compile the data, produce and distribute them. Many online databases are updated daily. This can be very useful but can also lead to a false sense of confidence. Newspaper databases have dated articles; however a major flaw in business databases is that they might not say how up to date they are. Even if the database you are searching is updated daily, that does not mean that *all* of the records are kept totally up to date. Some may be very old. How can you compare the figures of two companies when you do not know which years they are taken from? One might be affected by inflation or a collapse in the market. Even if the figures have been updated, when did they last check the directors' names? Books which are published quarterly might well have an advantage over online databases. However the online database is invaluable for recent press coverage.

## Obsolescence

Some types of information become out of date very rapidly while others retain a value for years. Company information can be out of date by the time it is published: there are always new profit figures and boardroom changes. Thus if you invest in books or CD-ROMs you must be prepared to update them regularly. Biographical information does date: there can be a new marriage, a change of address, etc.; however, much of it will always be true, e.g. names of parents, where educated, career history, etc. Thus you can get away with not replacing who's whos every year, especially if you supplement them with information from the press. The ideal is to replace them all, but if you cannot afford this you might choose to rotate purchases. If you cannot afford company books, rotating them is not so effective, so it might be better to go for the online version.

## Frequency of use

If you use one source all the time it might be cost-effective to buy it as a book or CD-ROM rather than pay by the minute to use it online. If, however, it is important that you should have as wide a range of sources as possible (for example, if you are covering many different countries) then you might well be unable to afford your own copy of everything that you want. If you did buy them they would probably sit unused on the shelf for much of the time. It would be better to dip into the less frequently used sources via an online host and pay only for what you use.

*Characteristics of the users*

Do other staff use your resources? This should probably be encouraged unless it is too much of a hindrance to you. It is costly to waste the time of a highly trained specialist on endless routine requests which could be answered by an untrained person. If the information is in book or simple database form then your clerical assistant can deal with these requests. Alternatively, you might encourage other departments to answer their own basic queries. Even the most senior people are often not averse to taking a quick look in a book so long as they do not have to go too far to do it. If it would take as much time to ask the researcher to do it as to do it themselves then why waste the researcher's time? Alternatively, secretaries might appreciate being trusted to do basic research themselves. Tasks which the researcher sees as a chore, others might enjoy for the variety and sense of achievement.

If you want to free yourself from routine checks then you must provide information in an easily accessible, and non-frightening form. This often means books. Even with simple instructions, CD-ROMs can seem intimidating to someone who is not accustomed to them, and it does not take much to persuade people that it is too much trouble for them. There is also the cost of keeping a spare computer to bear in mind. It is less likely that you would want to have an online database on open access as the costs are so high and even the most user-friendly require a minimum level of training. Books, however, are part of everyone's life. Although you might end up with several copies of the more popular works (e.g. *Who's Who*), so that everyone has one within easy reach, this can still be cheap in relation to the salary of the person who would have to answer endless queries. It then leaves the researcher free to make a much more valuable contribution to the office.

*Costs*

CD-ROMs still tend to be more expensive than books, though they are becoming cheaper. Some online hosts provide break-downs of their bills by database, so in theory it is possible to compare it with the cost of the book, though it is difficult to place a value on the flexibility of the online version. Online sources can be risky as an inexperienced user can inadvertently run up a huge bill: in some databases a single document can cost £50 or more. This can often be avoided by setting up the system to warn you in advance how much each item will cost (the host will advise you on whether this is possible). It is often possible to obtain the information more cheaply through other databases. Online databases require extra equipment (e.g. modems) and entail costs in attending training courses (even if they are free you must pay travelling expenses and allow for the value of time lost). Since online hosts provide so much choice you will probably end up attending courses not only on how to use them, but also on the contents and relative merits of the various databases. Finally, in the UK you do not pay tax on books, but you do if you retrieve the same information online.

*Size*

Even CD-ROMs have a limited storage capacity. If you are searching for an obscure prospect you could end up inserting and removing a whole series of CDs in order to repeat the same search on each. An online host would enable you to enter your search terms once and check literally hundreds of databases in a matter of minutes.

Paper sources are even more cumbersome than CD-ROMs: searching a physical newspaper index would involve much lifting up and down of volumes. They are also much more demanding of physical space, and there is the slight risk of a back injury in using them. You should always treat the larger volumes with respect, even if it is well within your strength to lift them. Don't jerk them suddenly or hold them awkwardly, and try to ensure that the most commonly used or most awkward books are on the middle shelves where you don't have to reach up or down to them. If your shelves are very high it is essential to have a stable stool or set of steps so that the shortest user can reach the top books safely and easily.

*Availability of the information*

Company and news information is widely available in electronic form, but biographical and foundation information tends to be restricted to books. The Reed/Marquis group is beginning to make its biographical works accessible online as is the US Foundation Center (both of which can be found on Knight-Ridder's *Dialog*), but these are still relatively unusual.

*Conclusion*

You will probably have little choice but to buy much of your biographical and foundation information in hard copy. Business information is a different story: it is readily available online, while books and CD-ROMs are expensive and can rapidly become seriously out of date. If you are concentrating heavily on one country or if you want to make the information available to as many users as possible then a book or CD-ROM might be worthwhile. If you need to cover a large area then it is probably cheaper to go for the online version. The optimum will probably be a mixture of the two.

# Which online host(s) should you choose?

## Factors to consider

### *Availability*

Some hosts are only available in their home country, unless you wish to make an international phone call each time you use them.

### *Minimum annual charge*

Some insist that you should commit yourself to a minimum level of usage per year. This can be very high if you are on a tight budget or if you want to make use of more than one host. Some hosts might waive this for charities.

### *Start-up costs*

These are not normally too high, but might include training, a manual, and the annual fee for the password.

### *Usage costs*

It can be difficult to compare prices because there are so many ways of charging. It is likely to be a combination of a charge per minute plus a charge per article or per line (and don't forget that there is likely to be tax on top). Different hosts might offer exactly the same database at different costs or they might have alternative databases which are just as good. If appropriate, remember to ask about discounts for charities or educational users. There are also bulk discounts, but usage must be high to qualify for these.

### *Degree of complexity*

Most online hosts are moving towards more user-friendly screens, though the more complicated searches still often require quite detailed knowledge. Arrange for a demonstration so that you can judge for yourself whether you can handle it.

### *Range of databases available*

Hosts are increasingly marketing themselves overseas but their database ranges might retain a bias towards the country of origin. Some specialise in business, in newspapers, or in scientific databases. A database (or acceptable alternatives to it) might well be available on several different hosts, allowing you to choose the cheapest or easiest to use. Do not be overwhelmed by a list of hundreds of databases as many will be irrelevant to you: state what you want and ask for a list of databases that will suit. The most useful ones are likely to be company and newspaper databases, though there are occasionally foundation and biographical ones.

31

Many business databases are designed to be used by researchers in institutions such as the big banks. For these companies money is no object and it is very easy to end up paying tens of pounds for one analyst's report. If your budget is not this big then make sure you look carefully at the contents of the various databases before going online and if possible set up your system so that it warns you how expensive each request will be. It is much cheaper to use factual company directories like Dun & Bradstreet's than the ready-made analysts' reports (which are not always as good as you might expect and might be totally out of date). The basic facts can then be enhanced with newspaper reports and your own analysis. See chapter 9 on company information for a description of how to write your own reports.

*Can the database be accessed through another host?*

Some databases can be obtained direct from the supplier and also from hosts which supply many other databases too. The multi-database host gives you more choice and the advantage of a uniform layout and billing system. Obtaining several databases direct from the suppliers means they all look and act differently which can easily become very confusing. However prices vary quite widely, even for the same database, so it might prove cheaper to go direct.

Some information providers are hosts in their own right yet also available through other hosts, an example being *FT-Profile* which is available through *New Prestel*. Sometimes these retain their own identity: they are kept separate from the rest of the service and use their own distinct format and search language. This is known as a gateway. The only difference between obtaining it direct and via another host is that there might be a different pricing structure. Alternatively, some hosts become nothing more than a set of databases within the parent host. They take on the other host's format and language and can be searched in groups with its other databases. This makes life easier for the searcher who can search more databases at the same time and without worrying about remembering different formats.

*Completeness of the information*

Where there are alternative databases which will do the same job, check how complete they are. Some newspaper databases cover a wide range of papers, but only take a limited range of articles from each, which means that if you are searching for a more obscure prospect the relevant information is likely to be missed out. They might also provide only condensed abstracts rather than the full articles. When looking at company databases check the cut-off point for inclusion, as there is a remarkably wide variation in the number of companies they cover. Also ensure that they have the type of information you need: most will provide financial information, but some only give the name of one key director. You could also check the update frequency, though unfortunately this is no guarantee that any more than a few records are correct: much of the information might be totally out of date.

*Timeliness of information*

It is likely that the more up to date the information the more expensive it is. Many press databases take a day or two to be transferred online, though some are online before they hit the streets. Some hosts separate today's news into a higher charge band. The most up to date sources such as newswires and stock market quotes are likely to be quite costly. Stockbrokers might be willing to pay for this, but many other researchers can get by with news that was correct a couple of days ago especially if they regularly scan the papers.

*Alternative methods of obtaining the same information*

If the minimum charges are prohibitive or you know you will use the database only infrequently, a different method of obtaining the information might be more appropriate. Does any other department of your organisation have access to online hosts? Perhaps they can do the occasional search for you? Even though they might charge, you would still save on the host's start-up costs, minimum charges, and training time, and it might help your colleagues meet their own minimum charges. Alternatively you might go direct to the host or the database supplier and ask them to do the occasional search for you. A local library might also be willing to do this. If the host has only one database that you need you might consider buying a book or CD version of it. Alternatively, if you only want information on a particular subject you might ask a press cuttings agency to send you articles, though this is very inflexible in comparison with the potential of an online database.

*Superfluous information*

Some hosts sell themselves more on the basis of the user's personal interests than the institution's requirements. You might be offered information on anything from holidays to hobbies, which can sound very tempting. Don't be dazzled by this. The result might be that the researchers spend their time investigating discussion groups and planning their next trip, which could be costly in terms of lost output and online time. You might also find that a more popular service does not provide the same degree of support for the business and press files as a host which specialises in more serious research.

## Off-line linkage

Some hosts provide software which permits you to type in the instructions before you go online. This can be useful if you are performing a complicated search or if you are likely to receive interruptions in the middle of a search or even if you are prone to typing errors. It does not generally make a great deal of difference as searches frequently evolve in response to the results you find.

## Sources of information

Some information on specific databases is available in the later chapters on sources. To obtain an overview the following might be useful:

*Fulltext Sources Online* – BiblioData/Learned Information

This is a guide to which hosts cover specific periodicals, newspapers, newsletters, newswires and TV/radio transcripts. There are subject and geographical indexes, so if your interests lie in a particular area you can get an indication of which vendor will be most useful to you. Basic facts rather than descriptions. It can also be found online, e.g. on *Data-Star* (Knight-Ridder).

*The CD-ROM Directory* – TFPL

This claims to be a guide to all commercially available CD-ROM titles, whether in business, science, etc. Arranged by title and by company. Further information includes conferences and exhibitions, journals and books, and who's who in the industry.

*CD-ROM and Online Business and Company Databases* – Aslib

A guide to the most useful alternatives in this field including indexes to databases, subjects and hosts. Relatively cheap and user-friendly, and possibly easier to use because it concentrates on the major hosts rather than overwhelming you with choice. A sister publication, *Going Online, CD-ROM and the Internet,* Phil Bradley (Aslib, 10th edition, 1997) addresses the basic questions in electronic information: how to start, how they operate, which to choose, etc.

*The Instant Guide to Company Information Online* – The British Library

This aims to help you decide which database will best suit your requirements before you go online. Only around 100 databases and 30 hosts are covered, but they are the major European ones.

*Gale Directory of Databases* – Gale

Profiles of around 15,000 electronic databases, revised twice a year. Details include time span, content, geographic coverage, updating, rates, contact details, etc. Its immense scope might bemuse the first-time user. This is also available on *Data-Star* (Knight-Ridder).

*World Databases in Company Information* – Bowker-Saur

Descriptions and comparisons of databases as held on various hosts. One of a series of sources for different fields, e.g. medicine.

*Information World Review* – Learned Information

An informative, accessible publication in newspaper format. It covers online, CD-ROM and the Internet. Articles on the latest news in electronic information, advertisements from the major suppliers, hints for searching, forthcoming exhibitions and conferences, job advertisements, etc. More heavy-weight articles can be found in its many sister publications, e.g. *Searcher*.

## Membership or training organisations for information professionals

It is easy to become confused by the variety of databases on offer. You might prefer to ask an expert for advice at an organisation such as Aslib or TFPL. They might even have facilities for you to try out the various products for yourself (though they will charge for this).

## Online exhibitions

Information suppliers show off their wares at a variety of annual exhibitions and trade fairs. If you visit a large one such as that held at London's Olympia in December (organised by Learned Information), you can tour the stands and compare the products for yourself. If this proves too hectic at least you can gather their promotional material and possibly arrange for their sales teams to demonstrate the systems in your own office. Major suppliers will be able to give you the time and date of the trade fair closest to you as they will want to demonstrate their products there.

# 4. Ethics, Security and Confidentiality

Once the value of prospect research is understood it might seem that the only remaining question is how to do it. However there is a further matter which might not be immediately apparent, but will inevitably need to be dealt with at some point. Ignoring it can damage your reputation and even have major financial implications.

This is the question of how far it is reasonable for the researcher to go, and what controls should be in place to ensure that the bounds of acceptability are not crossed. The next chapters will explain how to find many types of information, for example clues to a person's wealth and family background. However, only you can decide which of these methods you wish to employ, what sort of information you are willing to look for, and how you keep it.

This question might appear superfluous to the European researcher who is struggling to find any information at all. Its importance becomes particularly evident in the US context where there is a huge amount of information that would not be available elsewhere. For example, in the US it is possible to obtain useful information from divorce records, such as age, birthplace, children's names, and assets. However helpful this might be, many researchers find it distasteful to read personal information which the parties would probably prefer to keep confidential. In the UK the question does not arise as divorce records are not made public.

This issue raises strong feelings in both researchers and prospects. The public consensus tends to be that privacy must be upheld, but in practice this is difficult. This chapter will do no more than raise questions to help you judge for yourself.

## Reasons for employing ethical restrictions

The prospect researcher is always under pressure to provide the fullest information possible: your boss might demand a specific piece of information, and you will probably want to impress by providing the best possible report. Everyone likes to be considered good at their job, especially if there is a chance of promotion. It is easy to discount ethical standards as a luxury which you cannot afford. However you should at least consider the advantages to be gained from employing some restrictions.

On the purest level, applying ethical standards to one area of your work encourages them to spread throughout the organisation. This can enhance the employees' self-respect and lead to a more committed, contented workforce. People who feel uncomfortable with what they are doing are more likely to be unhappy and look for other jobs.

If you wish to join a professional body, perhaps of prospect researchers or of fund-raisers, it is quite likely that this will have its own code of ethics. If you are discovered to be breaking it you can be thrown out, which might have unfortunate consequences for your career. Unless you work alone you are likely to find other members working side by side with you and though they might not report you, they are likely to be aware of what you are doing. Alternatively, your employer might have its own code of ethics, though unless you specifically ask about it you might be unaware that it exists.

But perhaps your conscience is not troubled. After all, the information you use is publicly available. It is also easy to become so caught up in the pursuit of information that you do not stop to think about whether you *should* be delving so deeply into a person's private affairs. This is a particular problem for researchers in the US where a great deal of personal information is available. You might be able to identify a person's social security number, check their income tax details, or investigate their divorce records. In most countries such information is considered confidential and there would be considerable outrage if it became public. Americans also have a more open attitude than the British towards information such as religious or political beliefs, but everyone likes to maintain some degree of privacy.

It is worth standing back for a moment and considering what effect your actions might have on others as the result can be quite damaging to yourself. While the researcher feels excitement at finding key facts and pride in producing a full report, the readers of that report might be shocked at just how much intimate detail is included. Even if the information is all publicly available, many people do not realise how much can be found. There is also a difference between it being available in various obscure locations where it might be hoped that few people would trouble to look, and seeing it written out in a single, comprehensive report which is readily available at a moment's notice. The reader might be the contact who will arrange the first meeting with the prospect; such a person will already be reasonably close to the prospect and might feel alarmed that their friend's privacy is being invaded in this way. Alternatively, they might be worried that you have previously compiled a report on them too, and wonder how many skeletons you have found in *their* cupboards.

One practical way round this is to provide the contact with an amended version of the report. It is up to you whether you choose to do this, and of course you must still rely on other members of your organisation not to inadvertently show the contact the original version.

Alternatively, the reader might actually be the prospect. The contact, who might not be as committed to your organisation as an employee would be, might decide to show the report to the prospect. Alternatively, the prospect might notice that their visitor is avidly reading something just before the meeting and demand to see it (which is not as uncommon an occurrence as it might sound). As prospect research becomes increasingly widespread, prospects are ever more aware of the existence of reports, and it is not unknown for them to demand to see their files. If a fund-raiser does not instantly show a prospect the file, that prospect is likely to decide it contains something unpleasant and be less willing to make a donation.

In some areas there are freedom of information laws which give people the right to see what information is held on them. In the US, state regulations could possibly give the prospect the right to see the hard copy file, especially if the organisation is state-funded. Some respond by keeping sensitive information on a computer. In the UK the opposite is the case: prospects do not have the same right to see the files (unless, for example, a libel suit is under way), but the Data Protection Act gives them the right to see anything about themselves which is held on computer. This Act requires every data holder to register its activities, and only hold that information which is strictly necessary. Subjective information is not permitted, which might be a problem if you routinely include wealth estimates. While people are aware of its impact on databases they do not necessarily realise that it can extend to word-processor documents such as your bank of research reports and file notes. While prosecutions under the Data Protection Act might seem a distant threat, libel actions are very real. In some countries, for example, France, privacy laws must also be borne in mind.

However, some cases are far from clear cut. What if prospects have shown themselves to be overtly racist or sexist? Unless you record this, your organisation might be wasting its time in sending certain members of staff to meet the prospect. More seriously, what if a male prospect is known to launch sexual assaults on females? If a female member of staff has already been assaulted you have a duty not to allow other females to be put at risk through ignorance. But what do you do? Even if the prospect were instantly dropped, it is likely that in a few years' time his name would be brought up again. If he seemed a good prospect once then he is likely to remain so. Some researchers would refuse to record the incident anywhere, relying on their memories to ensure that if the name came up again a man would be sent. Unfortunately, in many organisations staff turnover is so high that you cannot guarantee being there. You might return from holiday to find that the approach went ahead in your absence. Even if you state in the file that this person should not be considered as a prospect, unless you state the reason it is quite likely that your advice will be ignored. Another suggestion is to record in the file that this prospect would be best approached by x, y or z where x, y and z are male members of staff. Again, it is possible that these staff will have moved on by the time the prospect is next considered and with no clear explanation of the problem a woman might be sent. However, if you simply write that this prospect might assault a woman you could be sued for libel.

## Controlling the content of reports

The fear of libel causes some prospect researchers to refuse to hand over anything but raw information. This might be a thick pile composed of photocopies from directories and print-outs from newspaper databases. The recipient of this sort of research will have to spend a great deal of time sifting through it for key details, which is clearly unsatisfactory. Unfortunately, the task of condensing the information into a report involves the dangers of repeating someone else's libel and of creating new ones through faulty interpretation; however there are ways of reducing the problem.

Firstly, it is good practice to ensure that your reports are tightly sourced. Every section or paragraph – or sometimes every statement – should have a superscript reference to an item in the list of sources at the end of the report. This list should include both precise titles and dates of every source. Where a statement seems particularly dangerous it is safer still to place it in quotation marks. This discipline focuses your attention much more clearly on what was actually said in the original, rather than what you think it said after a quick scan. It also means that the reader can see the reason why you made a particular statement. If your source is a reputable newspaper then, although you may be at fault for repeating a libel, it would seem unfair to hold you entirely to blame.

Secondly, ensure that all researchers have a good understanding of the difference between fact and analysis. It might be worth sending them on a course on report writing to focus their attention on how far it is reasonable to draw conclusions from bare facts. The safest policy is to ensure that inferences are worded as possibilities and backed up by reasons. Wealth is a typical example of an area where it is tempting to draw unwarranted conclusions. There is no guarantee that people who are ostentatiously extravagant are able to afford the lifestyle they follow. You have no way of knowing how many mortgages and other debts have been accrued, nor whether they can afford the hefty tax bill that will arrive at the end of the year. Although you cannot state categorically that 'x is worth £50m' you can say that 'x is likely to be very wealthy because the *Sunday Times* rich list judges his wealth at £50m and he has three mansions and an impressive art collection including a Rembrandt and a Titian.' To be doubly safe it is a good idea for the head of research to check colleagues' reports before they leave the department as it is often easier to spot problems in someone else's work than in your own.

Thirdly, is the information relevant? Would it make much difference if it were not included? There is no point in spending time and money acquiring information which has little practical value, especially when it can have negative consequences. This is a difficult question to answer as it is so subjective. Some UK researchers might be cautious about writing profiles containing information such as religious beliefs or ethnic origins, as they might be criticised for marking someone out as different. In the US it might conceivably be considered rude not to acknowledge such characteristics. To some extent the prospect's own attitude must have a bearing. Is it something the prospect is proud of and views as an integral part of his or her personality? Admittedly this is not necessarily an easy matter to judge. However if the prospect gives press interviews discussing the fact that he or she is gay or has had a sex change operation why should you not mention it? Offence could be caused if a partner is not invited to a gathering because nobody realises the importance of the relationship.

Another example is a criminal record. Some institutions specifically forbid mention of it. However, if the press realises that you are linked with a convicted criminal it can seriously damage the reputation of your institution. Even where the person is unconvicted but considered suspect by the press, or totally innocent but the inheritor of a war criminal's wealth there is considerable potential for embarrassment. Many institutions would prefer to know this information so that they can decide whether they are willing to back the association in public.

## Restricting research methods

As well as the content of the report, there are questions about the methods of compiling it. For example, is it ever acceptable to obtain information anonymously? Often you will be in a position where you do not wish the prospect to be alerted to your interest until you have had time to prepare your approach. There is no sinister intention behind this, but simply the idea that the prospect might reject you out of hand without giving you the chance to put your case. The researcher is, anyway, not normally the person who is intended to meet the prospect.

If you are ringing for information, such as a company's annual report, is it acceptable to ask for it to be sent to your home address so that they do not realise who you work for? Large companies quite possibly take little notice of who requests information, but what if you ring a small company to find out what its line of business is? Should you lie about why you want to know? Should you give your name even if they don't ask for it? Some researchers make a point of announcing their name and employer at the start of any telephone call so that there can be no doubt. Perhaps it seems unimportant whether you give the wrong name, but what if you are found out? It is now possible to obtain devices giving you the identity of a caller, and if you are discovered to be lying then the valuable reputation of the entire organisation can suffer. You might program your telephone not to identify itself; however there will be occasions when your identity is discovered anyway and there will then be a question about why you tried to conceal it.

If you are using a source of information which it would embarrass you to reveal, are you sure that the information supplier will not identify you to the prospect? Some organisations, such as the European Foundation Centre, do this as a matter of course, horrifying researchers who simply assume that their confidentiality will be respected (though their motivation for privacy is slightly different in this case). Even if there is a policy of not identifying information users, good researchers will know well enough how an informal chat with a member of staff can elicit all sorts of information.

Even if you restrict yourself to sources that appear acceptable, such as newspaper reports, you might still run into problems. A US researcher who refuses to look at divorce records might find them summarised in the press. Does it become acceptable to collect the information if it comes from a respectable source? How does this differ from other press reports that give details of assets and family conflicts?

Another question is whether you restrict yourself to publicly available sources or whether you are willing to go beyond them. Will you seek out people who know the prospect, journalists, or those working in the same industry, and ask them for their opinions? People are often much less careful about what they say in a private conversation than what they put in print, so there is a much greater chance of major inaccuracies. Unfortunately a great deal of oral information is inaccurate, and even if it is correct it might be so personal that you have no way of checking it. Are you willing to put these opinions into your report? Will you keep them in your file or on your computer? Will you record the name of your informant, or take all the blame if the contact or prospect demands to know why you made such inaccurate statements? You will probably have no proof that your informant did actually make a specific comment, and if you insist that they did you could make yourself immensely unpopular with someone who could be very useful to you.

A related problem occurs when you have a contact who is very eager to help and volunteers large amounts of information which sounds worryingly subjective. You might simply thank the person politely but ignore it, which leaves you open to charges of incompetence when the contact realises you have not passed it on. You might instead state at the outset that you would rather not be given inside information. However this is likely to puzzle and upset the contact, who might conclude that you do not trust the accuracy of the information, or that you do not trust his or her judgement over where to draw the line in passing on sensitive personal information, or that you simply do not value the contact's help as you are prepared to go to great lengths to find information that could have been given you instantly.

# Copyright

Research departments tend to do a huge quantity of photocopying and can easily breach copyright, yet they do not necessarily take it very seriously. In the unlikely event that you do run into trouble with copyright it will be the researcher who is held responsible, so it is worth having some idea of what it involves. The rules are too complex to explain in detail here, but there are courses and publications that will help, for example *The Aslib Guide to Copyright*.

One major problem area is the distribution of press articles. You can cut out and keep the original, but there is only one of it, it is likely to be grubby because the print rubs off, and the poor quality paper yellows and disintegrates with age. Technically it is illegal to photocopy it, though it does not seem unreasonable to take just one copy and immediately throw away the original.

Photographs are another potential source of problems. If you stick a picture of the prospect on the front page of your report then every time you photocopy it you are infringing copyright. As scanner technology develops they might soon be able to reproduce pictures rather better than photocopiers, and actually incorporate them into the report. This would be just as bad. However, at present, scanning still tends to be rather slow, produce poor quality images and use up sizeable chunks of the computer's storage space.

## Protecting confidential material

Inevitably you will have information that is sensitive. It might merely upset a prospect to know that you have it or it might be downright libellous. You are unlikely to want to keep libellous material but the nature of the work means that you can easily inadvertently acquire it. Although you can take steps to ensure that your material comes from the best sources, you cannot be absolutely sure that every statement you make is 100% accurate. It is therefore safest to ensure that your work is kept as secure and confidential as possible.

What is the best storage method? The answer depends to some extent on where you are. In the US you have to be particularly careful about paper files because as prospect research becomes more widely practised the prospects are increasingly aware of their existence. It is by no means uncommon for a prospect to walk into an office and demand to see his file. If you refuse to hand it over he will decide that it contains something unpleasant and either break off relations with your organisation or even launch a court case to obtain access. In the UK there is a lower level of awareness of prospect research, but people are very sensitive about data held on computers. Under the Data Protection Act they can demand to see anything you hold about them on your database on payment of a small fee. As they probably do not realise that you are collecting such a large amount of information for your reports they will probably not ask to see the paper file or your word-processor file.

Aside from protecting yourself, you have a moral duty to protect the prospect. As well as publicly available information your report might contain comments made by contacts or your institution's confidential records about the prospect's relationship with it. The following suggestions might help to protect this information.

- Incorporate the words 'strictly confidential' into your standard report heading, or even place them at the top of every page.
- Consider starting each report with an inoffensive cover sheet so that sensitive information is not immediately visible. It might contain the words 'strictly confidential', the title of the report, the date, etc. It has the added advantage of making the report look more professional.

- Use special measures when a donor or contact requests anonymity. Simply writing that a gift is anonymous may not be sufficient if a report is scanned quickly. It might be necessary to use capitals, bold type or a red stamp, or to place a warning on the front of the report.

- Impress on the people who use your reports that they have a responsibility to maintain the confidentiality of the contents. This can be very difficult if they are of higher status than you, and is anyway likely to be ignored. Ideally you should consult with them about how they use the reports so that you do not try to insist on something which is not feasible. You might consider under what circumstances they can remove reports from the building, how you can work together to amend reports before they are seen by contacts, and whether the reports you hand over are kept in secure filing cabinets. You can then produce a written statement which will be harder to ignore than an oral request.

- Are your files secure? Can you see them from your desk, and are they locked up when you are not watching them? You might keep them in lockable filing cabinets or lock the door to your office overnight. This means keeping the keys somewhere secure, but ensuring there is access if you take a two week holiday or are run over by a bus.

- Attach electronic tags to files, similar to those used by retailers. This is very expensive and does not prevent the contents from being removed or photocopied.

- Access to the files. Some researchers refuse to allow any material to be removed from the research office, not even the reports. They provide a table and writing materials and may even insist on vetting any notes that are made from the files. For most departments this would be impractical. They produce reports which are designed to be read by highly placed colleagues who will insist on having the information on their desks. You can attempt to have a policy on who may read the files, but this is very difficult to enforce. If files are to be borrowed then you might consider the following measures:
  - Attach prominent labels to each file stating its owner, its confidentiality and the duties of the borrower. Alternatively acquire a large red ink stamp.
  - Place large notices above or on the filing cabinets stating that the material is confidential and responsibility for maintaining that confidentiality rests with the borrower.

- Maintain a log of borrowed files so that every so often you can round up outstanding ones. This helps guard against them being left around the office when the borrower no longer needs them.
- Tie contents into files. It is very easy for them to fall out or be deliberately removed and incorporated into somebody else's files. An alternative is to have a list of contents in the front of each file. These are time-consuming practices, and their value must be weighed against the importance of the contents. They do not prevent the borrower from photo-copying everything in the file.
- Separate confidential items from non-confidential. Users might not always need the confidential information. They might be quite content to browse through press cuttings, company announcements, etc., without seeing anything more. This is a laborious system to implement and main-tain, and might not prove practical if everyone wants the confidential information as well. However it can work if you regularly have visits from enquirers whose access should be restricted.

- Particularly sensitive information might be removed from the general files and stored in such a way that only the head of research has access to it. It might be in a password-protected file or in a locked drawer. This means its owner must always know which prospects are being consid-ered and must ensure that someone else can take over the responsibility in the event of a long holiday or maternity leave.

- Computer security. Even locking the door might not prevent access if your computer is networked. If computer hackers can gain access to top level military secrets then your system is not likely to be too much of a challenge. If the computer is not connected to anything else at all (in-cluding the Internet) then you are probably safe, otherwise it might be worth having its security features checked out. Even if you think you are only connected to an internal network, someone else on that net-work might be linked to the outside world. It is a good idea to change passwords regularly and not to stick them onto the computer itself!

- The photocopier. If your files can be borrowed it is difficult to keep a check on what is photocopied. Although there is little chance of it work-ing, you might wish to place a notice on or by each photocopier stating that research material should not be copied without authorisation. If nothing else, taking measures such as this raises the level of awareness amongst other staff and helps deflect the blame should a problem arise.

- When disposing of information such as draft reports or internal memos, shred it rather than throwing it into the bin. This is not to suggest that the cleaner will pull it out and sell it. The problem is that refuse is not stored safely under lock and key. A sack might split allowing your confidential report to float down the street. A scavenger might discover it at a land-fill site. Once it is out of your office you have no control over it whatsoever.

- Phone calls from friends. If you are known to hold a list of addresses, for example of alumni, you might have requests for details of long-lost friends. They are probably genuine, but you have no way of knowing who they are or why they want the information. It is safest to ask them to send a letter which you will forward, giving the recipient the choice of whether or not to hand over his address.

- Archiving. As a file becomes older will it be archived or shredded? Universities in particular might find that generations of the same family return as students. It might be tempting to keep old files, but you are unlikely to have the space for all of them with your active files. However, if they are handed over to an archivist outside your department you lose control of them. You might wish to insist that they are only viewed with your permission. Keep in contact with the archivist in case there is a change of personnel and the files are no longer given the security you would wish.

- Job changers. Be particularly wary of those who are moving to new jobs. They might wish to take some of the information with them to make their new jobs easier. This is totally wrong, not only because it was your institution which paid to gather the data, but also because contacts and the prospects themselves gave the information specifically to you and to no-one else. This is more of a problem in countries where it is standard to work a long period of notice. However there is nothing you can do about the period when you do not know that the employee is planning to leave.

- Swapping information with other institutions. Again this is not ethical unless the information is publicly available. It might be advantageous to both institutions but it breaches the individual's right to privacy.

- Temps and volunteers. Even those who are not full-time members of staff should be aware of and bound by the same ethical guidelines as you. The ideal is to prevent them from seeing anything which is at all sensitive, but this may well prove impossible. Even data entry provides access to personal information. Be aware of what they are doing, what access they have to sensitive information, and ensure they know their ethical responsibilities.

## Conclusion

After reading this list it might seem that some of the suggestions verge on paranoia rather than being reasonable precautions. It must be emphasised that the danger of a libel suit is not great, though the damage inflicted by one could be severe both financially and in terms of loss of reputation. Most leakages of sensitive information come from carelessness rather than deliberate intent. Non-researchers are less likely to be aware of, or concerned about, the dangers. It is simply more convenient to transfer information to your own less secure files and to carry a report with you so that you can read it just prior to the meeting. It is also very tempting to gather useful information to smooth the transition into a new job.

The ultimate solution to the problem of preventing the disclosure of confidential information is, of course, not to keep it in the first place. If you are a member of a professional body it will probably have an ethics statement, but little ability to enforce it. Ultimately these questions are matters for individual judgement. You must decide for yourself on the basis of your own morality, the degree of risk you are willing to take, and perhaps the advice of your organisation's lawyer.

# 5. Day to day Questions

## Forms

Research departments used to revolve around forms, but as computers take over there is less need for irritating mounds of paperwork. The database can contain basic factual information such as addresses, names of officers/trustees, giving record, turnover, cross-references to friends and family, etc. If everyone has access to it via the PC on their desk there is no need for them to be constantly rummaging in your files. If regular back-ups are made and the computer works well then the information will not be borrowed or lost as is frequently the case with paper files. It can also be manipulated to produce lists of major donors, most frequent contacts, people in your county, etc.

Similarly, when a phone call or visit is made brief details can be entered onto the database. Databases should be sufficiently sophisticated to grant restricted access to certain users so that they can enter data in some screens but not meddle with others. Nor should paper forms be necessary for research reports as the basic framework of headings can be stored on the PC and the report typed in around them.

In fact the forms still exist, but they are headings on a computer screen which prompt you to enter information via the keyboard. This means that responsibility for their content and structure tends to migrate to the database office; however there is no reason why the researcher should not be involved in their design.

Unfortunately many people are still nervous of new technology and are not proficient at using a keyboard. In the future it is likely that everyone will be computer literate, but for the moment you might have to accept the duplication of paper form-filling and data input.

### Research request forms

It is likely to be in your interests to insist that requests are made in writing, preferably on a standard form. (This can be a screen on your database or a paper form). The reasons are as follows:

- It makes the requesters think about precisely what they do want and why, rather than making vague requests on a momentary whim.

- It encourages the requesters to give you all the information they have about the prospect. If they are not specifically asked, every time, what they know, it is surprising how often they will not trouble to volunteer information. This might reflect laziness or a touching faith in your ability to discover anything for yourself, but it will generally make your job much easier to know everything from the start.

- There can be no dispute later about precisely what you were asked to do and when you were asked to do it.
- Requesters might like a copy returned with the finished report as they might well have forgotten what was asked for and why.
- It is more reliable than jottings made during a conversation, which might later mean nothing to you.
- A copy of the request can be kept in your file with the report, so that in future you will know what the report should and should not contain. Requesters might sit on a report for so long that it becomes out of date and then ask for it to be updated. By then they might require rather more information and you will need to know whether certain areas need more work than others.
- It is a record of how hard you work. If you produce reports for several people, each is likely to see only how slow you are at providing their work rather than how much work you do overall. Leafing through the request forms can counteract that impression.

A request form might ask the following questions:
- Who or what to be researched.
- Database reference if known.
- Type of detail required (e.g. full report, contacts and wealth, etc.).
- Name of requester.
- Purpose (e.g. prospect for a particular project, or contact for another prospect).
- Date requested (you might like to place this in a section for your own personal use if you find that forms are taking a long time to reach you, otherwise it appears that you have taken an inordinately long time).
- Date required.
- Degree of importance attached to it (urgent, moderate, low priority).
- Any information already known. This is very important. Leave plenty of room and suggest appending extra information if necessary. Otherwise you might spend ages in fruitless or costly searches only to find that the requester did not tell you a seemingly unimportant but vital piece of information.

At the end of the form you might like to have a section for your own use prompting you to enter details of interim action taken. If you have a large amount of work to do then not all requests can be dealt with immediately, but it speeds the process if you call straight away for slow-to-arrive information such as annual reports. You might also wish to have a section for date completed so that you can evaluate how well you are meeting the demand. It is useful to produce the form in a different colour so that it stands out in your files.

## Prioritisation

No matter how much you might want to meet the requirements of the requester, you are likely to be restrained by budget and time. Inevitably you will end up negotiating over the amount of time you can allocate and how soon you can do it. This can be very difficult when there are numerous people asking for work at the same time, as each does not necessarily understand or care about the priorities of the others. Questions to ask include:

- Who asked first? Your research request forms will give the date. Although seemingly the fairest way, other considerations might weigh more heavily.

- How important is the person who needs this work? If it is the head of the office she might not be willing to wait in line with everyone else.

- What is the likely return on the investment, i.e. is this a particularly important prospect, or is it a long shot with little money and no contacts?

- Does the requester normally ask for work without first considering how useful it will be? If so, this lessens the likelihood that any particular piece of work is very worthwhile.

- Would the requester be seriously embarrassed if he did not have this work by a certain date? From time to time anyone can be edged into a position where they promise something at short notice and it is in everyone's interests that you try to help them out. However if it happens frequently and is having a bad effect on the rest of your work then you need to put a stop to it.

- Would an abbreviated report do as a stop-gap until you have time to produce a fuller version?

The research request form is very useful in dealing with this problem. Each request should have been given a level of priority by the requester. This enables you to distinguish between those requests which are required for a meeting and those where the requester simply chose what seemed like a reasonable length of time for you to complete the work.

Another possibility for those who receive requests from several sources is to distribute a 'work in progress' list. The work is listed in the order in which you intend to do it, together with the initials of the requester, the date requested and the date required for. Ideally it should be distributed at a meeting where everyone has the chance to review it together. This has the following advantages:

- It enables everyone to see where their work is in your list of priorities and why they are not receiving it instantly. They would probably otherwise underestimate your total workload.

- It gives the requesters the option of upgrading the urgency of a piece of work if they can see that there is a lot ahead of it, or of downgrading it if there is more important work awaiting attention.

- Requesters are less likely to forget to tell you if they decide not to bother with a prospect after all.

- It helps the requesters to keep in touch with what their colleagues are doing. Some might feel uncomfortable with this, but they will probably find it difficult to provide an acceptable reason for not doing it. On the whole it should prove useful, especially where there is the chance that two requesters might have their sights on the same prospect.

- It gives others the chance to contribute information about prospects that are not their own. Neither you nor the requester may realise that someone else knows something about the prospect. They might be able to rule it out totally, saving you work.

- If the list is reviewed at a meeting the requesters must be prepared to justify their choice of prospects and priority in front of their peers. They might be willing to put pressure on a researcher in private, not caring that this will be to the detriment of work required by their colleagues; however when those colleagues can see what they are doing they tend to become rather more thoughtful. It is also possible that their superior will disapprove of their choice of prospects and veto some of them.

The main disadvantage of a 'work in progress' list is that it does not show the routine daily tasks which take up a substantial proportion of your time, such as press scanning and obtaining new resources. It can make you feel very exposed, as others can judge rather more easily how well you are performing. If you are about to try it for the first time then be ready for the suggestion that each piece of work is taking too long. Have a positive answer ready rather than a defensive refusal to change. Explain the scale of your other activities, that you are flexible enough to offer a choice of full or brief reports, and offer to reduce the quality in order to increase the through-put. This might seem a threat to your professionalism, but requesters who are used to high quality reports tend to like them and to prefer to keep them that way (provided they have the choice of shorter, faster reports when necessary). It also means that if (as inevitably happens) your research does not turn up a particular piece of information you can point to their preference for reduced thoroughness! You may well find that they complain about missing information and you end up returning to your original high quality reports.

## Presentation of reports

A well-presented report is more likely to impress its reader, whether that is a member of your organisation or an outside contact. The latter is particularly important: if the contact forms the impression that your organisation is professional and thorough then he is more likely to take it seriously. It is also likely that the better the report looks the more willing the reader will be to believe its contents are true. The following are matters you might like to consider:

- *Font* (i.e. shape of letters). The choice may be restricted by the capabilities of your printer. Remember that other people's eyesight may not be as good as yours, and choose a size they can read. If you have a laser printer look for a clear font that will permit you to justify the right as well as the left of the paragraph. This makes it seem more like a professional published work than a piece of typing. Some prefer to leave the right hand side unjustified as this makes it easier to read, but so long as you have plenty of breaks (paragraphs, headings, etc.) and a clear print it should be acceptable.

- *Headings.* These are essential to helping the reader find information quickly and very useful for forcing you to structure the information well. Similar types of report should use the same basic headings (so long as they permit some leeway for unanticipated peculiarities) as this makes them easier to use. Within the standard divisions you might like to introduce your own sub-headings which sum up the contents of each paragraph enabling the reader to flick through quickly. You might also use bullet points or pick out keywords in bold. However do not do this simply for the sake of it: if you are not good at picking out the key point of a paragraph then it is better not to use headings than to write whatever comes to mind. Readers can use a highlighter pen if they wish.

A common fault is to have so many headings that the reader loses the overall drift of the text. Ensure that major headings stand out from sub-headings and be prepared to abandon them if your readership does not like them.

- *Spacing.* This should be consistent, i.e. the same amount of space between similar sections, with extra lines to emphasise divisions between major sections.

- *Cover.* Unless the report is very short, a front cover is a useful means of protecting confidentiality. If it is left lying on a desk or carried to a meeting the cover ensures that the contents of the report are not on public display. If the report is for an important person a simple comb binding machine and board covers can produce a smart finish very cheaply. Beware of using the organisation's logo before you have checked that this is all right, as your report might look so professional that it could give the impression of having official top-level sanction. Alternatively you might simply use an ordinary piece of paper. This looks rather bare at first, but can easily be filled up with a picture of the prospect (if a person) or key directors. You should also include the following information:

  - *'Strictly Confidential'.* You are likely to include information which has been passed to you in confidence, or opinions which might embarrass your organisation or affect its chances of success with the prospect. You might also consider that you have a duty towards the prospect to ensure that he is not publicly embarrassed.

  - *The prospect's name.*

  - *The requester's name.* The prospect might come up in a different context, so it is useful to know who is dealing with him.

  - *Your name.* The requester can then come back to you if there is something which is not clear or a point which could be elaborated on. She might even wish to congratulate you on your work or fill you in on the progress of the approach. It is also likely to motivate your fellow researchers to be more careful and take more pride in their work if their names are on the reports rather than an all-embracing departmental name.

-     *The date of writing.* All information should be dated as it is constantly becoming out of date.

- *Endnotes.* As no information can be guaranteed 100% accurate, it makes sense to source your work as closely as possible. Every statement, paragraph or heading (as appropriate) can end with a superscript number referring to a list at the end of the report. This list should mention not only the source but also the date. This enables both you and the reader to evaluate the reliability of the information. A newspaper article might have been correct at the time it was written, but if that was three years ago you cannot guarantee that it is still accurate. You can make the source list more complete by adding a separate section for those sources which were checked but provided no information. This means that if you are asked to elaborate on or update the report you do not end up checking everything twice.

Sourcing also means that if the report does end up in the hands of the prospect it is possible to justify whatever you have said. Although this does not entirely absolve you it might mollify the prospect a little. If you are quoting a national newspaper then, although you might have repeated a libel, at least it can be shown that you had a reason other than maliciousness for what you have said. If a statement seems particularly likely to offend then quote the source directly within the body of the report so as to distance yourself from it further.

# Feedback

It can be very disheartening to feel that your reports disappear into a black hole never to be seen again. The requesters might be very appreciative of them, but not realise how important it is that they say so. It is therefore a good idea for researchers and requesters to have regular meetings. The requesters should be asked for feedback on the reports, good or bad, whether the structure is useful and the information correct, and whether contacts who have seen them have passed any comments. Although you might not like to hear bad comments, it is better to have the opportunity to put things right rather than have complaints behind your back. It is also important for the requester to update the researchers on how the approach is proceeding. After writing a report researchers almost feel they know the prospect and are likely to be fascinated to hear more and to know whether their deductions proved correct. They will then return with more enthusiasm to their work, feeling that they are making a valuable contribution.

# Press scanning

It would be easy for the researcher to allow this task to take over. It undoubtedly has its uses but should not be an excuse for not finding time to write reports. You might look for the following:

- *Updated information on prospects.* There is often a long gap between the preparation of the report and the eventual conclusion of the approach, during which time the report will need to be supplemented with updated information. If possible, obtain a regularly updated list of current and potential prospects. You can then send the relevant articles to whoever is interested in them. You might also send information to your database team.

- *New prospects for consideration.* This is often seen as one of the more important products of press scanning. You might send suggestions to the member of staff who is most likely to act on them, or build up your own file in anticipation of being asked to supply new prospects en masse. A prospect might be someone who has a tie with your institution and sufficient wealth, celebrity or power to be of use to it. Alternatively the prospect might exhibit characteristics or interests which match yours.

- *Potential prospects for your files.* You are unlikely to be able to anticipate the list of prospects two or three years ahead; however it would be nice when a new request comes in to have something already in the files. It might also be the case that requesters like to browse through files of press cuttings to see whether vague ideas are worth pursuing. You might even find that your information is used as a general resource by a much wider range of people (although they can get under your feet this is probably worth encouraging as it means your funding is safer). You might therefore wish to develop a policy of filing information on wealthy people and top companies which are not currently prospects.

- *Information on your institution and competitors.* This might be placed on a central noticeboard. If you choose to circulate weekly press cuttings you can be more certain that everyone gets to see them, but they will probably be out of date after sitting in someone's in-tray for too long.

If your time and storage space is limited and press scanning is taking over, what can you do about it?

- *Limit yourself to 10 articles per newspaper.* This will focus your mind on what is really important. You can easily become carried away with collecting information on any major company or wealthy person you come across, but the time and space cannot be so readily justified if there is no guarantee they will ever become prospects.

- *Is the balance of papers correct?* Ideally you probably need a mixture of heavy-weight company reporting, more light-weight interviews with people, and local interest. If you are reading similar papers you will find a great deal of repetition. Even the best newspapers cut costs by having a team of staff reporters re-write press releases. If you must read overlapping papers you might like to concentrate on analytical sections written by senior staff, e.g. the *Financial Times'* 'Lex' column.

- *Can someone else read them?* The requesters should read a newspaper themselves as no matter how efficient you are at sending them press cuttings they will gain something by looking through it too. Many people would consider it a perk to be expected to spend some of their working day reading a paper and would do it at home anyway. Moving from that to marking the occasional article for their PAs to cut is not a particularly difficult step. However they might cover only their personal set of interests and persuading them to think of other staff too might prove difficult. One solution is to have everyone reading a paper. Also be aware that they might decide they are too busy and tell their PAs to scan the paper for them. Even if the PAs are able to work out which articles are important, they might lack the overview to provide a useful service to the entire office.

- *Can you create a computer index instead?* (See the section on your own databank, below). This works better for journals than newspapers as the latter deteriorate, have shorter articles, and are more bulky. Ideally you should keep the original journal so that the index need only contain a basic reference directing you back to the original for the full details. This means an overall heading giving name and date of the journal, followed by a list of relevant names with page numbers and possibly 'p' for photo. It can be tempting to summarise the article; however if you spend too much time reading and abstracting articles then you do not gain anything by not cutting and filing them. You might never need the article again, and if you do you are likely to be doing detailed research which involves reading it thoroughly making the summary worthless.

- *Would it be sufficient to use online sources instead?* Many papers (though less frequently regional and gossipy ones) are available almost immediately through online databases. There is sometimes a day or two delay, though some are online before they are on the streets. (CD-ROMs are much slower because of the time taken to produce and distribute them.

They also contain a relatively narrow range of information.) You must be very sure that no-one is going to object to you not maintaining all the files before you take this step as it is difficult to change your mind once committed. Is anyone interested in parts of the press which are not online? Sometimes items like obituaries and announcements of marriages are not included. You must also be willing to respond quickly to an increased volume of requests for online searches which would previously not have been referred to you at all. How large will this be? There are cost implications in using the online databases more often. These should be set against the cost of hiring another person or the value of the increased number of reports you are able to produce once freed from press scanning.

## File maintenance

- *Who does it?* This is a task for which you should have clerical assistance. A properly trained researcher's time is too valuable to be spent on routine filing, and it would be demotivating to do it.

- *Photocopy or cut?* You might decide to cut out the articles and paste them onto a sheet of paper (press cuttings would otherwise crumple and become difficult to store); however this method has the problem that the paper deteriorates and the newsprint comes off on your hands. Photocopies are much cleaner and easier to handle; however you must be aware that unless your organisation has an arrangement which permits it to do this you may be in breach of copyright (which is illegal). There is some leeway, for example educational establishments have more scope for copying. If you make one photocopy per article and then throw away the original you might argue there is little effective difference between this and cutting the original. If you make several copies you have no excuse. Although copyright law is not easy to enforce, you must be conscious of the potential consequences. There are various books on the subject, e.g. *The Aslib Guide to Copyright*.

- *Method of storage.* Insufficient storage space is frequently a problem. The most space-efficient method is high banks of suspension files, though these pose more of a fire-hazard and often cannot be locked (though some can). If they are too high there is the danger of injury to staff who may be shorter or less physically able than you and find difficulty in reaching the top. You must also be sure that the cabinets will not topple over through filling them from the top or clutching them for support when on a stool. Old-fashioned filing cabinets take up more space and are more laborious to open and close but enable you to lock away confidential information.

- *File organisation*. You might decide to arrange files by number, giving each new one the next number in the sequence (possibly its database reference number), and simply slotting it in at the end. This means you do not end up trying to squeeze them into the middle and periodically respacing the entire series; however it slows down routine filing. It is probably easier to have straightforward alphabetical sequences for people, companies, industries, countries, etc. There will probably be numerous solitary items which do not merit their own file and these can be placed in an alphabetical sequence at the beginning of each letter section.

  Binding each sheet into its file means they are safer from deliberate or accidental removal but takes longer to do. You might decide to save time by simply leaving them loose within the file and if something is missing searching online, especially if you would anyway always look online when you write a report.

## Company financial statements

Most public companies will happily add you to their mailing list in the hope that you will invest in them. These financial statements make the task of writing reports much easier and as they might take a couple of weeks to arrive it is a good idea to build up a library of them in anticipation. However, although they are generally free they are not inexpensive to collect. It can take a long time to send out requests, even if you set up a mail-merge with a standard letter. It also costs a fair amount in terms of postage, telephone costs, and stationery. Once you have received the first report you cannot simply hope that they will continue to arrive in future years. Some companies do not keep mailing lists, some insist that you regularly confirm you still want the report, and some simply lose your details.

## Updating the information on the database

The actual inputting should be the responsibility of someone other than a trained researcher, though it is helpful if you have the ability to update occasional items as you come across them. Where you can have a role to play is in providing sources of new information for the database. These might be any of the following:

- *Research reports.* Only some of the information can be stored on the database. Databases require factual information which can be placed under standard headings. Research reports contain a lot of detail and analysis which would not fit. The only possibility is to insert large amounts of free text, which is generally not feasible. Many systems insist that each record must be of the same length, so in order to accommodate the information known about a few prospects the majority of records would end up with large amounts of unused space and the system would run out of storage capacity. In the UK, as in several other countries, there is the added problem of a Data Protection Act. Owners of databases must justify the type of data they hold to the Data Protection Registrar and may not hold anything which is opinion rather than fact. Anyone may ask to see the information which is held about them. Although this affects your word-processed documents too, your database manager is likely to be particularly careful.

- *Directories.* You might perhaps obtain who's whos, business directories, etc., with the intention of enhancing your database. The inputters would systematically work through them looking for, for example, alumni of your university, or people who are already on your database in case you do not have an up-to-date address. However the wholesale transfer of data might provoke the publisher to complain that you are in breach of his copyright. Some publishers specifically reassure their biographees that they will not sell mailing lists, knowing that they might otherwise not receive the information. Some insert phantom entries and wait to see whether they receive any junk mail.

- *The press.* You might come across obituaries, changes of directors, detailed interviews, etc.

- Asking your constituents to fill in *biographical forms.* One way of doing this is by straightforwardly sending out a form to everyone on the mailing list. You must judge for yourself how much information you can reasonably ask for. This depends on the strength of the tie with your institution (e.g. university alumni might fill in quite a detailed form, while people whose details were obtained by buying a mailing list might be quite insulted by it). It also depends on national attitudes towards privacy, especially in areas such as wealth. If your database is complex enough to distinguish between sources or types of record you might send out different types of forms to different constituencies. One way of encouraging the return of these is by providing a useful service, such as a free catalogue, social events, information pack or glossy magazine, which might be partially funded by advertising or sponsorship. It is probably worth making it clear that this information will not be sold to any other organisation as a mailing list.

Once you have a reasonably informative database you can analyse it. You can pull out those who look wealthy for special attention, target a specific industry (since key players are likely to know and even be influenced by each other), and segment the remainder of the list so that your mass mailings are more precisely targeted (e.g. people in their 50s are asked to give more than those in their 20s, while people in their 60s are offered help in making their wills). You could also employ a profiling company to match your database against its own and provide a list of people who share important characteristics with your supporters (e.g. some occupations might be considered to indicate a greater interest in the environment). See chapter 6 for further information on using a database to find prospects.

## Creating your own databank

There are numerous sources which are not indexed and other pieces of information which could usefully be pulled together into a single source. If you have the resources you might wish to create your own personal databank of information. This is not an essential task, and should only be considered if you have a clerical assistant with sufficient time to spare. The sort of material you might include is up to you, but the following are suggestions:

- *Charitable donations to other organisations.* This helps you gain an idea of the prospect's charitable interests. In the US there are publications which will cover this area quite well, but for most countries these do not exist or are far from complete. Details can be found in a variety of publications: fund-raising magazines, the local press and the mainstream press. However not all of these are available online and finding them again could be laborious. You could cut and file every single reference, but this is laborious in comparison with simply indexing them on your computer. The index need only be a basic list, each section headed with the name and date of the source, followed by a list of the prospects and organisations mentioned. Ideally you should keep the original journals so that you can refer back to the full details.

- *Society press.* Magazines which specialise in glossy pictures of society ladies attending parties might seem at first sight to be a waste of time. However they can provide a picture of the prospect, an indication of who she knows, and details of her interests or which charities she supports (though they might merely be along for the party). They might even have a large spread on your prospect's home and family. These magazines are rarely available online and are unlikely to have their own indexes. It is thus worth creating your own.

- *Book indexes.* Some books, notably biographies, foundation directories and company histories, contain references to large numbers of potential prospects. Although they have their own indexes, it would take a long time to pull them all off the shelf, and you might not remember to do so. If you scan these indexes onto your computer you can search them all quickly and effortlessly, referring to the books only if a reference comes up.

- *File indexes.* You are not likely to remember every file you have, so end up trekking to and from the files to see whether there is anything there. An alternative is to keep lists of your file series on the computer so that they can be checked quickly along with everything else in the databank. You might include the name of the prospect together with the date of any research report and, if a company, the date of the most recent financial statement received. This has the added benefit that you are sure to notice when a file is missing.

- *Named posts.* Universities often commemorate their donors by appending their names to the posts they have funded. These named posts frequently crop up in job adverts in the educational press (e.g. *The Times Higher Education Supplement* in the UK and *The Chronicle of Higher Education* in the US). They do not generally give more than the name of the post, the institution, and the field of work, but over a number of years it can build up to a useful overview of philanthropy in the educational sector.

- *Event attendees.* Some institutions hold large garden parties, dinners, etc., and it is important that good records are kept of who was invited, whether or not they accepted the invitation, and (if possible) whether they actually turned up. Ideally this should be on their main database records rather than your databank.

- *Information from your own institution.* Before the arrival of the prospect research team it is unlikely that all relevant information was kept in one central location. It is therefore a vital part of your job to find and collate this information. It might consist of records of regular employers of graduates, gifts or other contacts dating back many years and possibly held by whichever section of the institution happened to have been involved, without any central co-ordination. This might involve acquiring other departments' file lists and scanning them into your computer, or even indexing some of their old files. It is always immensely embarrassing to meet a prospect and discover that you are unaware of his previous contacts with your organisation. It leaves the prospect with the impression that your organisation is either incompetent or ungrateful.

Do not forget to collect information from those you work with most closely. Anyone who meets prospects will gather further information, for example they might suggest new lists of prospects and provide useful details. It is no use leaving this information in someone's head or buried in the files, even if both seem accessible. In a short while memory will fail or the person will move to a new job and you will have nothing to remind you that a prospect has been considered before and that there is a good contact. Ideally every letter, phone call, meeting or fax should be logged on the relevant prospect's database record, and everybody should provide you with a list of prospects and any new names which have been suggested.

- *Lists of famous graduates.* A university would find it useful to build these up over the years as they can be used for publicity, fund-raising brochures, etc. A long-established university might have separate lists for living and dead graduates and possibly for women (as it is often harder to find notable women). The draw-back of these lists is that they are very difficult to keep up to date, so they might be best viewed as a list of suggestions which should be checked before use. They might be compiled from histories of the university, directories, press scanning, comments from contacts, etc. Although they are not of a huge amount of use when searching for other prospects, the tendency for families to have a tradition of attending the same university might mean you come up with notable relatives.

- *Names in published lists:* rich lists, highest paid directors, etc. These can refer you to the actual article which will give the full details, e.g. level of wealth.

How should you structure your databank? If you have a good word-processing package such as WordPerfect or Word and a reasonably modern computer then this is very simple. Each list is placed in its own document within one huge directory. In WordPerfect you would call up that directory and use the 'find' command listed at the bottom of the screen. In Word you would use 'find file' within the file menu, and the 'special search' option. Either will permit you to scan the entire directory in a single search. In both cases you have to ensure that you are searching all files and the entire contents of those files rather than their names. Alternatively you might choose to create a spreadsheet. Rather than straightforward lists you might wish to place donations under headings to bring together all those connected with medicine, welfare, etc. You can still search this sort of list for individual names, but you have the option of searching for potential prospects with an interest in a particular field.

## Getting out and about

Who should speak to the contact? In a larger office there is likely to be a division between researchers and the solicitation staff who are responsible for liaising with the prospects. Volunteers have valuable information to give, yet they are often prospects in their own right. Like any other prospect they need to be 'chatted up', encouraged and entertained, which is more the solicitation staff's area of expertise.

One solution is for solicitation and research staff to visit the volunteer together, however this involves costly duplication of effort. The researcher loses a substantial part of the day in travelling and listening to general chat which prevents him from doing desk research. As there are likely to be more solicitation staff than researchers, a task which takes a reasonable proportion of the former's time could totally swamp the latter.

It must be asked whether there is any reason why solicitation staff should not be capable of questioning and recording information themselves. They have to see the volunteer anyway, and if they are sent out with a series of questions and a notepad they should be able to manage. As they are the users of the research they should have a good understanding of the information required.

Perhaps the researcher could meet the volunteer occasionally so as to establish a relationship which enables him to ring and clarify or enlarge on comments recorded by colleagues. Alternatively he could prepare an interim research report and send it to the volunteer for corrections and additions; hard facts often provoke more useful responses than open-ended questions.

Researchers might feel that they will find themselves redundant if they take this line, but that would be to devalue the highly skilled desk research that they should be doing and which certainly could not be done effectively by the solicitation staff. Even the most willing volunteers tend to make vague statements and have faulty memories, which means that their information needs to be distilled and verified by thorough desk research before it can be used. It is pleasant to escape the office, travel and meet people, but time is limited and should be used to best effect. However, if the solicitation staff prove to be unreliable at recording information (and they might justifiably feel that they cannot develop the relationship properly if they are scribbling furiously all the way through a meeting) then it might be best to send a researcher too.

## Keeping up with change

You can never stop looking for new resources as sources and techniques change so rapidly. You might also find the requirements of your job alter as a new geographical area is taken on. Keep up to date through fund-raising magazines and by putting yourself on the mailing lists of major publishers. You might also pay the occasional visit to major libraries to see whether they have any interesting new books.

There is a great temptation to sit back on your laurels when a long search for a particular foreign who's who is eventually successful; however this is not a good idea. Unfortunately who's whos are often produced by small national publishers and it is by no means uncommon for them to go out of business, or simply decide to stop publishing because the first edition was not profitable enough. Look out for small distributors in your own country as they too will feel the difference when a book disappears and try to replace it. They might also recommend similar books.

Electronic information is particularly fast-moving. The major online hosts acquire new databases virtually every month and are constantly improving the facilities available on their systems. The Internet is likely to change dramatically over the next few years; already it is possible to see the beginnings of many services which will shortly be of tremendous value, especially if its speed can be improved. Try to attend electronic information exhibitions, such as the one held at London's Olympia every December, to ensure that you are up to date with all the latest products.

## Obtaining books

This might appear straightforward, but is a little more complex than might be anticipated. Should you obtain your own books or let someone else do it for you? How long will it take? How do you distinguish the good books from the bad?

Obtaining books is time-consuming. Even if you have the publisher's details, you have to check when the next edition is due out. If you are in fund-raising you might negotiate a discount or ask for damaged copies. You might also need to wait for the postage costs to be calculated (which for overseas books will often have to be worked out especially for you). Unless you go to the expense of airmail, postage from overseas can take several weeks. This is on top of the publisher's normal despatch processing time which is likely to be a week or two.

Rather than order direct you can arrange for a bookshop or agent to obtain the books for you. You may well have to provide details of the publishers yourself as prospect research books come from such a wide range of obscure sources. Even so this can save you large amounts of time and eliminate costs such as postage and obtaining cheques in foreign currencies. However you lose contact with the publishers and the opportunities to ask for discounts, suggest improvements to the books, and find out about new books they publish.

It is this last point which really matters because finding information sources is as vital a part of prospect research as any other. The range of books available is constantly changing: not only are there new books which could save you a great deal of research time, but existing ones can cease publication, publishers go out of business, etc., leaving you to find replacements. The demands on the prospect researcher are constantly changing: a book which once you discounted as irrelevant might two years later be just what you need, yet how do you find it again if you don't have the publishers' catalogues? Because the prospect researcher's needs are so unusual and there are as yet few departments geared up to international research there is not likely to be any publication or agent that will suggest anything other than the more obvious sources. It is thus very important to be constantly looking for new sources yourself.

It is also important to be aware that not all publishers have the same goals in mind. Some set very high standards for the quality of their reference materials, while others are more motivated by profit. First editions are often not as good as updates. There is far more work to be done in producing the first edition, and the length of time it takes might be underestimated. There is also no certainty that the book will make a profit, so the publisher might be less inclined to take a risk and go over-budget in producing it. It is not unknown to find a who's who that starts off with large numbers of As and Bs, but tails off towards the end of the alphabet because there was not enough time to finish it. Rich lists are likely to provoke rather more complaints in their first edition because subsequent versions are corrected in response to the outcry. However it is often the case that there is no alternative to a particular book, and as there is never any guarantee that there will be a second edition you cannot afford not to buy it.

Another problem is the existence of publishers which play to the vanity of the public. They make money by selling who's whos and associated products to the people listed in them. This means that their selection criteria are unlikely to be as rigorous. They ask that you state whether you wish to buy the book at the same time as you send in your biographical details, which makes it difficult to tell on what basis they decide to include you. Once you have appeared in one publication they might deluge you with offers to be included in other books, to purchase certificates, plaques, medallions, etc. You might be awarded the title 'Ambassador of the World' or invited to a conference, all at considerable cost to yourself.

If you are not a biographee and wish to avoid buying such books it can prove difficult to work out in advance which they are. Reputable publishers try to dissociate themselves from their less rigorous colleagues by stating that they have independent selection boards and never link inclusion with payment. Unfortunately there is nothing to stop anyone else from saying this too. They are more likely to encourage people to be included and buy the book if they say that each person was specially chosen and that it is a great honour, rather than that inclusion depends purely on payment. Finding the book in a public library is no guarantee either. Being offered inclusion when you ring up to ask the publication date is one clear signal (though this is by no means always the case). You might get an impression by looking at the occupations of a sample of the entrants. Less reliable is checking for people who you think ought to be included; their presence might be a deliberate ploy to add credibility to an otherwise poor selection, while their absence might mean that a reputable publisher has respected their wish for privacy. Another potential indication is that a series of books is cumulative, i.e. that the majority of people in one edition do not appear in the next. There might be a genuine reason for building up a series in this way, but it might also be connected with the fact that buying a copy of a book which mentions you is a novelty the first time, but less appealing the second.

Becoming a biographee in one of these books has its merits, such as the amusement value of their latest sales gimmick and the opportunity to buy the book at a reduced price. Despite their faults, these books do have some value. If you have a limited budget and need information on the top people in society, then they are not the first books to choose. However, if you have the standard reference works and wish to broaden the scope of your library, they will contain many otherwise unknown people, which can be particularly useful if you are involved in mass mailings. Alternatively, you might be interested in a section of the population which is not so heavily represented in other publications, for example, women, musicians or writers.

In some instances there are alternative who's whos which claim to cover the same ground. If your budget can stretch to it then it is probably worth either obtaining all of them or else rotating your purchases in successive years rather than ignoring some altogether. This is because publishers are likely to use different selection criteria and have differing degrees of success in implementing them. How would you find the 10,000 most interesting people in Europe and how would you persuade them that they wanted to be listed in your book? Something as straightforward as a different language can be a real barrier for some publishers. In reality publishers appear to sneak a look at competitors' books in case they have missed anyone, which means that once someone appears in one book they will appear in others.

It is frequently the case that a who's who will have a bias towards one nationality or racial group. This might be explained by the fact that this group is economically and politically dominant, hence viewed as more important. In an international publication it might be that there is more information available from a particular country or that it is easier for the publisher to obtain (and understand) information from its own country. One of the more commonly seen biases is towards the US.

No matter how large your budget it is most unlikely that you will be able to afford every book you see. If you are starting a new library it is vital that you plan your purchases carefully as you could easily find that your money has totally disappeared and you are left with patchy coverage. In the first year you might wish to focus on your home country or region and buy some more overarching books for the rest of the world. In subsequent years you can build on this foundation by allowing the less essential books to become slightly out of date while you extend the range. In the meantime you can fill in the gaps by dipping into online news and company databases.

Unless you must have the book instantly then check when the next edition is due out as this information might not be volunteered. The combined delay of requesting and obtaining a cheque (pre-payment is the norm) and waiting for the publisher to process the order and despatch the book might mean that by the time you obtain it there is only a short wait before the next edition becomes available.

The final prices should be checked before purchase. Some prices are inclusive of postage and packaging while others might add on 20% or more of the cost, and all will vary depending on which country you are in. You might even find that the book is cheaper for you as an overseas purchaser because you do not pay the local tax. Prices also vary (sometimes quite dramatically) as exchange rates fluctuate.

Some publishers demand payment in their own currency, while others will convert the price into sterling or dollars which means you don't have to pay for a foreign cheque. Some countries, notably continental European ones, might confuse you by using a full stop rather than a comma between the thousands and hundreds.

It is important to keep good records of what has been ordered as by the time it arrives you are likely to have forgotten the details. It is extremely unusual for publishers in any country not to send the books you order (though they can take a very long time about it), but as you normally have to pay in advance it is sensible to have a system which enables you to check that everything paid for is received.

# Being 'pro-active'

If prospect researchers are to be viewed as respected professionals rather than clerical support it is important that they make a positive contribution to the development of strategy. Researchers should not simply do as they are told without question; they should be constantly evaluating their performance and whether improvements can be made in their methods or those of the office as a whole.

However the term 'pro-active' has become so popular that a manager may demand it without knowing what to expect. The result is a puzzled researcher and a dissatisfied manager. If you are faced with this demand it is possible that you are already pro-active, but that it has not been recognised as most of your colleagues do not have a very clear idea of the full extent of your job. Exhortations to be pro-active might reflect the frustration of colleagues who are unsuccessful in dealing with their existing list of prospects or in finding new ones. They are turning their attention on you to solve their problems because they cannot do so themselves. If this is the case then focus for a while on finding new prospects (see chapter 6 on this). It might alternatively simply mean that the term sounds rather good and your manager hopes that invoking it will somehow provoke a magical change, though without knowing how.

The best response to problems is often to be positive. Rather than worrying fruitlessly about what is wanted make a list of what you are already doing. Submit this to your manager, asking for any suggestions that you have not considered. You might include items such as the ways in which you find new prospects (see chapter 6 on this for ideas), work on upgrading the content of the database, the steps you are taking to find new resources and improve the training of your staff, and how you liaise with colleagues to ensure that the department is as responsive to their needs as possible. Also include on-going links with colleagues such as discussing approaches to prospects or keeping them up to date on press coverage of prospects. The reports themselves are pro-active in suggesting projects and avenues of approach.

Don't get carried away with providing impressive services without analysing their value in comparison with alternative ways of spending time and money. For example, there are services which tell you when people have sold a huge volume of shares. In theory this provides a pool of prospects who have suddenly acquired a lot of money. However have you actually checked how many of these people are approached, or how many approaches are successful? Perhaps your colleagues prefer to use different sources so that they can be sure of having contacts? In this case you might redeploy your resources into an area they do find useful. Perhaps they need you to analyse the names further and provide an easy list of the ones in their geographical or business area, or those with whom there are good contacts? Similarly you can do surveys of how much use is being made of other types of information. Showing that you are performing cost-benefit analyses can look impressive (so long as it does not become too costly of your time to be worthwhile).

# Matching your output to the requirements of the requesters

From the beginning you should aim to be constantly responsive to the needs of the requesters. It is no use producing a beautifully prepared report if all they wanted was a quick response about a small piece of information.

There are advantages to designing a standard report layout. It helps the researcher organise the information, ensures that different researchers are producing similar reports, and helps the requester to go straight to the required piece of information. However standardisation should not go so far that it becomes inflexibility. The requester is likely to have different needs in different situations.

Does the requester want an in-depth analysis of the prospect prior to a carefully planned approach? Or is an overview of numerous guests at a reception required so that key points can be quickly assimilated just beforehand? Is it certain that the prospect is a good one, or is it just one of many vague suggestions to be checked out quickly? If the latter is the case it might be worth providing basic run-downs of who or what the prospects are, whether they have the capacity to be of use to you, and what contacts you have with them.

If the requester thinks these brief reports look hopeful then you might go on to produce full reports. It might turn out that the requester was thinking of someone else or was totally misinformed, and you would thus have saved yourself valuable time.

One solution might be to group the reports into categories. You might thus have a standard set of headings and procedures for a full report on a person, a set for a brief 'contacts and wealth' report, etc. There might also be the option of a booklet of briefing notes for occasions when the requester has to meet numerous prospects in a short space of time. This does not rule out the need for flexibility when a specific request does not fit into any pattern, but it helps both researchers and requesters to know what they are doing.

Patterns should be agreed with the requesters. Once set they should be re-viewed regularly to ensure that they are as good in practice as they were in theory and that there are no new requirements or amendments that would suit better. The requester might have realised that contacts prefer the information presented in a slightly different order, or might like to give more prominence to a particular section.

There should also be the option to amend reports for different readerships. This involves considering whether parts are too confidential or too blunt for a particular reader, who might be a friend of the prospect. The requester might prefer that all such material is extracted and placed in an appendix for the requester's eyes only. If so this is better placed at the front of the report, as if it is at the back it can easily be forgotten and handed over with the rest. Alterna-tively you might be asked to adapt the report at a later date. This is an impor-tant consideration and is better viewed as a challenging opportunity for you to practise your tact than as a nuisance.

# 6. Finding the Prospects

If you already know who or what you wish to research then this section is not for you. However, if you have been asked to find a list of the 50 best prospects and do not know where to start then read on.

The first thought of the inexperienced prospect-seeker is likely to be along the lines of: "Bill Gates has a lot of money – let's approach him". It is easy to find a list of wealthy people (e.g. the *Sunday Times* rich list), but everyone else knows the same names. These people are bombarded with approaches so are less likely to respond. This does not mean you should give up with them, but they are not necessarily the best prospects.

Some researchers distinguish between prospects and suspects. The latter are those who you suspect might become useful prospects. Rather than complicate the issue, the distinction is not used in this book.

## What is a prospect?

Ideally a prospect should have some or all of the following characteristics:

- Wealth, power, or influence
- Celebrity status (their influence can make up for lack of money)
- An existing link with your organisation (e.g. a business partner, a graduate of your university, a donor, etc.)
- An interest in your organisation's aims and activities (even if the prospect has never heard of you, attitudes and activities can suggest a possible interest)
- A desire or need that you can meet (even if it is merely a desire for social acceptability).

## Contacts and advocates (volunteers)

When looking for prospects you should also be looking out for contacts. These are friends of your organisation who are willing to help by suggesting new prospects, providing inside information about prospects, arranging introductions, and ideally approaching the prospects themselves. It is likely to be much easier to gain access to a prospect through a personal introduction, while if the approach itself is made by a respected friend an audience and a favourable

71

response are more likely. Contacts might be major donors, members of a fund-raising committee, or business associates.

It takes rather more than wealth or prominence to make a good contact, there must also be commitment. This might be exhibited by attendance at your social events, or donations (even if small) over a number of years. People who do not show these features might still, with encouragement, make good contacts; however it would take more time and effort to find these people amongst the mass who are too busy or uninterested, and time is not necessarily in plentiful supply.

There is no clear distinction between a prospect and a contact. Contacts are generally supporters in their own right, and indeed the more they have done for you the more effective they are in approaching others. One of the first questions prospects are likely to ask of the contacts is what commitment they themselves have made. Some organisations will not use contacts who are not themselves committed to helping in a major way because they do not consider that prospects would take them seriously. The larger the commitment, the more they can ask of others.

Contacts need to overcome the reserve that many people have when talking about money or asking for favours. This is more of a problem in the UK than the US, especially in the field of fund-raising. It can surprise Americans to discover just how embarrassed the British can become even when attempting to advocate an indisputably good cause. The result is that good intentions can evaporate when the moment arrives or the message can become lost because it is not stated with sufficient clarity and force. Coaching can help, and the spread of modern professional fund-raising is creating a pool of effective volunteers who are picked up by one charity after another. Even so, it is worth looking at the attributes of successful contacts and seeking similar people; for example, some of the best advocates are self-made men who are not afraid to be seen as 'pushy'. They might have undergone some life experience (such as war or the death of a loved one) which imprinted itself so deeply on them that your cause is an integral part of their life. Alternatively they might be society ladies who make good causes their life's work.

## Sifting through your database

Your organisation's existing network of contacts can generally throw up some useful names. Even if they have never before been considered as prospects, they are probably the people who will most readily give you some time when you are starting from scratch. If they are no use as prospects in their own right they should be able to suggest new prospects and advise on the chances of success.

When faced with a huge database of names how do you extract the most interesting ones? This depends on the type of data you already have, the tools which are available for your geographical area, your budget and the amount of time available. Some very elaborate ways of screening have been devised, for example checking every name for hits on online databases and filling in a form for each, then an overall spreadsheet. This might be satisfying, but it is very costly and time-consuming, not to mention mind-numbing. Always keep in mind that an outside company might be able to do a mass screening faster and cheaper than you.

Scoring them on wealth might seem an obvious starting point. However you should also take into account factors indicating a likelihood of success, e.g. attendance at receptions, donations, committee membership, age of prospect, or your ability to acquire an introduction. Some examples of useful factors and how to obtain them are given below.

- *Commercial screening.* In the US this is a relatively easy and common practice. Various companies or fund-raising consultants maintain their own databases of lifestyle or personal information. They might be facts about named individuals or assumptions based on the expenditure or socio-economic profile patterns of the neighbourhood. They might be drawn from mailing lists gathered for direct marketing, or from public record information, e.g. the census (typical education level etc. in a neighbourhood), court records (divorce, inheritance, bankruptcy) or car registration lists (scale of expenditure). Some lists claim to contain just millionaires. The screener will cross-refer your names and addresses with its own list and pull out those it considers the best prospects.

  Such companies can be found through advertisements and product listings in prospect research, direct marketing or fund-raising journals. They are more widely used in the US than elsewhere as there is more statutory disclosure, research budgets are bigger, and more companies are willing to gather and sell information.

  Although screening is a useful way of deciding where to concentrate your effort, the data should not be used without further research to check which prospects are unsuitable. Someone who is being sued or is approaching bankruptcy might appear on such lists because widespread press coverage has made his database record easier to fill in. There will also be potential prospects who are missed because they give a business address rather than a home address (which unfortunately often tends to be the case with wealthier people). Do not do a screening before you obtain a major batch of new addresses, e.g. from the latest intake of students.

A slightly different version of this technique is to pull out those people who are both on the commercial database and notable donors to the client. The database will contain tens or even hundreds of characteristics for each person, and it will amalgamate them to come up with a typical profile of the ideal prospect. This profile can then be matched with other people on the database and everyone who looks similar can be extracted. These should then be good prospects. This profiling technique is probably more suitable for mass mailings than for finding a small number of prospects for special attention.

Because the amount of information is so great and it was often gathered for a different purpose some prospect researchers consider this technique unethical.

- *Screening using characteristics from your own database.* If you have a sufficiently large and detailed database with good quality information you can perform the screening process yourself. You can analyse the data on the good prospects, for example those who have donated over £5000, and try to come up with a list of characteristics, for example people who live in the South East, studied Classics, have job titles of director or barrister, are mentioned in *Who's Who in the City*, etc. You can then compare this profile with the overall database, giving each record a score for the number of characteristics it matches. Those non-donors with the highest scores should be worth considering more closely.

- *Screening by your contacts.* Your contacts can provide much useful information as well as introductions. There are various ways of approaching this:

     a) *An informal "who do you know?"* This is necessary for those contacts who do not wish to pore over long lists. It might produce useful and unexpected results; however it might equally result in a baffled expression as the contact attempts to work out what type of person you want then struggles to remember names.

It is possible that your contact will point you in the wrong direction. Perhaps his opinions are unreliable, or his memory is vague. Maybe his circle of friends is restricted or has a strong bias in a particular direction (for example politically). Unless you do some research of your own you might find that you have been led in the wrong direction by someone whose eagerness to help masks the shortcomings of his information.

     b) *A questionnaire.* You might take names from a commercial screening or compile your own list, e.g. the top three directors of each of the top 50 companies, names from rich lists, people who were in the same year or subject group at university, parents of current students, or people from your database who look particularly interesting. Alongside each name and company name have tick boxes for different degrees of friendliness. A sample key might be as follows:

A – known very well

B – known moderately

C – known by sight

D – not known or not on good terms (two alternatives save the potential embarrassment of admitting openly to a disagreement, but you might prefer to separate them).

This key contains no reference to whether or not the contact would be willing to approach these people on your behalf. Moving from being prepared to provide information or a letter of introduction to actively lobbying on your behalf is a major step. If you are sure of your contact's willingness then you might amend the key appropriately, otherwise it might be better to leave the extent of involvement to a later stage in case it frightens the contact into refusing to do anything at all. If you do have different keys for different people make sure that you know which one they used (e.g. by using different letters). It is very easy to overlook this and confuse yourself totally!

If you have a particularly good relationship with your contact you might ask him or her to fill in more detailed screening forms with questions about types of wealth, giving capacity, etc. You can then develop a more complex rating system, for example 1A for very wealthy people with a strong contact. This is more likely to work in a country like the US where people are more used to and accepting of this strategy. In many other countries there is a danger that the contacts might be shocked at you asking for such detailed and personal information.

The information should be cross-referenced on your database (or card index if you have no database) against the names of both people, indicating which one filled in the questionnaire (perhaps by using upper case letters). You should also ensure that each reference is dated because questionnaires should be repeated every few years, and if the contact has changed from A to D you need to know which entry is the more recent.

- *Wealth or giving potential.* This might seem the most obvious code to put on the database and use for ranking. In the US it is not too difficult to do this. You might have access to ready-made mass information such

75

as credit ratings or questionnaires filled in by the prospects themselves. Alternatively, if you have regular volunteer screening sessions at which people are invited to give a rough score to people they know you can get an idea of how wealthy they appear (though they may in reality be living off an overdraft). Ideally, you would also be able to refer to the full information so that you can judge how many people gave a figure, how close the figures were, and how well each screener knew the prospect. If you like statistics you might construct a system which builds in these reliability measures, though be sure that everybody who uses it understands it. A simple figure is often more effective.

However, researchers who do not have access to these sources may feel they ought to manufacture wealth figures themselves. This involves guessing on the basis of one or two indicators such as job title and inevitably produces inaccurate results. Guessing at wealth requires careful research, and even then there may be insufficient information to obtain even a rough idea. Even when you are reasonably happy with the figure, the factors in the decision can rapidly become out of date, and because of its judgemental rather than factual nature this information does not sit well with data protection regulations. It might be better to code a limited number of interesting people as prospects so as to exclude them from mass mailings and study them each in depth. Alternatively you could forget about wealth codes and rely instead on occupation codes.

- *Interesting occupations.* Your database should contain far more than simple names and addresses. It is useful to have job titles and employers' names, but these mean little to a computer. Thus you should go a step further and include job classifications so that, for example, you can pull out a list of people with the code for company director. Equally you can exclude people who are not of interest, such as teachers and social workers who are not likely to be immensely wealthy. One way of doing this is with SIC codes (widely used and printed in company directories by publishers such as Dun & Bradstreet). There are different versions of these (notably UK and US variants) but they share the disadvantage that they are designed for classifying industries rather than job titles, different parts of the same industry are listed under widely separate codes, and they are rather confusing to use. The accuracy of your data will suffer if the system is too complicated to be used with ease by the inputters. Your database supplier might have an alternative system or you might design your own by studying the range of occupations in careers literature.

- *Good prospects that have turned you down before.* All approaches should be recorded, even if the outcome is 'no'. It may be that a person is tied up with personal problems or a company is going through a difficult trading patch. A new chief executive might have been appointed, personal circumstances might have changed, or there might be something about your new approach which strikes a chord. However, make sure you know why the approach failed last time so that you do not simply annoy the prospect.

- *Donors to your organisation.* Those who have given already are more likely to give in the future than those who have not. This is one reason why good reciprocation is vital. You should be able to pull off a list of donors for different gift ranges. This list will be particularly valuable in an organisation that does not routinely return to previous donors. It is also useful to consider the lower level donors who might be persuaded to give a major gift.

- *Contacts.* Those with the most recent, numerous or important contacts with your institution are more likely to make good prospects. At least you will not have to struggle for an introduction. They might be members of committees, business associates or regular attenders at drinks parties, but they have already shown a commitment to your organisation. Ideally your database should have codes for specific types of contact (e.g. member of fund-raising committee, attended gala evening in 1996, etc.) so that you can readily print out lists.

- *Questionnaires filled in by prospects.* Some US universities ask the parents of their students to fill in forms with questions about their occupation, income or wealth. Other fund-raisers ask their constituents for their own salaries, perhaps within certain bands. Beware that in some countries this would be considered shockingly intrusive and could damage your reputation. However where it is practised it can be very useful. The result is a steady flow of questionnaires which are scanned by the research team for anyone who might be interesting. This is done partly on instinct and partly looking for specific things like job titles, known family names, or home address.

## Rating systems

Trying to juggle all of these different factors can be difficult. One solution is to focus on one factor at a time, for example, start with a list of people on your database who are wealthy then pick out those who are also donors.

Alternatively you might devise a numerical scoring system which allows you to take all of the factors into consideration at the same time. This involves giving each person a score for each factor (e.g. 1-5). However this is not sufficient: the factors might have different degrees of importance. If you consider that a good contact is the most important factor then you might multiply the contact scores by two or three so that it weighs more heavily than the other factors in the final score. If you have several similar factors (e.g. attendance at dinners and membership of committees are both indications of an interest in your institution) then you are giving that element a heavier weighting. Thus, if you have five factors related to interest in your institution and one wealth factor then you might decide to multiply wealth by five to even up the balance. How you weight the different factors might depend on factors such as the prestige of your institution (a respected name might make it easier to achieve an audience), your degree of optimism, and the personal style of the people who will make the approach.

Having got a list of top prospects you might choose to investigate the top tier in depth and produce a full report. The lower tiers might be quickly checked in biographical or business directories, to get some indication of who they are and the sort of contacts they might have. If you can afford it (and a suitable product is available) you might run their names against a commercial database to gain information on wealth, occupation, etc. If they seem particularly interesting you might write a full report on them, either as prospects in their own right or as a route to prospects.

The bottom ranks should not be ignored. Rating systems only give an indication of the more likely route to success; they are not infallible. For this reason prospects who have some points in their favour but not sufficient to merit a personal approach could be invited to less labour-intensive social gatherings, just in case.

## Beyond your database

Where do you look when you feel you have exhausted your current pool of prospects? Do you feel that there are many excellent prospects that are being ignored because they have not found their way onto your database? Consider some of the following ways of tracking them down:

- *Foundations and trusts.* An easy starting point for a fund-raiser is to work through a book of grant-giving bodies. This is effectively a ready-made prospect list, though not all entries will be appropriate to your needs. A variant on this theme is the national lottery, which in many countries disburses money to good causes. See the later chapter on foundations and trusts for further details.

- *Published rich lists* might seem an obvious starting point. The American business magazines *Forbes* and *Fortune* publish annual lists of what they consider to be the wealthiest people in the world. Lists for specific countries are given in the later chapters on sources.

The major drawback of the rich lists is that everyone else has seen them too. They can also never be 100% accurate. Personal wealth is a very private and complex matter. Many wealthy people would not themselves venture to place a figure on their wealth as it is tied up in property or investments whose price fluctuates all the time. Someone looking from the outside can never know precisely what a person owns or what his income is. Even access to the tax records cannot help much as wealthy people are unlikely to keep all of their wealth in countries with open tax regimes. Inevitably they much prefer to keep it shrouded in secrecy in tax havens.

Even in countries where there does not appear to be an established rich list, the occasional one might appear in the press. This sort of rich list can be rather more useful as fewer people are likely to have found it; however a one-off is unfortunately more likely to contain uncorrected mistakes. If you have contacts in the country, particularly contacts in the press, you might ask whether they have come across such a list. If you speak the language you might ring one or two of the main newspapers and ask whether they produce a list, or if not whether they know who does. Even if the newspaper does not have its own rich list it is likely to write articles about ones published elsewhere because of the interest they arouse.

Otherwise you can try searching an electronic database. Choose a news database which has a good coverage of the country. Reuters *Textline* is one example of a good international news database. It attempts to include at least one or two major newspapers from as many countries as possible, supplemented by reports from the Reuters newsagency and the BBC Monitoring Service. The latter two might pick up stories from local papers which are not themselves available online. If you are using other databases remember that the *Forbes* international lists are available on some of them. These are very long and mostly irrelevant to the country you want, and if you decide to print out the full text without looking at the contexts first you can become immensely frustrated watching page after page of unnecessary information scroll by. The suppliers' best attempts at removing duplicates are frequently unsuccessful, so you end up with the same annoying list repeating itself over and over again.

This sort of search is very hit and miss, but the possibility of impressive results makes it well worthwhile. It involves fishing around with words which might appear in a rich list. First you need to specify the country: Poland or Poles or Polish. Add this to useful words like richest, billionaires, millionaires, wealthiest or rich list. Until you find it, you will not know whether the list is called '50 wealthiest Poles', 'Polish rich list', 'Poland's millionaires', etc. (NB – As a word like 'Poles' can have other meanings, you might wish to reduce the number of false hits by limiting your search to the headlines of the articles.) Even if there is not a fully fledged rich list, there will at least be the names of individual millionaires.

If you already know two or three of the wealthiest people (perhaps from *Fortune* or *Forbes*), but wish to find a fuller list, there is an alternative method. You can enter those names you do know (in the form x+y+z), assuming that they will figure in any rich list, and see what you come up with. Although there might be articles which simply mention them as business partners or rivals, you might also find both straightforward rich lists and articles which you would not otherwise have found, such as 'the most powerful families in South East Asia'.

- *Buying in lists*. There are research companies which specialise in collecting lists of wealthy people to sell to charities. You can buy (often at considerable cost) a list of names of those whom they consider to be the most likely to support your activity. This is different from screening because you actually buy the list rather than that part which matches your database.

Outside the US they may well obtain much of their information from press scanning. Each day they add to their databank of names and interests by extracting key points from the standard daily newspapers, a few 'society' journals (including topics like beautiful homes), and the fund-raising press. There is nothing special about these publications. You can obtain them for yourself (as can anyone else working for an organisation in the same field). The research companies have the advantage of sufficient staff to read a wide range of publications and a database going back over several years, but if you are more interested in an on-going supply of names than an initial large input then you might wish to build up your own databank.

While some vendors are entirely reputable there are concerns about the methods used by others. You cannot guarantee that the list is not based on information acquired illicitly (perhaps from another organisation's database), that it is accurate, or that the vendor will not take your money without sending the list. Some charities refuse to buy certain lists because they are not happy about the way the information was obtained. Once they have bought the list the vendor can mention their names to potential customers, possibly tarnishing their reputations. It is difficult to keep track of these vendors as they might go out of business then start up under a different name. They may be reluctant to disclose their sources and their products may look unprofessional, but there is no guarantee one way or the other. The fact that a product is advertised in a major fund-raising magazine is no guarantee that it is reputable.

- *Private companies.* A list of the top privately-owned companies should be quite easy to obtain (e.g. from Jordan's in the UK). The people behind these companies are likely to be very wealthy, unless the company is failing.

- *Press scanning* is another potential source of prospects. You might find people or companies that are interested in your field. There might be alumni you did not know existed, supporters of causes in the same field, or companies which have just experienced a major jump in profitability. Don't rely solely on the financial press. There is a great deal to be found in the local press (as prospects tend to feel a particular responsibility towards their own region) and even in society magazines. Reading magazines like *Vanity Fair* and *Tatler* might seem frivolous, but they can yield in-depth articles on the rich and famous, as well as telling you who is supporting which charity. Unfortunately they can also threaten to bring an office to a stand-still as everyone else wants to read them too!

- *Directories.* If you have sufficient staff you might consider plodding through biographical directories. This works for universities which have numerous notable alumni as it is easy to spot those with a connection to the institution. Other fund-raisers might look for people with related charitable interests. Alternatively, you might be looking for people who work in a specific job, such as politicians. In this case you can narrow down the search if you can find either a list of the top people or a directory devoted specifically to that job such as *Dod's Parliamentary Companion.*

- *Favourite places of the wealthy.* Wealthy people tend to congregate in certain areas, so it is worth putting particular effort into gaining access to their social circles. Some areas have obvious climatic advantages such as the south of France. There is often a strong element of tax planning, for example wealthy British people might head for a tax haven such as the Channel Islands, while Americans might go to the Bahamas. The US is considered particularly tough in taxing its citizens even if they live overseas, which encourages some to change nationality. One man's high tax economy can be another's tax haven, for example there is a sizeable community of wealthy Greeks in the UK. One reason for the UK's popularity has been its policy of allowing the wealthy to live off capital tax-free, whereas an income would be taxed. A contact in the midst of such a group is well worth cultivating.

There are noted financial centres such as Switzerland, Liechtenstein and Jersey where money can be handled efficiently and discreetly without losing too much in taxes. The fact that a person's financial affairs are handled there does not mean that it is her home base. Because of the concentration of wealthy people who pass through the hands of lawyers in such countries a charity might consider it worth cultivating the legal profession. Someone involved in drawing up a will is in a position to suggest a donation. Although he might not wish to sell a particular cause directly, he might be prepared to keep a stock of brochures so that the client can choose for herself.

- *A foreign country.* You may be setting up an overseas office or launching a campaign in a new country. See the later chapter on researching a new country.

- *The government.* There are numerous government schemes aimed at providing grants. One particular area of interest is the European Union, for example, the European Social Fund (see publications such as *Grants from Europe* in the general Western European section). The body's own information service should provide information, as might a local chamber of commerce or business advice centre.

- *An industry.* There can be advantages in targeting an entire industry. They might share the advantages of a particularly favourable trading environment. You can design a marketing strategy that will appeal to all of them and save on the costs of producing plans, forecasts, etc. It is likely that your contact will know people in several of the companies. There can be an element of competition between them if you can offer something they value, though equally, once you have won over one company then its competitors might not like to be seen to be copying someone else and might turn to another institution.

It is relatively easy to find a list of the top companies in a particular industry. Some publishers specialise in producing industry reports in book form, examples being Jordan's and Euromonitor. The top 40 US businesses in 50 sectors are provided in *The National Book of Lists* from the Reference Press. Alternatively you can find brokers' reports online. Either way they are quite expensive. From time to time lists of the top companies in an industry appear in the standard press. You might like to build up industry files as you come across these or search for them online, or you could use the *Directory of Business Periodical Special Issues* from the Reference Press. However they rapidly date so you might prefer to build your own list from an online or CD-ROM company database, such as Dun & Bradstreet's or ICC's on Knight-Ridder's *Dialog.* This sort of database is a directory of companies in a particular country or region. You must first select all of the companies in the appropriate industry, probably using an SIC (industry classification) code. Then rank them by turnover and print them out in the form of a table. This is quite effective for countries such as the US and UK where a great deal of information is readily available. It is much more difficult in many other countries as there can be huge gaps in the database's coverage, especially where private companies are common. It might be advisable before going to the expense of displaying the results to check what proportion of the turnover fields are greater than zero.

- *Contacts of members of staff.* Scientists within your own organisation often know fellow professionals who work in the same field, and they might even have persuaded companies to sponsor or collaborate in their research. Solicitation staff might themselves have come from industry. Even if they do not wish to trouble their friends with requests for help they can better understand and command greater respect in their own field.

- *Donors to other organisations.* People who are already committed philanthropists or serve as trustees on boards of other charities are likely to make good prospects, especially if they have a link with your organisation. This might seem too much like poaching from another deserving cause, which is a matter you must decide for yourself. People who are already heavily involved with a charity frequently have the time and inclination to help others as well. They also know what is required of them, which is a great help. Ideally the two organisations should not be incompatible or in competition with each other. Even so the volunteer will have a limited pool of friends that they can call on to support these causes, and extending the range of causes might dilute the level of giving to each. If they give because their friend asked them their tolerance of such requests might wear thin (some people find themselves shunned because they have asked for too much!). If they give because they genuinely support the cause their pockets might be empty. In reality the motivation is probably a combination of the two. These reasons, together with volunteer fatigue, help explain why some fund-raisers rest or rotate their volunteers, and why charities launch major campaigns every so often with quieter periods in between. However, if you are not careful your volunteers might become bored and look elsewhere or be poached by other fund-raisers.

- *Major families in your locality.* In some areas it is clear that certain families feel a duty to their community. Their philanthropic activities are likely to appear in the local press, or their names might be on major buildings.

- *Top people's banks.* If you routinely receive mass donations it might be worth looking for cheques which are different. Wealthy people are likely to use banks which offer a more personal service than the standard high street banks. There is no guarantee that the person is very wealthy, but the chances are higher. Even if the cheque is only for a small amount, a more personal approach might yield a major gift.

- *Clubs.* Private clubs, golf clubs, yacht clubs, etc., are often exclusive haunts of the rich and well connected. The cost of membership or the need to be recommended by an existing member often debar all but the top strata of society. An introduction to a member of such a club can be a useful way of networking. Although you are unlikely to obtain a membership list from the club, people often list their clubs in biographical entries.

# 7. Marketing Your Organisation to the Prospect

Prospect research involves more than simply finding out about the prospect. It should go on to draw conclusions about the best means of approaching the prospect and which aspects of your organisation's programme would most appeal to him. Some researchers are unwilling to take this further step, but they should at least understand the principles if they are to be capable of distinguishing between necessary and irrelevant information. Points which appear trivial might actually be of considerable importance.

## What do you want from the prospects?

The first step is to obtain a clear idea of what your organisation wants from its prospects. This might initially be presented as a single, straightforward goal, such as £40m. The ideal is to subdivide the target into a range of smaller goals, such as a building (or individual rooms), items of equipment, staff posts, etc. This provides a range of selling points which will appeal to a wide variety of interests and pockets.

Prospects like to think that however little they can afford it has achieved something material, rather than being swallowed up by a seemingly bottomless pit. They also shy away from an association with failure. If you have a long way to go before reaching your overall target then there is no guarantee that you will reach it; however if they can give you something relatively small which appears an end in itself then it might not matter so much what happens to the rest of the programme. This approach is particularly important for prospects who are not already heavily committed to you. They can more easily be enthused by one small area of activity, which either fits in with their existing interests, or which they can feel would not have come about if it had not been for their input. There is also room for reciprocation: the project can be named after the donor, and she can visit and inspect it. This should give greater satisfaction, and possibly encourage donors to give again, or else persuade their friends that they wish to give too.

This approach has the draw-back that some projects are very popular while others attract no support at all. If this is the case you might ask your firmest supporters to help out, explaining that the more attractive projects are likely to be funded anyway, especially if you can show the less popular ones have attracted support. Alternatively costs can be built into each project, for example a professor would need a secretary, travel allowance, office space, etc., which could come out of an enlarged endowment. Another possibility is to use mass appeals to fund the less attractive aspects of the programme as many small donors are happy not to specify where their money goes.

There is also the possibility of non-monetary help. A company might be able to offer office space (especially if you want a small overseas branch), training, its own product, or introductions. Some companies prefer to offer their goods or services free or at cost price, for example, a construction company might have a quiet period yet prefer to keep its employees occupied rather than lay them off and have to recruit new ones next time they are needed. A retailer might have surplus goods, for example, unbought food is often given away to worthy causes. Large companies might second staff to help a charity for a short period.

## What can you offer the prospects?

There is always something you can offer. It might appear that philanthropy involves giving something for nothing, but this is not the case. Reciprocation is a very complex matter, encompassing both material and psychological rewards. The return must be designed to suit the person and the situation, and you must be clear about the range of possibilities before you start. To follow are some examples of motivations. It is by no means an exhaustive list: others will suggest themselves as you consider a prospect's individual characteristics. A single prospect might be swayed by different ones, or respond to a combination of several.

Companies and foundations should be viewed at least in part as groups of personalities. You should therefore consider them (or your targets amongst them) in terms of the personal motivations as well as looking at the company itself.

### Companies

- *A business transaction.* This is a straightforward exchange where both parties obtain something which is of financial value to them. It might be investment in a company in return for a share of the profits. Alternatively it might involve paying a university to undertake research which has commercial benefits for the company which sponsors it.

- *Recognition.* A company can raise public awareness of itself or one of its brands through a link with a high profile organisation or event. This is what lies behind a number of sports sponsorship deals. A company might also sponsor a fund-raising event or fund a named university post or scholarship. If you are offering a sponsorship deal you should be prepared to organise press coverage of the donation or event. The more positive and extensive the coverage the better your chance of obtaining further deals. You should also consider what audience you can reach and whether this ties in with the prospect's desired audience. Do their social and economic characteristics match? What number of people is involved? What is their spending power? They might be customers, a specific target group of customers, or potential employees (this last is particularly relevant to universities). Marketing budgets have the potential to be much larger than charitable budgets, so this line might be more profitable.

- *Approval.* This is similar to the above. A company can improve its public image by helping the local community or popular charities. It might wish to counteract a tarnished image, perhaps through support for environmental research. This will impact both on sales and on recruitment.

- *Corporate hospitality.* If you have an interesting venue, such as a museum or architecturally interesting hall you might permit the company to use this on certain occasions.

This illustrates that you should look beyond the charities budget when approaching a company. You might obtain direct investment from its research and development budget. You might approach the public relations department offering good publicity or the marketing department for sponsorship or promotions. The Corporate Affairs Department, which considers matters such as corporate identity and public perception of the company is another possibility. The personnel department might be interested in access to graduates if yours is a university with high prestige or one which runs a relevant course. It is also a route to the employees, i.e. payroll giving, secondment, employee fund-raising, etc. Alternatively some companies make a point of supporting the community in areas where they are based so you might more profitably approach the local branch. Finally, there is the standard fall-back of the charity budget.

## People

- *Personal beliefs.* Some religions encourage the donation of a certain proportion of income to charity each year, for example the Christian tradition of tithes. Quakers are one example of a group which actively maintains this practice, though often anonymously which means they attract little attention. They are particularly strong supporters of education. The companies they founded may show their influence. Political beliefs can also have an effect on donations (though frequently a negative one). Are the prospects noted campaigners for the environment or do they consider it a costly encumbrance on their business? Are they firm believers in the need for private investment in formerly public spheres such as education? A strong social conscience is a good indication of a willingness to help, but it might mean the prospect is already heavily committed elsewhere.

- *Gifts.* These might range from a diary to a model of a building. The more expensive ones might have a prestige value and might be exhibited proudly in the prospect's office. The less costly ones also have a value in making the prospect feel a tie with the organisation and as a continuing reminder that the input is valued and remembered. This sort of recognition occurs after the gift has been received, but might provoke further gifts or encourage the prospect's friends or colleagues to become donors.

- *Access.* If you have something which interests the prospect and access to which is normally restricted in some way, you can offer it as a privilege. This might be a reader's ticket for a library, a special tour of a museum collection, or updates on the progress of scientific research.

- *Honours.* Some institutions are capable of awarding honorary degrees; however do not assume that they can be used as an incentive, as the institution might insist that they can only be conferred in recognition of genuine achievement rather than as rewards for gifts. An alternative is membership of a body designed specifically for donors, such as a council of benefactors.

- *Meeting celebrities.* You might have supporters who would be willing to attend a dinner with the prospect. They might be public figures such as royalty, politicians or film stars, or their prominence might be in a more restricted circle, such as astrophysics. The prospect might wish to discuss interesting ideas (e.g. new computer applications), gain access to an elite social circle, or have a photograph taken with the person. All that matters is that the prospect should be impressed by them. Whatever the original motivation, the prospect might be drawn into a rather deeper interest in your affairs than would otherwise have been the case.

- *Social standing.* This might be linked with the previous two points. Although it is not often openly discussed it is frequently a motivating factor, especially with the upwardly mobile. It is a widely held (though unproven) belief that you can purchase honours such as knighthoods by performing the requisite number of good works. Prospects might also feel that by linking themselves with an august institution some of the prestige attaches itself to them. Even amongst the more established rich it is often expected that everyone will make some contribution to charity, sometimes to such an extent that a married woman makes a career out of philanthropy. Although wealth alone can bring some degree of social acceptability, it is difficult to ignore the opinions of your peers. There is also sometimes an element of reciprocation: if you ask for a donation to your pet project then you must be prepared to give an equivalent donation to your friend's favourite charity, unless your friend is much wealthier than you.

- *Naming opportunities.* Prospects might be attracted by the idea of having a permanent reminder of their investment in the form of a named building or post. This does not appeal to everyone; however if the prospect does not want his own name used he might be more willing to name something in honour of a (possibly deceased) parent or spouse, or a respected mentor.

- *Publicity.* Public figures, like companies, sometimes need good publicity. If their business or personal activities are frowned upon they might attempt to build up a stock of goodwill through positive coverage in the press. They might simply thrive on the attention. Alternatively they might loathe publicity, perhaps through modesty or because one gift can provoke a flood of applications from other fund-raisers. It is therefore wise to ask their opinion and take it very seriously when anonymity is requested, even if it means your organisation itself loses out on a valuable piece of promotion.

- *Personal satisfaction.* This might be derived from the knowledge of having made a difference in an area which matters. Alternatively it might be pleasant to be treated like a VIP and to gain influence in a nationally-recognised institution.

- *Progress reports.* Apart from the occasional foundation which is too bound up with administration and correspondence, it is an almost universal truth that prospects like to be kept up to date on the use of their funds (unless the gift is so small that this would seem an excessive expense). This might involve visits to inspect work, press releases on the latest activities, or personal letters from the people who are benefitting from their money.

- *Loyalty.* If this is your college then you should support it.

- *Fulfilling duty to the local community.* Some prospects will only co-operate with local projects as they feel a sense of paternalistic responsibility.

- *Reaffirmation of own identity.* Prospects like to see themselves as certain types of people, and a link with your organisation can strengthen this. They might like to see themselves as a supporter of ecological projects or the relief of poverty. They might be alumni of your university who want to maintain an association with it. This feeling tends to grow stronger if they live overseas so are physically and culturally separated from it. People who are born to wealth are possibly less likely to feel this need as they are more confident of their own identity.

- *Helping others similar to the prospect.* Prospects often like to help those with whom they identify. They might provide funding for research into an illness which has affected their family, scholarships for those struggling to gain an education, or investment or training projects for their home country.

- *Helping an admired or respected individual.* This might be a scientist whose work the prospect will fund, a programme head whose commitment is admired, or a friend who has asked for support on behalf of a chosen charity.

## Conclusion

Only after reaching a clear understanding of what you want and what you can offer should you actually start researching a specific prospect. The researcher should be in a position to suggest the optimum achievable goal for each particular prospect and the pros and cons of the ones most likely to appeal to that person. If during the course of a meeting it becomes obvious that the prospect will not meet the prime goal, then the fall-back positions should be ready prepared. No matter how detailed the research, prospects will always be capable of surprising you. Research should prepare the requester for all likely outcomes, but point out which seem the most likely and explain why.

# 8. People

Personal information is one of the most sensitive areas for the researcher. You should be sure of your stance regarding ethics and confidentiality before you attempt to write your own profiles. In particular, are you infringing privacy or data protection legislation, your own institution's guidelines, or the policy of your professional association? The following shows what you can do, but not what you ought to do.

## Basic resources

At the most basic level there are four major sources for profiles of people: rich lists, who's whos, the press and biographies. As these will depend on the country, see the geographical sections towards the end of this book for more precise details. This chapter provides a general overview.

### 1. Rich lists

If the person you are researching is wealthy then you can start off with one of the published rich lists. These are generally published by the press, though there are also some books available. The press versions generally have the advantage of appearing annually but books can often provide more detail.

You can hope for an estimated figure for wealth and a brief description of the person's business interests along with general comments and often a photograph. These lists, though very helpful as indications, cannot be viewed as a cast iron guarantee of wealth. It is impossible to say for certain what people are worth, partly due to the privacy which surrounds their assets and partly because you cannot give a precise monetary valuation for possessions without actually selling them. However so long as you accept this they provide a good starting point.

Ideally you should obtain as many as possible. In many countries you will be lucky to find them at all, but in the UK and, in particular, the US there are numerous versions. See the chapter on finding prospects for further details of how to find rich lists for other countries.

### 2. Who's whos

These give the bare bones on which the profile can be built. Most developed countries have at least one who's who, though it might take a while to find it as it will often be published and distributed only within that country. There are also who's whos for particular jobs, such as politicians, scientists or musicians. No matter how out of date the book, there is always information which should not change, such as date of birth, family, education and early career.

### 3. The press

Large research departments generally maintain files of press cuttings on people who might prove to be useful. There are also newspaper indexes in book form, which can often be found in libraries. However these are rapidly becoming superseded by electronic forms of access. You can now buy old editions of newspapers stored on CD-ROM, though the price can be rather high. More flexible are online databases, which give you the same information on a pay as you go basis. This means you can access a wider range of the press which is particularly useful if you are covering several countries.

### 4. Biographies

Libraries or book shops should be able to tell you whether one exists. Alternatively there are indexes of books in print available through online databases or the Internet as well as printed ones (e.g. from KG Saur, part of Reed).

Autobiographies are clearly likely to be subjective. However you should also be wary of biographies. If one was written with the subject's help it means the subject is likely to approve of the author's line possibly because he or she influenced it or because the author had to keep the subject happy in order to gain the information. If it was written without permission the author might have little inside information and might have strong views on the subject.

Some people have several biographies written on them. More recent biographers are likely to have read the earlier books and assimilated the information into their own. However their interpretation and opinions might be very different. Do not become carried away with reading these books. Attempt to summarise the key points, but add a 'further reading' section to your report mentioning their existence. Readers might prefer to read them themselves or might consider they have sufficient information already.

## Working through a report: stage by stage

The following demonstrates section by section how a detailed report might be compiled. The subdivisions of the report are as follows: title page (including photograph), address, wealth, biography (family details, childhood, etc.) career, personality and interests, contacts, likelihood of success and suggested projects.

There is one more aspect of the report which is not listed below as it is too important and possibly too sensitive. It is by no means unusual for the super-rich to have murky backgrounds. They may even be involved in war crimes, arms dealing or corruption. While some make their fortunes through sound business sense, novel ideas and good luck, others do so by ruthlessly trampling on others along the way. Unfortunately the more unsavoury elements might be attracted to worthy causes partly because it provides them with a legitimacy and social acceptance they crave and partly because their money is new so not tied to crumbling ancestral mansions.

If you do not pursue and pass on this information your organisation's interests might be seriously harmed by a link with someone whom other prospects find unacceptable. In-depth press articles might provide hints, though others will ignore them for fear of a law suit. If such information comes to light you might wish to put the report on hold while you try to discover, perhaps through personal contacts, how serious the matter is. However, this should be done carefully as it might spread an unsavoury rumour more widely and provoke a problem before your organisation has had time to consider how it should respond. Such information is best kept out of the standard report as it is likely to be too sensitive. It should be handled with great care because of the libel implications.

## 1. Title page and photograph

The purpose of the title page is to explain clearly what the document is whilst retaining the confidentiality of its contents. It gives added protection in case the report is left out on a desk or read on a crowded train on the way to a meeting. It also gives a more professional feel to the document than would launching straight into the text. This is especially important if the report has to impress a volunteer.

The title page might contain the following:

- Large, clear statement that the report is strictly confidential.
- Possibly the organisation's logo if you have this in electronic form and want to make the report look impressive. Be careful about using this without obtaining permission as it might give the impression that the report has the approval of the entire organisation, when in fact it is only your work. Whether a charity or a company, your employer is likely to place a high value on maintaining its reputation, and the sensitive nature of research reports makes them potentially dangerous. If you cannot use the logo then settle for the name of your department or simply 'research report'.

- Name of the prospect.

- Name of the person for whom the report was written. This should always be recorded in case another member of staff decides to approach the same prospect. A wealthy person might also be considered from the point of view of his company and foundation, resulting in three approaches from different angles. If they were all channelled through research it would be possible to point out that someone else got there first.

- Name of the researcher who wrote the report. If the requester has queries or amendments (or even praise!) she knows who she should contact.

- Date of the report. Reports are liable to become out of date very quickly. You need to know how reliable they are.

- Photograph. A first meeting is likely to be a little awkward, and anything which makes it easier will be appreciated. If there are several new people to be met – perhaps at a dinner – then it is well worth studying their photographs first. This prevents embarrassment over introductions: you can work out which people know each other already, and focus your attention on the guest of honour. You can also avoid warmly greeting the prospect's assistant rather than the prospect himself. It also ensures that they stick in your mind as distinct personalities, giving you a better chance of remembering the conversations you have had with each. People can be either very annoyed or deeply flattered by the extent of your recollection of their names and past conversations.

Seeing a photograph also provides information about the prospect, such as age, and possibly a clue to his character. It can make it easier to prepare yourself for the meeting, especially if there is something unusual about the prospect. The last thing you want is to crush an arthritic hand or stare in awe-struck horror at the prospect's bright pink hair.

To follow are potential sources of photographs. Decide for yourself which seems most appropriate to the particular situation, bearing in mind that most are covered by copyright.

— *The prospect's secretary.* Many important people keep a stock of biographies and photos of themselves in case anyone requests them. It might be surprising to learn that this practice extends beyond the pop and political worlds into the upper reaches of business. There is no guarantee that the prospect will have a public photograph, and it is not wise to assume that she does as she might feel she has to obtain one specially. A discreet enquiry to her secretary is probably the best approach, though make sure that no other department of your organisation has already obtained one. This type of direct approach will not be suitable for all reports. It will be more acceptable where the prospect has already accepted an invitation, and where the person you are briefing is of a relatively high standing, such as the head of your organisation or a celebrity. It will not be acceptable where no contact has yet been made as the prospect might be disturbed at your interest in him and has in any case no reason to send you anything.

— *Arrange for your own photographer.* If, for example, you are holding a dinner to honour key contacts, you might ask them if they would each care for a photograph to commemorate the occasion. Ideally you should have someone who they would wish to be photographed with, such as the head of your organisation or a celebrity who supports your cause (having checked first that they are agreeable to being photographed). If the photograph is considered impressive enough it might be displayed in the prospect's office, providing you with a form of unofficial advertising. You should therefore try to obtain a professional photographer so that the end result is of good quality and does not merely embarrass the prospect. The result should be a happy prospect with something solid to remind him of your organisation, and a photo for your files.

Even though the prospect is already known to your organisation, the photo is still of use if a different member of staff needs to meet her, which becomes increasingly inevitable over the years. You should bear in mind that even though you commissioned the pictures to be taken, the photographer is likely to retain the copyright, so must be paid for each copy you need. Clearly you must negotiate such charges in advance.

— *A biography.* It is unlikely that a biography would not contain photos of the subject, though they will be covered by copyright. Ideally you should obtain the most recently published book and check the date of the photo in case the prospect has changed very much over the years.

— *Who's whos*. Most do not contain photographs, but there are a few which do.

— *A company's annual report*. Companies are increasingly adopting the practice of providing pictures of their directors in their annual reports. They do not have to do this, but they probably feel that it reassures the shareholders if they can fit smiling, confident faces to the names. The pictures will not be identical in succeeding reports so if you are throwing away old ones it might be worth tearing out the photo pages in case they are clearer than more recent ones.

— *The press*. Pictures might be culled from the business sections of newspapers or from the society press such as *Tatler* or *Hello*. You can either cut out the photos and file them or you can keep the whole magazine and create your own index by listing every interesting person on a computer (ensuring you head each section with the date of the issue). The latter is probably quicker, though it does take up more space and it does require absolute accuracy if you are ever to find the photo again. A computer will not find a name which has one letter wrong. As ever, remember that the photographs are subject to copyright. You should not make copies of them; you should only keep the original.

— *Photograph libraries*. These are companies which specialise in collecting and leasing photographs. Their customers are likely to want to publish the photographs in advertising, the press, etc. They are therefore likely to be rather expensive for the prospect researcher. Prices must be negotiated individually, but it is not unknown for one photograph to cost £100. Libraries tend to be organised into topics, such as 'dogs' or 'weather'. By no means all will have pictures of people. If you wish to pursue this avenue you should consult a directory of photo libraries to find those that cover your area.

## 2. Summary

You might like to use this prominent position to give a very brief summary of how useful this prospect is. It might include wealth, giving capacity, whether any contacts exist, and whether there is a strong chance of an interest in a particular project.

### 3. Address, telephone number and title

It is worth listing as many addresses as possible. The requester then has the choice of whether to approach through the office or the home, and can track down those people who move between several homes. If possible acquire telephone numbers, fax numbers and secretaries' names to go with the addresses.

The most likely sources for the address and telephone number are biographical directories. The more exclusive the publication's circulation the more likely it is to contain otherwise confidential information as it is not anticipated that a very wide audience will see it. Thus in the UK many otherwise unpublished addresses are available in *The City of London Directory and Livery Companies Guide* as at first sight this publication is of no interest to anyone other than a fellow member of the livery companies.

If your prospect is a company director then, depending on the country, you might find that it is one of the details to be supplied to the official registrar of companies. Similarly, trustees might be required to file their addresses along with information on the foundation.

Telephone directories are another useful and widely available source. If you wish to check your database records en masse then there are companies which specialise in data collection that will verify addresses for you, for example telephone companies. If you are looking for a wealthy person who could live anywhere in the country it might be worth checking the capital's telephone directory as she is likely to have an address there too (though it could be ex-directory).

A wealthy person is likely to have several addresses and move between them at regular intervals. If this is the case you cannot guarantee that he will receive your letters for some time. If there are children then there might be a stable home base unless they are at boarding school. Similarly, business interests might keep him in a certain country for much of the time. Different homes might be used for different purposes, for example some people will not respond to 'business' correspondence when they are on holiday. If they are tax exiles meetings must be particularly carefully planned because they will only be allowed a limited number of days in the country before they become liable for payment.

If you have an overseas address which appears to be out of date check with someone who knows the country that you have the correct spelling and format as this might prevent mail from being delivered. A publication that might help is *The Guide to Worldwide Postal Code and Address Formats* (Marion Nelson).

If you really cannot discover where a person lives, but have received a small donation from her, you can ask her bank to forward a letter using the details on the cheque. Alternatively, if you know what company or university she works for try looking for her email account on the Internet. If you work for a university try asking a contact in the same year and subject group.

It is very important to ensure that you are addressing a person correctly, as they can be very sensitive on the subject. This can be difficult, as even the person's compatriots might not understand the complexities of the system. An English person who does not mix with the nobility is unlikely to know precisely how to address them. However amongst the nobility themselves this can be a matter of extreme importance. Each rank (dukes, earls, barons, baronets, etc.) has its own specific form of address, and there are variations within them according to the person's status. Thus 'Margaret, Lady Smith' is not the same as 'Lady Margaret Smith'. If you are not careful you might find yourself implying that the lady is a widow, ex-wife, etc., which could be confusing or even gravely insulting. Even if you do not know the difference, the lady and her immediate circle will be very conscious of it.

The respect accorded to the nobility varies from country to country. Hereditary titles are very common in many countries, even though new ones are no longer so readily created. The fact that there are so many people claiming titles can devalue them. Where there has been insufficient regulation of titles it is known that some were adopted fraudulently which causes them to be viewed with suspicion. In some countries (such as the US, France and India) republican sentiment, or even legal prohibition, discourages the use of titles, though the practice might persist in limited circles as a form of courtesy. If you want the goodwill of a person who is strictly speaking not entitled to a title, but still uses it, you would be well advised to use it too. It can also work the other way. Post-war, many Germans living overseas have dropped their titles and made their names less Germanic in an attempt to assimilate into their new environment. Names which incorporate 'of' (e.g. 'de' in French or 'von' in German) might indicate an aristocratic pedigree, and this word is often dropped. Sometimes members of the nobility drop their titles for business purposes, though continue to use them socially.

Even republics which disapprove of hereditary titles generally have some form of honours system. These might be military awards or recognition of distinguished service to the state. It might surprise Europeans to learn that the US grants the title 'the honorable'. This is held for life by someone who holds or has held high office whether at federal, state or city level. It can be difficult to identify such people as it is a title used by other people but not by the holder herself (i.e. it does not appear on her business cards, letters, etc., though it is correct to use it when addressing her).

Even untitled people require some care in address. English-speaking countries consider it acceptable to call an older unmarried woman 'Miss'. In some other countries it would be impolite to do this, thus in Germany any woman from her twenties onwards might be called 'Frau' ('Mrs') rather than the diminutive 'Fräulein'. It is worth getting into the habit of describing the prospect as 'Mr Bloggs' rather than 'Bloggs' as this creates a much better impression when it is read by outsiders. These are likely to be contacts who are quite friendly with the prospect and who would prefer you to be respectful, both for the prospect's sake and their own.

In the UK it is common practice to drop one title when you acquire a similar one of a higher order, thus someone with both a BA and an MA would mention only the latter. It would be considered 'bad form' to boast of too many qualifications or to use letters after your name which had been purchased rather than earned. In many other countries people enjoy acquiring letters after their name and will list as many as possible. It is not a good idea to neglect to use them.

To add to the confusion, a member of the nobility might have numerous titles each of which is valid. A duke might also be a baron, though he will be known by the former title as this is more important. Thus the Prince of Wales is also Duke of Cornwall as well as having a different surname. This creates great confusion when trying to find a biographical entry. Each publisher will have its own standard way of organising entries. Members of the royal family might be listed under their country, their surname, or placed in a separate section at the front of the book. In the UK a duke is likely to be under his title. The eldest son of an English nobleman is likely to be under his father's second most important title, as it is the tradition that the eldest son uses this as a 'courtesy title' during the lifetime of his father. Second sons will be under the family surname (which is quite possibly totally different from the titles). Some books list the nobility in strict alphabetical order, while others place them before or after others of the same surname (thus Lord (John) Smith could come before Mr Alfred Smith).

Some people use patronymics rather than standard inherited surnames. Muslims are particularly likely to insert a word like 'bin' or 'ibn' which means 'son of'. Women might keep their own family names when they marry. It is also sometimes the practice to refer to the mother's family name as well as the father's.

Faced with this minefield how can you determine which is the correct mode of address? It is no use hoping you can get away with saying anything because you are a foreigner if you need the person's goodwill. You will need to discover not just the full title, but also how to address the person (e.g. 'your grace', 'your lordship', 'your honour'). Yearbooks and who's whos sometimes explain the rules. The country's embassy might be able to help out, for example, with top level politicians. Some countries have directories of the nobility, and these might either give the rules or the specific mode of address for each person.

In the UK it is possible to buy entire books, such as Debrett's *Correct Form* or A&C Black's *Titles and Forms of Address* to explain the rules. However these can be difficult to apply and do not allow for exceptions where personal preference overrides the rules. If a lady remarries she should cease to use her former husband's title; however it is not unknown for a lady to decide that she prefers the sound or higher status of her former husband's title and continue to use it. Conversely, some people prefer not to use inherited titles. Whatever the reason, it would be rude, not to say strategically unwise, to ignore the person's wishes. For this reason a book such as Debrett's *People of Today* which gives each entrant's preferred mode of address (or 'style') is a useful acquisition.

An international guide to titles, table seating, etiquette, etc., drawing on experience in the White House, is *Protocol: The Complete Handbook of Diplomatic, Official and Social Usage* (Devon Publishing).

### 4. Wealth and giving capacity

Americans often calculate a rough figure for maximum giving capacity to be 5% of assets. This might be amended to liquid assets to exclude the prospect's home as that might be a large proportion of net worth but is not likely to be sold. If you are thinking of a will then a larger sum is possible. An alternative is to calculate annual giving capacity as 2% of income. However these are no more than very rough indications and the two calculations could well produce very different figures. The amount will vary according to personality, type of wealth, national patterns for each country, etc. Similar figures for other countries can be derived from charitable statistics; however this would not take into account the extra returns which you might hope to obtain from using new techniques such as prospect research which are already in use in the US.

A figure for giving capacity is not sufficient alone. Regardless of how much prospects can give, they might prefer to invest their money, give it to their children, or give it to another institution. It has been estimated that for every gift you get you need three very good prospects. This will be considered later in the report.

Furthermore, wealth can only be estimated using a variety of potentially unreliable indicators. In most countries it is impossible to obtain access to tax records and people are very sensitive about revealing their true wealth. Many of the super-rich do not even know how much they are worth. Values are constantly fluctuating and can only be known for sure by selling everything to see what the market is prepared to pay.

Although rich lists are avidly studied, wealth is too complex and subjective to be reduced to a simple figure. You should always try to analyse its various components. The wealth that is tied up in property is different from cash-flow. Income must be set against outgoings. After performing various objective calculations, you might find that the most important factor is subjective: how wealthy the prospect feels.

To follow are some clues to a prospect's wealth. More country-specific sources are listed towards the end of this book. These are particularly important for the US where the range of sources is unusually wide.

- *Rich lists.* These can be very useful indications, and a great deal of work has often gone into them (especially as the penalties for publishing untrue information can be unpleasant). However they do have their limitations. The notorious press baron Robert Maxwell featured regularly as one of the richest people in the UK until after his death it was finally proved otherwise. It is often the case that competing lists will provide quite different estimates for the same person. Sometimes you can work out why by checking the introduction for details of how they were compiled, but often there is no reason given. One particular area of disagreement is reigning monarchs, who might claim that their apparent wealth actually belongs to the country.

  Like anyone else, the compilers base their conclusions on publicly-available information as it is extremely unlikely that the subjects will provide accurate information on their wealth. This might be supplemented by inside information from people who know the person, but compilers generally like to be able to verify facts. Some journalists also have the advantage of being able to call on the services of a professional valuer for works of art or real estate. This is inevitably subjective: two experts will disagree, and in reality no-one can be certain how much a piece of property would fetch if brought to the market. The longer established the list the better it ought to be, as complaints from the people concerned should ensure that errors are not repeated. However, complaints do not necessarily mean that errors exist, as wealthy people have their own reasons for wishing to over or under-state their wealth, and may not even know their true worth.

- *Shareholdings.* If your prospect is a director or one of the very largest shareholders then the company's financial statements might disclose the size of the stake. In many countries this is a legal requirement, and the information is reproduced in books and electronic sources. This is so that the other shareholders and lenders know who has influence over their investment. Unfortunately today's public companies are so large that even a hugely valuable stake can appear small in comparison and so escape mention. However if the prospect is a director then even the smallest stake might have to be recorded.

Discovering which companies a person holds shares in can be very difficult. Sources are generally set up the other way round, that is, they list the shareholders in a particular company. Not all companies have to list their shareholders, particularly those that are small private ventures or partnerships. Databases tend only to cover the largest shareholdings in the largest companies or possibly just public companies. Those databases which allow you to look up a person's shareholdings are likely to exclude overseas companies, such as those based in tax havens which are particularly favoured by the wealthy.

You can obtain clues to shareholdings from directorships. These are much easier to track down, for example through directories, online databases or company registries. You might also find press articles linking your prospect with a company, or a volunteer might know.

If you do discover the number of shares held in a public company then you can multiply them by the current price per share (which can be found in the financial press, e.g. the UK's *Financial Times*) to find the current value of the holding. If it is a very large stake (e.g. 25%) then you can never guarantee the price, as the fact that such a large stake is being sold can in itself destabilise the market. Shares in public companies appear relatively liquid (i.e. they can be turned into cash easily); however it is less likely that they will be sold when their price is low as this might incur a loss. In reality most people are unlikely to sell up unless they wish to swap them for other investments or pay off a large bill.

You might come across companies which will provide you with weekly or daily information on directors who have sold shares in their companies. The idea behind these services is that such directors will temporarily be sitting on a large amount of cash and if you approach them quickly you might be able to relieve them of it. This assumes that the directors are selling their shares because they believe the price has reached its highest level. In fact they might have other reasons, such as the desire to buy a new house, pay school fees, or switch into other investments. It also assumes that your colleagues are willing and able to respond instantly the moment you inform them of a sale. If they have several prospects underway already they might be reluctant to take on new ones where they don't even have a contact. If you wish, try out a trial subscription; however as this might be very expensive you must be sure to evaluate the results before renewing.

As well as looking at overall value, you might consider the cash-flow generated by the shares. A profitable company will normally pay out a dividend, that is a certain amount of cash for each share held. This might be once a year, once a quarter, or not at all if the directors don't feel it is justified. The size is supposed to depend on performance, but this is not always the case, for example, companies which fear takeover might pay higher dividends at the expense of investment in the hope that this will maintain the loyalty of their shareholders. Again, the financial press will tell you the size of the latest dividend and its frequency. You can then estimate how much the shares would have brought in over the course of the year. It is likely that the prospect will to some extent have anticipated this income and how it should be spent, but as trading conditions fluctuate they might be either pleasantly surprised or somewhat disgruntled.

Another figure which you might come across is the number of options. Share options are an incentive to directors, rewarding them for improvements in the performance of the company. Directors are entitled to buy a certain number of the company's shares at a fixed price, and if the market value of the shares climbs above that price they can make a profit. If it does not then they do not have to take up the options. Unfortunately the purchase price of these options is frequently not published which makes calculating their value difficult. In a good market, exercising share options can bring in nearly as much money as the annual salary.

- *Private companies.* These can be very difficult to value unless a figure is given when they are sold. One solution is to compare the private company with a similar one in the public sector, though this is a very crude method. No two companies are identical, and sale prices are subject to rather more influences than a straightforward assessment of profitability. By chance there might be few people willing or able to invest in that particular area at the time of sale. It should be remembered that public companies grow by selling shares while private ones are more likely to invest by taking out loans. When a company is sold these debts will be taken into account in the price, though offset by saleable investments such as property. Private companies are likely to show lower profits than public ones as the incentive is to invest in the overall value of the company and avoid tax rather than show a constantly high return in order to impress shareholders.

In many countries it is not even possible to discover how much the various members of the family own. In the UK it can be found through Companies House so long as it is not a partnership. Another potential source is the Dun & Bradstreet report. You can also look at wills and probate to discover who inherited a company and what value was placed on the estate at the time.

- *Age.* Younger people have children, homes, etc. to establish and might wish to invest in a business to increase their future prosperity. Wealthy people nearing retirement have a choice: they can spend their money or allow someone else to inherit it. Although people are living longer which can mean high medical and care bills, the elderly are conscious that their days are numbered and more likely to dispose of their money one way or another.

If they wish the money to be inherited then tax planning becomes a vital consideration. In many countries inheritance tax can make a substantial dent in the fortunes of wealthy people. There are ways round this, for example in the UK by passing on the wealth seven years before death (which means that unexpected early deaths can have a major impact on the family's finances). It is also possible to place the money in a family trust and live off the interest without touching the capital.

Alternatively, childless prospects might be planning disposal to charities. If this has already been done then it might be too late to change their minds. Charities are increasingly taking an interest in helping people write their wills, which means they might be told how much they stand to receive. Although this is not a legally binding agreement, the prospect will feel duty-bound to carry out a promise. Alternatively people might be prepared to make gifts before their death; however unless they are terminally ill or very wealthy it is more likely that they will prefer to make provision in their will in case they find a use for the money in the meantime.

- *Family matters.* Does the prospect have ex-spouses to maintain or children to educate and establish? Has a divorcée accrued considerable wealth from former husbands? A divorce might also mean that you no longer know which partner owns a piece of property. In some countries (e.g.

the US, but not the UK) it is possible to see records of divorce, but it is often considered unacceptable to intrude in this way. Alternatively perhaps there is a family member who needs expensive medical treatment?

- *Property.* Directories will list the prospect's various addresses, giving an indication of the wealth required to own these properties. You can, if you think it is not too intrusive, ask an estate agent or auctioneer to suggest a value for a property. However it is dangerous to put too much emphasis on this as you would need to account for fluctuations in the property market, state of repair, and whether the house was heavily mortgaged.

It is also possible that the prospect is no more than a tenant, and the true owner is his employer, a family trust, or a charity. As an example, in the UK, death duties and running costs have forced some stately home owners to hand over their properties to the National Trust on the condition that members of the family are allowed to live in a small corner. It is easy to distinguish these by acquiring a guide to National Trust properties. This fact is also likely to appear in press articles about the family. Alternatively, the property might have been placed in a family trust, possibly based overseas. A trust is not considered to be private property, though it can provide an income. This is a confidential matter, though it can be guessed at if the value of the property does not appear to be included when a will is published.

Ownership of an extremely valuable stately home can actually be an indication of poverty rather than wealth. If it has been newly acquired the prospect is probably very wealthy, though it is always possible he has been overstretched; if, on the other hand, it has been in the family for generations it can be viewed as a major burden. It will incur large expenses in running costs and repair, although the family's original source of income might be long gone. Although the owner might wish to sell it this might be impossible because of the feeling of betraying the trust of ancestors and descendants alike. In the meantime the family could be incurring hefty income and inheritance taxes. Despite the Rembrandts and Titians on the wall, such people will have very little disposable income and feel relatively poor. They are likely to appear in the press from time to time when selling off works of art to keep their heads above water.

The ownership of other valuable items, for example stables of racehorses and art collections, should also be taken into consideration. It is important to notice whether the prospect is buying or selling them. The sale of works of art might indicate a worrying need for ready cash, which is often the case with the landed aristocracy. It might alternatively mean that the prospect has plenty of money but prefers not to liquidise long term assets at this moment. It could even mean simply that the prospect has decided he or she does not like modern art after all. Contacts might have some idea of the reason. You might also gain an indication by considering how attached the prospect is to this piece of property, for example jewellery is not often voluntarily sold within its owner's lifetime.

- *Hobbies.* Some require a fair amount of money, for example polo suggests the ownership of ponies and sailing suggests ownership of a yacht. Some US states permit access to registration records of yachts and aircraft, while biographical directories will often list membership of yacht clubs. The press and biographies are also sources of information on hobbies.

- *Inheritance.* Copies of wills and probate are often held in official repositories where anyone can gain access to them. The information they contain varies widely. There might be a full inventory listing all items of value. More likely there will simply be an overall figure for the value of the estate. Check obituaries or a who was who to find out when your prospect's parents died and where they were living at the time, and this will probably lead you to the will.

- *Taxation.* In those countries where you cannot obtain access to tax records you can at least gain a vague indication of wealth through the lengths to which the prospect will go in order to avoid paying tax. Some live in tax exile or own companies based in tax havens. Where inheritance taxes are substantial some people avoid them by placing assets into family trusts as these are not, strictly speaking, personal property. This cannot normally be done on the deathbed, indeed in the UK it requires seven years' foresight. When a wealthy person suffers an untimely death it is quite possible that the family will have been caught out and will face a large tax bill.

- *Fluctuations.* A person's wealth can fluctuate rapidly as the rich tend to be willing to accept higher risks in the hope of higher returns. Rather than placing their money in a fixed interest account they will invest it in business ventures whose fortunes may be good or bad. If their wealth has fallen dramatically due to a drop in the value of their shares or a fall in the value of their property investments there are further questions to ask: is the fall due to a general fall in the equity or property markets? In this case when the markets recover the value should be back to normal. More worrying is a situation where only the one company is affected as this indicates an underlying problem that might not be resolved. However, even if the drop is due to the business cycle, can the company hold out until the market returns to normal? Although all their competitors are likely to be in the same position, some have higher borrowings than others and are more likely to collapse. Does the person's wealth depend very heavily on a single investment? If not then there is more chance of recovery, and a comparison with previous years' figures should provide a better idea of the normal level.

Even those investments which appear to be risk-free can occasionally turn sour. An example of this recently occurred in the UK when the Lloyd's insurance market dramatically ended its long run of success. It was only then that its many ordinary backers began to take seriously the theoretical unlimited liability which could push them into bankruptcy. These people come from all over the country and all occupations. Although they would normally be anonymous, some have been mentioned in the press, especially those who have been vociferous in demanding compensation.

- *Salary.* In some countries it is necessary to provide figures for the pay of the most important – or even all – directors in the company's annual report (or in the US the proxy statement). You should also look for bonuses, retirement benefits, etc. If the person is a government employee, such as a judge, MP or top civil servant, it is likely that they are on a published scale which might appear in an almanac (see *Whitaker's Almanack* in the UK). There are also publications which provide average figures for different industries and occupations (e.g. *IDS* in the UK).

The economic cycle can result in large-scale cut-backs in managerial and financial staff. Companies within the same industry (notably banks) tend to reduce staff numbers at the same time making it difficult for them to find new jobs, especially if they are towards the end of their careers. However when times are good banking staff can earn huge bonuses, occasionally becoming instant millionaires.

- *Credit ratings.* There are companies which specialise in scoring people for their reliability in repaying credit. You might require a licence to gain access to these figures. They also tend to be relatively costly and do not explain the basis for their decisions. There are many similar databases based on census results, lifestyle analysis, buying power, postal codes, etc. If you are prepared to pay a lot for a mass screening they can save your time, but they are probably more of a likelihood than a precise measurement.

- *Control over other funds.* Prospects might not own a company but their position within it might give them influence in the disposal of its marketing or charitable budget. Similarly they might be a trustee of a foundation which was not set up by them but whose donations can be influenced by them. Although not part of their wealth, this affects their giving capacity.

- *Donations.* If the prospect has given away large amounts of money it might indicate great wealth. Alternatively it might mean that it has already all been given away!

- *Formulae.* Some researchers like to use rough estimates of asset values to calculate even rougher estimates of overall wealth. Here is one example of how this might be done. Research into the wealth of American millionaires has produced figures for the average proportions held in various types of assets. Two of the largest asset types tend to be real estate and stock in public companies. Someone who is barely a millionaire might have around 30% of wealth in real estate and 15% in stock before deducting debts in the region of 9%. By $10m there might be real estate and stock levels of about 20% each with debts closer to 7%. Bearing in mind that these are only rough guides, if you can guess at real estate or stock figures you might like to use it to estimate the overall wealth.

## 5. Biography

Under this heading would be information such as family (names and occupations of parents, spouses, children, etc.) date and place of birth, and education.

Checking through the whole family can provide a variety of useful insights. You can tell what sort of background the prospect comes from. The spouse is quite likely to have a say as to the size or possibility of a gift, so it is worth knowing who that person is, and even writing a detailed profile. Children might be a drain on resources, they may be a useful topic of conversation, or if you are fund-raising for a university they might be studying (or hoping to study) at your institution. Cousins can be checked out to see whether you know them already (in which case they are potential contacts to approach your prospect), or else maybe they could be prospects in their own right once you have brought the current prospect on board. You might even decide to launch a joint approach: they might join together in creating a fund to commemorate another member of the family. Antecedents are important either as people who might be commemorated by a named gift, or as indicators of the interests of your current prospect. It also pleases people if you are aware of the achievements of their parents or grandparents.

Place and date of education and subjects studied are particularly valuable if you work for a university. If not it can still be a useful source of contacts as you might know other people in the same year, or simply from the same institution. Some institutions have more prestige and higher entrance requirements than others (e.g. the French *grandes écoles*, the Ivy League, Tokyo University, or Oxbridge).

The basic sources are who's whos supplemented by press articles (probably via online databases). You might even be lucky enough to find a published biography.

## 6. Career

A chronological list of the prospect's business career can be taken from biographical directories. If the person is not covered then a quick search of an online database such as *Textline* might provide news articles about their career. If there is still no sign then extend the search, possibly to all the databases on the host e.g. through *Dialog's Dialindex* (file 411).

Current directorships should also be listed. They can both show the range of business interests and suggest contacts. If there is no biographical entry then look in company directories which provide an index of directors, or check on online company databases. The registrar of companies is another source of lists of directorships. In some countries (e.g. the UK) directors are required to list all their other directorships within that country in each company's official return. If you find one directorship then you can find the others (unless they are overseas).

Check out each company's performance via investment publications or online databases (except where it is one of a multitude of non-executive directorships as these are unlikely to take up much time). This affects the prospect's wealth particularly closely when it is a private company, though even directors of public companies may have share options and profit-related pay. Sometimes the location of private companies and the continued funding of them despite heavy losses indicates a loyalty towards the prospect's home region and the desire to create jobs for it. It is useful to be aware of potentially time-consuming or worrying business problems, for example the presence of a hostile predator. The prospect is also likely to be impressed, or at least more sympathetic, towards someone who understands these business activities (unless there is something embarrassing about them!).

If the prospect does not have business interests then explore whatever he or she does do, whether it is charitable activities, farming or politics. These could also appear under the next section.

## 7. Personality and interests

This is often the section where online databases can be most helpful. Who's whos will list hobbies (American ones even extend as far as political and religious convictions, and occasionally a personal life statement); however these are uninspiring in comparison with what can be found in the press. Contacts can also be very helpful as can biographies, though these sources share the problem of subjectivity.

Does your prospect have major likes and dislikes? Are there subjects which are best avoided, or where you should be particularly tactful? Will he react badly to someone who is not immaculately dressed, or feel more comfortable with someone who will chat about sport over a beer?

What spare time activities does he have (if any)? These might indicate a preference for a particular type of project. If his hobby is painting then it might be wise to prepare a few comments on watercolours, still lifes, etc., as appropriate, and be aware of the possibility of sensitivity to criticism. Discussing a common interest might simply be a useful way of breaking the ice on a first meeting.

What type of person is he? Is he absent-minded, and so likely to miss a meeting or need to be reminded of what he promised to do? Does he rapidly become impatient with people who do not get straight to the point? Does he dislike flattery? Perhaps he enjoys socialising or is always seeking to extend his network of contacts?

On the basis of what you have discovered it might be possible to suggest the type of cultivation or reciprocation which should appeal to your prospects: are these people who would prefer to keep their generosity or business dealings a secret, have a large photograph published in the papers, be introduced to a prestigious supporter, or receive lots of technical information on the activities of your organisation?

## 8. Contacts

People who are both friendly towards you and know the prospect can be useful in two ways. Firstly they can give you additional information, such as suggesting the best method of approach and warning if they think it will be a waste of time. Secondly they might be persuaded to undertake the approach themselves.

The ideal is to find someone who is respected by the prospect and who will agree to approach the person on your behalf. This is a great deal easier in some countries than in others. It avoids the delay of working to build up a relation-

110

ship from scratch (which might anyway prove impossible), and it means that your own staff can oversee far more work than they would be able to manage in person. Such approaches are also more likely to succeed because you can be sure that the prospect will at least listen to what a friend has to say, and might agree to support your project simply because it was the friend who asked.

Contacts might be found amongst the prospect's relatives, or by scanning the names of colleagues on boards of directors or trustees, fellow members of a club, or perhaps people who share the same interest. Whether or not you are writing a report for a university it is worth looking for people who were educated at the same place. Does the prospect already have some link with your organisation or an existing interest in your field of work which might suggest appropriate contacts? If you have had your contacts fill out questionnaires (see the chapter on finding prospects) then the results might reveal further links, or else rule out those who you thought might be useful. Not all of these people will be respected, or even liked by the prospect, but they do at least give you a starting point.

It would also be appropriate to list under this section any previous meetings or even rejected invitations, as well as past donations to your organisation.

## 9. Likelihood of success and possible projects

At this stage you can analyse the factual information built up above and provide suggestions of the type of approach that might work. Using the suggestions in the chapter on marketing together with your own ideas, you can judge which of your own particular menu of projects would best suit what you know of the prospect's career, personality and interests. The section on wealth and giving ability should give some indication of how much the prospect can afford to give, bearing in mind other commitments. The aim of this section is not to decide on one project for each prospect, but to suggest a small number which might suit so that the person is not overwhelmed with literature.

The factors which influence the decision to make a gift are very personal and vary over time. Here are some suggestions which might affect your chances of success:

- *Links with other organisations.* These might show a pattern which the prospect might wish to continue. Alternatively the prospect might have decided that enough has been done in that area and refuse to be involved with it again. If the other organisation is rather more successful or better known in this field, it might be wise to steer clear of a competition you are likely to lose and think of an alternative proposal instead.

Information on previous benefactions might be available in published sources, especially in the US. Large donations will be mentioned in the press, and smaller donations might appear in local papers, though as these might not be indexed it can be difficult to find them. If you ring a local library you might find that the staff have some personal knowledge of the prospect's donations. Alternatively, you might find details of gifts recorded in the annual reviews of charities. If you have the time (and if there are no publications which already do this), it might be worth collecting and indexing these reviews.

No matter how assiduous your research, you can still find yourself blocked when the prospect prefers anonymity. You might not be able to find anything at all, but sometimes there are ways of obtaining clues. One starting point is asking volunteers who know the prospect. Alternatively you might check the boards of fund-raising charities, since people who sit on them have generally given donations. For most countries you will probably have to create your own index of charitable trustees because they will not be available. (In the UK an unindexed book is published by Hemmington Scott.) You should also check whether the person is a trustee of a grant-giving body. This might be her own or her family's money (look for fellow trustees with the same surname), and if not might at least give an indication of the range of her personal charitable interests.

• *Ties with your organisation.* Is the prospect a graduate of your university, someone who has been treated by your hospital, had correspondence with you, sent in donations, offered to help, etc? If so it makes it more likely that this person will be responsive, and the existing interest should suggest the type of project which will appeal. Sometimes it can work against you, for example if the prospect has children attending or about to arrive at your university he might be unwilling to make a large public donation for fear of prompting suggestions that he has bought their entry.

The most useful tie with your organisation is probably a previous donation. Donors tend to give again and there are plenty of excuses for contacting them under the guise of reciprocation. However there is no guarantee that it was not a token gift to excuse themselves from further involvement.

• *Influence of the contact.* A good contact who is both capable of putting your case forcefully and well respected by the prospect can make a great deal of difference to the success of the approach.

- *Momentous events.* People often make a donation when something unusual has happened. This might be the death of a relative, which has resulted in a surge of cash through inheritance, a desire to commemorate the deceased, or a re-evaluation of priorities in life. Overcoming a serious illness might have a similar effect as the prospect might wish to contribute to research into the illness or help those who are suffering in the same way.

- *Sudden wealth.* This might come about through the sale or flotation of a company, a huge increase in the value of shares, or an inheritance (all of which might be discovered through the press). People frequently adjust to their level of wealth so that their spending is on a par with their income. However large the sum, they might feel that they have little left over. Exceptions are those whose typical expenditure includes an allowance for charitable activities and who have not already committed themselves to a specific cause (these are often wealthy wives whose 'occupation' is charitable work). When prospects suddenly find they have more money than they are used to they feel rich – they have more than they need. It is this subjective feeling which frequently causes people to dispose of large sums of money. This may well be a temporary phenomenon, lasting only as long as it takes them to adjust their expectations of expenditure into line with their new-found capacity. It is important to approach them quickly, especially as plenty of others are likely to have the same idea.

- *Age and family commitments.* Young prospects are likely to have plenty of plans of their own, such as a home, a family or investment for the future. However when they have young children they often write a will, and it is worth encouraging them to include a donation, even if the pay-off is uncertain and a long way in the future. Retirement often provokes a reassessment of the financial situation, which might result in an off-loading of wealth or again the writing of a will. If the prospects are elderly have they already arranged for the transfer of wealth to the next generation, possibly to avoid inheritance tax? Perhaps there is no-one to inherit, in which case they might like to give their wealth away while they are still alive; however you cannot guarantee that they have not already done that.

- *Business interests.* People can never be entirely divorced from their business interests. Even if they do not wish to make a personal commitment they might be willing to consider the potential advantages to their company. This is more true of private companies (which might be used as an alternative route for handing over essentially personal money), but it can also be the case where the prospect is an employed manager.

- *Hobbies or interests that tie in with your projects.* If you have a project which is a major interest of the prospect then there is a much greater chance that you will engage the person's interest and eventually obtain a donation.

## 10. Sources and appendix

As discussed above, reports should be tightly sourced so that the reader can check how recent or authoritative each aspect is. If there is extra information which would be rather bulky to put in the report or is not of prime importance it can be appended so that the reader can look at it if she wishes. This might be a detailed list of donations from a personal foundation or a particularly detailed article on the prospect's art collection. Such information should also be briefly summarised in the main body of the report. Do not fall into the trap of appending large numbers of press reports: it is your job to condense them for the reader.

# Briefing booklets

If several people are to be met in a short space of time, for example at a reception or on a foreign tour, a different type of document should be prepared. You will probably not have time to produce a full report on each of them, and even if the requester has the time to read them all, he is unlikely to remember the entire contents. It would therefore be better to summarise the salient points in an easily digested briefing which can be scanned quickly immediately before the meeting. These briefings can be bound together in a booklet so that they are less likely to be mislaid.

Useful contents might include:

- Itinerary / agenda / seating plan
- A picture of each person opposite a one-page summary, as follows:
  - Aim of meeting, i.e. what should be discussed with the person
  - Previous contacts (they would not be impressed if everything they said last time had been forgotten)
  - Occupation
  - Family details, e.g. name of spouse, occupations of children (this personal touch is generally much appreciated).

The format depends on the preferences of the requester, but is probably easiest to take in as a series of bullet points. Whatever format is chosen, ideally each briefing should follow a similar pattern and be confined to one side of paper.

If there is any chance of a briefing being extracted or photocopied it might be worth ending each one with your initials and the date. This is because there is no overall heading to give this information. It is particularly useful if individual briefings are compiled by different people within the team.

## Sample report on a person

To follow is a report on a fictitious individual to show how the results of the research process might look. It is written as if for the fictitious Dorchester University's fund-raising department. Being only an example it is relatively brief; it might be useful, for example, to describe in more detail the applications of the miniwidget. If Sir Whipsnade Figgins were to be given a copy of the report it might be better to amend the mention of him in the contacts section.

The sources listed are not extensive, but should serve to illustrate how you might discover this type of information. Their random order is the result of compiling the report as you work your way through the sources. This is the easiest way to do it, though it is not necessarily the best. You might prefer to arrange the sources in a consistent order, e.g. biographical works first, press articles next, etc. Alternatively you might arrange the numbers so that when reading through the report the first you encounter is 1, the next 2, etc. You then have the dilemma of what to do when you reuse a source later in the report. Do you give it the original number again and mess up your sequence or do you accept that you must repeat the same source several times in your source list?

If you are not willing to accept a random arrangement of sources you must wait until the report is finished before assigning numbers. If you do this there is the danger you will forget which piece of information came from which source. Alternatively you can give numbers then rearrange them at the end, but this method is very likely to result in errors. The best solution is probably to assign letters then replace them with numbers at the end. Although this works well it is so time-consuming it might be considered not worthwhile.

# STRICTLY CONFIDENTIAL
## THE HON JOHN XYZ SMITH

*Picture of the prospect to be inserted here*

REQUESTER:      SUSAN MARSHALL

RESEARCHER:     VANESSA HACK

DATE:              30 JUNE 1996

## Summary

Mr Smith would make a very good prospect in the £5-10m range. He has considerable personal wealth, the likelihood of a major inheritance, and strong ties with Dorchester. He also has influence over Giant Industries. With retirement looming he might also be willing to act as a contact, both for prospects in the engineering world and possibly also in the solicitation of his brother.

## Addresses

NB – Mr Smith enjoys the title 'The Honorable' due to his father's life peerage. He does not himself stand to inherit any greater title.[1]

### Home address[2,3,4]

The Old Manor House,
Downtown Road,
Hamborn,
Essex
ESX 9XY
Tel: 01234 567891

### Business address[5]

Giant Industries plc,
1-5 Plymouth Street,
Hamborn,
Essex
ESX 3BA
Tel: 01234 567999
Fax: 01234 567888
(Secretary: Miss Jean West)

# Wealth and giving capacity

Mr Smith appears to own a large and growing fortune. The 1996 *Sunday Times* rich list assessed his wealth as in the region of £65m. He might inherit as much as £40m on the death of his father, Lord Smith.[6]

Much of the family's wealth came from taking Giant Industries public; however it retains a valuable, though relatively small, stake in the company. At 31.12.95 Mr Smith owned 3,999,001 shares in Giant Industries.[7] At 30.06.96 these shares were valued at £10,546,222. In 1995 they provided dividends of £399,900.[8] Mr Smith, as Chairman and Chief Executive of Giant, was paid £755,000 in 1995.[7]

At the core of these companies is the patent for the upturned miniwidget, which was invented by his father. Demand for this item is buoyant, so it is likely that he has a strong, steady flow of income.[9]

Mr Smith also owns a network of small private companies involved in the acquisition and management of real estate. It is difficult to place a value on these as they are constantly borrowing and lending to one another and some are based offshore. The slump in the UK commercial property market does not appear to have caused them significant difficulties, though it must have affected their rental income. At present they appear to be absorbing money for investment and producing relatively low returns. However as they are investing in prime properties they should be well placed to benefit from an upturn in the market.[10,14]

Aside from his substantial residence in Hamborn, Mr Smith has renovated a castle in Scotland and owns houses in London, Paris and New York.[3] These contain a valuable art collection including Rembrandts and a remarkable Titian which alone is thought to be worth about £6m. He also runs a stable of racehorses. Despite a recent and costly divorce (a precise figure for which is impossible to calculate) he gives every impression of being exceedingly wealthy. However, his new wife's tastes have been described as extravagant, and he has a young child to raise and provide for.[6,11,12]

Mr Smith's giving capacity is currently limited by family expenses and a costly lifestyle. Although Giant is doing well his private companies are probably providing relatively low returns. However the possibility of an inheritance and an upturn in the property market makes him potentially capable of giving £5-10m.

# Biography[1,2,3,13]

| | |
|---|---|
| Born: | 30 December 1930, Hamborn, Essex. |
| Father: | Alfred XYZ Smith, Lord Smith of Hamborn |
| Mother: | Jane, née Watson, former secretary to Lord Smith, died of cancer 1985[19] |
| Brother: | Hon Walter Smith, MP |
| Sister: | Duchess of Wessex, currently divorcing the Duke on the grounds of adultery[11] |
| Education: | Eton; Dorchester University, 1948-52, Modern Languages |
| Married: | 1960-91, Susan Edwards, a former actress |
| | 1991-, Marina Lightbody, 35 years his junior |
| Children: | Jane (Mrs Percy Potter), b 1962, ed Dorchester (1980-83, Journalism), editor with the BBC |
| | James, b 1965, ed LSE, working at James Capel |
| | Jeremy, b 1966, ed Dorchester (1984-87, English), actor |
| | Jessica, b 1970, dropped out of a secretarial course, unemployed |
| | Pumpkin Petula, b 1992 |

## Lord Smith

Mr Smith's father is a noted engineer, much respected for his pioneering work on the miniwidget. The son of a miner, he received little formal education. After an apprenticeship in a small engineering firm he managed to persuade a bank to back his revolutionary design and created Dwarf Ltd. This proved so successful that it took over several competitors, ultimately evolving into Giant Industries. Lord Smith was honoured with a life peerage by the Labour Party and holds political views which are opposed to those of his two sons. Now in his nineties Lord Smith is increasingly unwell and is thought to be confined to his bed.[11,16]

## Hon Walter Smith

Mr Walter Smith is well known to the press for his firm anti-EU comments. He represents Essex Mid-West in Parliament, which includes Dorchester. He is married to the American heiress Mitzi Belle who is the largest shareholder in Belle Oil International of Texas. The couple have no children.[1,3,6]

# Career[2,3,11]

After national service with the Coldstream Guards Mr Smith joined the family firm. His father, having himself worked his way up from the bottom, was insistent that he should experience all aspects of the business. His first job was therefore sweeping the factory floor. Having learnt most aspects of upturned miniwidget manufacture Mr Smith's progress to board level was rapid. When in 1965 his father retired Mr Smith succeeded him as Chief Executive, adding the title of Chairman in 1970.

Under Mr Smith's guidance Giant Industries has expanded its overseas markets, notably within Europe, the Middle East and North America. He has successfully switched the more labour-intensive aspects of production to the Far East, enabling him to undercut competitors. Notable amongst these is Supawidget Ltd whose inverted miniwidget is gaining ground in the market. Although the inverted miniwidget lacks the finesse of the upturned one, its innovative 'easistart' feature has proved popular. Giant is thought to be researching the possibilities of incorporating a similar feature into its own product.[9]

Aside from Giant, Mr Smith owns a network of private companies. It is difficult to evaluate their success as some are based offshore and they repeatedly invest in each other. They appear to be buying prime properties and renovating them in readiness for the next boom.[10,14]

Mr Smith is close to retirement age. He has not actually declared his intention to retire, but since his second marriage he has spent less time at Giant. It is widely anticipated that he will be succeeded by his second in command at Giant, Mr Paul Scott, rather than a family member. This should be a reasonably smooth handover as Mr Scott has worked at Giant for 10 years and is thought to share Mr Smith's vision of the future. This means that investors are reasonably content that the firm's direction and profitability will continue as before.[9]

# Personality and interests[11,15,16]

Mr Smith is a firm supporter of the Conservative Party, to which Giant Industries gave £100,000 in 1995.[7] He has been described as a frequent guest at the Party's fund-raising dinners. Unlike his politician brother he often speaks favourably of the European movement. His views on this cause are strong, and he would be unlikely to draw back from a forthright discussion should the opportunity present itself.

Mr Smith used to be an active sportsman. He was particularly fond of hunting until he received a serious injury during a fall. He now enjoys golf for which he uses a buggy since standing for too long can be painful. Should Mr Smith be invited to Dorchester it would be important to ensure that his programme does not involve too much standing and that transport between sites is provided wherever possible.

Mr Smith is known to appreciate good food and describes himself as a connoisseur of fine wines. It is of paramount importance that if he is invited to dinner the menu should be considered carefully with a view to exploiting the chef's strengths, as Mr Smith is a man who is not afraid to express his opinions on this subject. Mr Smith is not known to have any particular dietary requirements, but is believed to be a heavy smoker which might limit the range of fellow guests.

Until his second marriage Mr Smith kept a relatively low profile. The present Mrs Smith is very fond of lavish parties and regularly appears in new and costly jewellery. She has said that she is rapidly bored, so any invitation which involved her would have to be particularly entertaining.[12] Mr Smith appears to be devoted to his new wife and to their daughter who already has her own stable of ponies. He is particularly interested in Pumpkin's progress at reading, which he believes to be above average.

Little is known of the extent of Mr Smith's philanthropic activities. He paid for the Jane Smith wing at Hamborn hospital following the death of his mother. This is a general purpose intensive care unit with 12 beds.[19] Otherwise he does not appear to be publicly involved with any major charity.

## Contacts[17]

Mr Smith and two of his children attended Dorchester University. Mr Smith has been quoted as saying that it provided him with "a good grounding for life in the modern world", though he has also complained that the food was rather poor.[16]

He was a member of the rugby club, through which he knew **Sir Whipsnade Figgins**. This friendship continues to the present day, though at a slight distance. Sir Whipsnade has indicated his willingness to approach Mr Smith on behalf of the University, though as President of the Old Dorcestrian rugby team he might be tempted to mention the hole in the clubhouse roof before other University needs.

Until recently Mr Smith proved elusive as he travelled a great deal. Since his second marriage he has spent rather more time at home in Hamborn, which is within easy travelling distance of the University. He attended the 1993 performance of The Yeomen of the Guard, the 1994 grand dinner and the 1995 summer picnic. On these occasions he met the Vice-Chancellor and discussed the state of the miniwidget market and the difficulty in recruiting speakers of foreign languages.[18] He declined invitations to the open day and the recent cricket match. It is possible that Mrs Smith has some impact on his choice of events.

## Likelihood of success and possible projects

A donation could come from two possible sources. Mr Smith is personally very wealthy. He also has access to the resources of Giant Industries. As he is well known to the University it is likely that a small gift could be relatively easily obtained. However the main objective should be a longer term solicitation for a multi-million pound gift preferably within his lifetime but possibly in his will.

Since Giant Industries went public the Smith family's shareholding has been much diluted. Yet although the major pension funds are now the largest investors, they seem content to leave management decisions to Mr Smith. There seems little doubt that Mr Smith's position at the firm is so dominant that no-one would question his decision to make a multi-million pound gift to Dorchester. However this should be done before he retires.

From the company's point of view collaboration in the field of **Plastics** might prove useful. If it is to maintain its leading position in the miniwidget market it must stay ahead of the competition. Professor McNabb's work in mini-plastography is world renowned, yet the department is under threat of closure by the health and safety inspectorate unless it can find sufficient funds to upgrade its facilities. Giant could not only afford to install these facilities, but could even erect a new, purpose-designed building which could carry its name.

Mr Smith studied **Modern Languages** at Dorchester. He has put his skills to good use in expanding the business into Europe, and believes that there are too few well-trained graduates to take full advantage of the opportunities.[18] He might therefore be interested in a post or scholarships either in this faculty or jointly with **Management Studies**. It might be appropriate for the Vice-Chancellor to approach him on this matter as they have discussed it on previous occasions.

Mr Smith might consider commemorating the achievements of Lord Smith through a **naming opportunity**. Although Lord Smith does not have any personal links with Dorchester, nor did he attend any other university. On his death Mr Smith is likely to inherit several million pounds, and as he does not appear to have urgent need of this himself he might consider a significant donation. Mr Smith's brother might like to co-operate in this project. Although he has no personal link with the University, it falls within his political constituency and he is known for his comments that universities must support themselves through fund-raising. As he is very wealthy and has no children he would make an ideal prospect.

Alternatively, this would be a good time for Giant Industries to name a post in honour of Mr Smith himself as he reaches retirement age. It would mark a fitting conclusion to a successful career.

**Rugby** is another possibility given his interest in his youth, especially if Sir Whipsnade Figgins is to be involved in the approach. However this is not an ideal project as the cost of repairing the roof is relatively low and the money could probably be obtained from other sources. If he is unwilling to look at the other projects it might be worth putting together a package involving a whole **new clubhouse and gym**.

As Mr Smith's only other known donation is to a hospital he might take an interest in medicine. **Cancer research** might be worth trying as his mother had this disease and it was to commemorate her that he built the new wing.

Finally, given Mr Smith's obvious devotion to his youngest daughter and new wife, he might be swayed by a project which appealed to them. One possibility would be the creation of the Pumpkin Smith **nursery** for the children of academics and students. The ladies of the nursery fund-raising committee would no doubt wish to repay such generosity with invitations to social events of a type which might appeal to Mrs Smith. Mrs Smith herself might like to join the committee and widen its horizons in the direction of a second nursery and after-school care.

As well as being a prospect in his own right, Mr Smith is well placed to be a contact for other prospects. Although he retains the private companies and has a young daughter at home, retirement should mean he has more time to devote to other activities. His wide range of business contacts and respected position within the industry mean he could be very useful. However he has not actually announced his retirement so it should not be assumed he will be ready just yet.

# Sources

1. *Debrett's Peerage and Baronetage,* 1995

2. *Who's Who,* 1996

3. *People of Today,* 1996

4. British Telecom telephone directory

5. *Directory of Directors,* 1996

6. *The Sunday Times* rich list, 14.05.96

7. Giant Industries annual report, 1995

8. *Financial Times,* 30.06.96

9. *Investors Chronicle* survey of the miniwidget market, 01.05.96

10. Companies House

11. *Independent,* profile of Mr Smith, 12.12.95

12. *Hello,* 29.02.96

13. Dorchester University central records

14. *Engineering and Building Weekly,* 16.04.96

15. *Business Monthly,* top industrialists, 18.10.95

16. *Daily Mail,* profile of Mr Smith, 02.04.93

17. University alumni database

18. Vice-Chancellor's file notes on meetings with Mr Smith

19. *Hamborn Advertiser,* 01.08.90

**No reference found**

*The City of London Directory and Livery Companies Guide,* 1996

*Directory of Charitable Trustees,* 1996

*Gardens of England and Wales,* 1996

Appendices

Financial tables for Giant Industries (taken from its annual report)

# 9. Company Information

Fund-raisers often look upon a company as a form of foundation. They consider only its charitable budget and send in an application along with all the other charities. However it can be much more profitable to look at other parts of the company's budget, which can be tapped by providing something which the company wants such as advertising opportunities (sponsorship), good publicity (a strong public association with a good cause) or services (universities might offer training courses). As well as different sources of funding you can aim to expand the amount of funding available by delivering a strong sales pitch to a top director. For this reason companies might be looked at as collections of individuals who share some common interests.

## Basic resources

Directors are naturally reticent about their companies' finances and activities. Where the founder's family retains control it can seem an invasion of personal privacy if others are given details of the company. For any type of company there can be important business implications in revealing information. A competitor might find their plans very interesting. If profits are poor, investors will lose confidence and credit might not be so forthcoming. It is also costly and time-consuming to meet auditing requirements and produce glossy annual reports. It is thus hardly surprising that companies are unlikely to volunteer much information unless forced by regulators or enticed by money. Some examples of pressures which force information into the public domain follow.

### Government registries

Each country has its own rules regarding the type and quantity of information which must be disclosed. These protect investors and trading partners from potential fraud. They thus promote investor confidence and encourage the expansion of business, hence increasing the country's wealth. However these measures can meet resistance from companies which prefer to keep their business dealings to themselves. They are costly in terms of creating and maintaining a regulatory body, and poorer countries may have more pressing problems such as famine and political unrest. Some countries have such an ingrained habit of non-conformity and corruption that even where attempts are made to obtain information it cannot necessarily be trusted. You should therefore be prepared for wide variations between countries in both the amount of information available and its reliability.

The first step in obtaining this information is to work out where it is held. There are books which can help such as *International Company Filing Requirements* (Informed Business Services) and *European Companies* (CBD). Another route is to ask the information department of the country's embassy; promoting business is likely to be one of their key concerns, so they should be able to help.

The country might have a central registry or a range of regional ones. If the latter is the case then you must know where the company is based before you will be able to find its records. If possible you should also try to discover what type of company it is. If it is private then it is quite possible that there will be no records anyway, especially if it is small.

Although you might be given the impression that you have to visit in person, information can often be obtained by post or fax, though you might have the delay of payment in advance not to mention communication difficulties. Some of the more advanced countries are beginning to provide electronic access to their records. The European Union has the patchy beginnings of an online service, some countries being better than others.

If you do a great deal of work on a particular country (especially if it is your own) then it may well be worth setting up an access route to the national registry (i.e. establishing an account or obtaining an online service). For large public companies other sources, such as books, are frequently easier to obtain and use; however in some countries (such as the UK) the registry might have advantages when researching private companies.

### The desire for investment

In order to expand or invest in new technology a company needs cash. One way of raising this is by going public, that is, selling shares on the stock market; however stock markets too have their own rules on disclosure. Investors will not hand over money without information to confirm that the company is a good investment. It is therefore forced into giving full details of profit, turnover, etc. The largest world stock markets, such as those in London and the US, have some of the best standards of disclosure. This information can generally be obtained quite easily by anyone who chooses to ask for the company's financial statement or annual report. If you have a problem obtaining it that way there are equivalents available online, or you can pay a company such as *Disclosure* to obtain it for you.

Annual reports are summaries of the trading year. They may be supplemented by smaller interim reports at the half year or even every quarter. There tends to be a gap of two to three months between the announcement of the results at the company's financial year end (which might be at any time but is often 31 December or 31 March) and the publication of the annual report. Rather than waiting for the publication of the annual report you can obtain more up to date information through the press or stock exchange announcements. The latter might be available online; alternatively most stock exchanges produce an official newsletter.

The annual report is normally a glossy document following a fairly standard format: a description of the company's performance throughout the trading year in the first half and financial tables in the second half. Requirements might include names of directors, a sector by sector description of performance, a five-year overview of financial performance, a figure for charitable and political donations, numbers of shares in the company held by directors, etc.

It should be borne in mind that the annual report is effectively a sales document, designed to keep existing shareholders happy and encourage new ones. It often has attractive pictures and although it cannot lie it does its best to present a good image of the company. In countries such as the UK it must present the bad as well as the good, but in other countries you can be less certain of this. There are many ways that companies can manipulate their accounts to make them look better for the brief snapshot taken at the year end. Accounting regulations are constantly being updated to ensure that the investor cannot be misled too much, but the best financial experts are normally one step ahead.

Annual reports might add relatively little to the material in the registry; but they are more user-friendly, easy to obtain and useful for building a library of ready information. They should, however, always be supplemented with more up to date information from the press or other publications.

Annual reports can be particularly valuable when a company's home country does not require it to disclose much information. Foreign companies are drawn to the major international stock markets as these can provide high levels of investment. They also demand high levels of disclosure which means the company provides far more information for the US market than it does at home. It is a good idea to obtain a list of the foreign companies registered on the major international stockmarkets such as those in London and America. One cheap source is *The Complete American Depositary Receipt Directory* from Reference Press which lists all ADRs by company name, industry group, and country of origin. This will tell you that a foreign company is listed in the US though not give much detail about that company.

As well as annual reports, companies will produce brochures when they wish to take over another company or make a new issue of shares. They are also likely to be required to issue public statements whenever anything significant happens, for example a major drop in profits or a takeover bid.

Alternatively, companies can raise money on the bonds markets. The UK's *Financial Times* has daily coverage of Eurobonds, with a weekly summary on Mondays. The managing bank will be listed, and this can be approached for a public prospectus. The bonds might be issued in the name of a subsidiary or project.

In those countries which do not have strong stock markets it is likely that there will be a tradition of raising money privately. It might come from banks, other companies, or private investors, but whatever the case it is unlikely to result in disclosure to the general public. Although the players on stock markets are avidly searching out new investment opportunities overseas there remain many parts of the world where raising finance is a private affair.

### The need for credit

Companies need to be able to acquire raw materials before they sell the finished product, which gives them cash flow problems. They therefore ask the supplier for credit, that is a certain period of time before payment becomes due. The supplier will decide whether or not to agree on the basis of a report from a credit reference agency which specialises in gathering information on the credit-worthiness of companies.

These agencies obtain information on private companies which would be difficult to find elsewhere. This can include not only the company's record of paying former debts, but also basic financial figures like turnover and pre-tax profit. They use both official sources and straightforward approaches to the companies concerned, which have a powerful incentive to comply.

Credit reports can be expensive, but if you only want the basic financials without the credit rating you can obtain it from a company like Dun & Bradstreet. As well as credit reports this American giant produces an international range of books and online services which give basic facts such as turnover, number of employees, etc. Unfortunately it takes a while to compile such comprehensive figures so as with any source check how recent each entry is.

### Secondary sources

These are sources that gather information from elsewhere and present it in a different format, e.g. directories. They might be more user-friendly but they can also be less reliable. They include books, online databases and CD-ROMs.

Publishers will frequently offer the same information in all three formats, so see the chapter on electronic information before deciding which to use. Although publishers frequently obtain their information direct from the company or the national registry there is no guarantee that they have reproduced it accurately or kept it totally up to date.

The standardised format of business reference sources might lull you into a false sense of security. It gives the impression that the information contained within it is also standard: that it is all equally reliable, no matter which country it comes from. In fact some countries have stricter standards and better enforcement than others. It might be in the companies' interests to inflate their figures to encourage investment or to minimise profits to reduce the tax bill. In some areas, such as the former Soviet Union, accountancy is a new concept and one which is not yet perfectly understood. There are also quite legitimate differences between countries in their accounting standards, which means that figures are by no means comparable.

The publishers might adopt various measures to counteract these problems or they might be content with the data in its raw form. They are not normally very good at explaining either what the differences are between countries or what adjustments they have made in response. Although there is no way that the prospect researcher can be an expert in the accounting and regulatory environment of every country, it is at least worth noting that these problems exist.

It is also worth being aware that online company databases can be very out of date. Press databases, however, are likely to be correct to the last day or two. It is therefore worth supplementing a check of a company database with press coverage to ensure that there have not been any new profit announcements or changes of directors.

Beware of trusting press reports, even when it seems that everyone is saying the same thing. Newspapers keep costs down by using press releases and briefing sessions provided by companies' public relations departments. Relatively untrained reporters can thus turn out large quantities of articles on a wide variety of topics. When reading several papers you become aware that they are essentially rewriting the same information without analysing it in much (or any) depth. They might emphasise different parts of the story, but they do not necessarily think much about what they are writing. There is also a tendency for errors to be compounded in more in-depth articles because the journalist has researched the topic by reading earlier articles. The fact that everyone appears to be saying the same thing does not, therefore, mean that it is correct.

If there is a great deal of coverage of a particular company you might choose to narrow an online search to a particular newspaper, so as to avoid duplication. You might also wish to do a search specifically of those columns devoted to more thoughtful, individual comments, such as the *Financial Times*'s 'Lex'. These tend to be written by senior journalists who will go out of their way to provide a new angle on a story. Alternatively you could print out all of the headlines and scan them for those which contain some element of analysis (e.g. 'Can XYZ Co sustain the momentum?' rather than 'XYZ Co sales up by 50%').

Stock market reactions should also be viewed as potentially unreliable. Although banks employ trained analysts and huge research departments they still exhibit a strong herding instinct. They rely heavily on what other people think, and try to anticipate what other people's reactions will be. If they think the other players in the market will react badly to an announcement (even if they think everyone else is wrong) they might still fall into line. This is a strange environment where objective reality is not necessarily important: if everyone decides to sell then the price drops and it was a bad investment, even if on trading performance it should have been a good one. The market makes its own objective realities. Thus it is quite possible that your analysis of a firm's trading prospects could be more accurate than the stock market's.

As well as directories there are business histories. The author might have obtained access to rather more information than is available to other sources, but might have a bias in a particular direction. In order to obtain the information he might have had to convince the company that he would present it in a favourable light. Alternatively he might wish to obtain more publicity and higher sales by claiming to have discovered scandals.

# Non-standard companies

### The obscure small company

This chapter deals primarily with large companies. Small companies can be much harder to research and you should not be too concerned if you do not find anything. They are not likely to be quoted on stock exchanges so try company registries, contacts and mass trawls of online databases. It might help to search on the telephone number rather than the name in case the owner is running several businesses from the same address.

Although they are too small to be prospects in their own right they are likely to be researched as part of the private wealth of individuals. They might be means of negotiating tax and might be part of a network, part of which is based offshore. The fact that they appear to be doing little or even making losses does not necessarily mean anything if you cannot see the full structure.

### Partnerships

These might look like ordinary companies, but need to be treated rather differently. They frequently operate in professional fields such as law or accountancy. Some partnerships look very much like a single, large company because they share the same name and co-operate in their activities; however if one branch dislikes what the others are doing (such as merging with another partnership) it might vote to secede.

The partners tend to be well-educated and articulate, and each owns a stake in the company so likes to have a say in everything that happens. This could make the larger ones unwieldy, so they might have senior partners who operate rather like a board of directors. Even so some decisions might only be decided on a ballot of all the partners.

Charitable donations are a particularly awkward matter. It is very difficult to get everyone to agree on a large donation, especially when it is to a university that only some of the partners have attended. The partnership's money is effectively the private wealth of its partners, and they are much more careful about giving it away. The solution might be to treat them as a collection of individuals, perhaps holding a presentation for the entire group, but asking them to contribute on a personal level rather than as if they were a standard company. Alternatively they do sometimes appreciate marketing opportunities, e.g. in sports sponsorship.

Partnerships are generally difficult to research. In many countries the only information they have to provide is to the tax office. However their professional bodies often produce directories which will give information like address, names of partners, qualifications and specialisations.

# Which type of company report?

The rest of this chapter describes how to produce a detailed report; however this is not always appropriate. It is important to ensure that your commitment of time and resources is in proportion to the likely returns. Work closely with the requester to ensure you understand what precisely is required.

If the requester is merely surveying the territory to find worthwhile prospects then it might be more cost-effective to provide a survey; for example, you might consider an entire industry or the top companies in your region, and focus on factors such as previous contacts or level of profitability or extent of involvement in a specific sector, as seems appropriate.

If the intention is purely to approach the company's charities fund then the likely return is possibly not sufficient to justify the production of a full report. Higher returns can be obtained by providing something that the company wants, such as marketing opportunities or skills in research and development. It may not be aware that it wants these things until you put your case, so do not be put off by the absence of similar deals in the past. If, however, the charities budget is the target then it might be adequate to hand over a copy of the company's annual report, its guide for applicants (if one exists), and photocopies from publications that describe companies' giving records (e.g. those of the Directory of Social Change in the UK and the Foundation Center in the US).

The full company report would be appropriate if a full-scale approach is to be made to the main board. This will require substantial planning as it could potentially have significant returns and must be right first time. One of the purposes of such a report is normally to give an indication as to whether the approach is likely to be successful. If the research throws up what appear to be major problems then discuss these with the requester at once rather than wasting time in completing the report.

# Working through a report: stage by stage

## 1. The company's name

Although this seems obvious, the vital importance of identifying the correct company can easily be overlooked. Corporate families often contain numerous companies with only slight variations in their names. Although these might seem insignificant to you, employees of the group will be very well aware of the differences. If you are not careful you might end up providing contact details for a subsidiary rather than the parent.

Unfortunately the person who requests the report is quite likely either to give an ambiguous name or to give the name of a subsidiary when he means the parent. Unfortunately even the most prestigious newspapers are capable of making the same mistakes. It is not uncommon to find press articles that use a generic company name when in fact they are confusing two distinct subsidiaries, or occasionally two totally different companies. One frequent source of confusion is General Electric of the US and GEC of the UK.

Before you start, make sure that you check in a book such as Dun & Bradstreet's *Who Owns Whom* (as this provides very full listings of companies with similar names) and if necessary go back to the person who requested the report to make sure you are researching the right one. The name should be written out in full at the head of the report, and if necessary any potential confusions should be carefully explained.

## 2. Confidential information

Whether or not you wish to extract this from the body of the report depends on who will read it. If your reports are of a good quality it is possible that they will regularly be handed over to a contact on the inside of the company. The report might be one of the means used to persuade a contact that your organisation is serious and professional, and hence worth helping. Reports must also convince contacts that by linking themselves with your organisation they are not likely to suffer a damaging loss of face through your incompetence.

The type of information you extract is up to you and the person who requested the report. It should be appended to the report for the requester to read, and, if appropriate, convey to the contact. The following are suggestions:

- Adverse comments about other people in the company, e.g. mistakes they have made or personal characteristics such as meanness with money. These people might well be friends of your contact, and such comments might instantly alienate them. Even if they are not particularly friendly with them the contact might well feel embarrassed on their behalf or even on his or her own behalf if there is a suspicion that you are compiling similar material concerning him or her.

- Adverse comments about the company. Mistakes made by the company might reflect on your contact if nothing was done to prevent them from happening. You might be totally unaware of how large your contact's role was. This is a difficult area as you do not wish to appear ignorant of key facts, such as problems with a particular business area or an acrimonious court case. If these are stated in the report in a brief, factual, non-judgemental way the contact is likely to accept their presence as a sign of your thoroughness. You can still elaborate on them in the confidential section.

- Charitable gifts or refusals to donate from other people in the company. Such matters are often seen as confidential. Even if people do not request anonymity, they probably do not anticipate you discussing them with their colleagues.

- Contacts with other members of the company. It is possible that there were various alternatives who were considered as key contacts. If your contact realises that someone else could have done the job he or she might decide to drop out and leave it to that person. However, it is important that he or she is not totally in the dark, as it would be embarrassing to appear not to be fully briefed.

- Opinions as to the likely success of the approach. There is something to be said for mentioning points for and against in the report itself so as to show that you understand the company's point of view. However, your report is in some ways a sales document, and if you manage to convince the contact that it is not in the company's best interests to help you or that the approach is not likely to succeed then there is little point in writing it. If you really think that the approach will fail then stop writing the report at once and speak to the requester, as this will save everyone's time. Generally the outcome is not so clear cut and you can present a reasonable argument for success.

## 3. Key data

The front page of the report itself gives brief at-a-glance information.

- *Summary.* This must be brief: no more than a few lines giving the key points of the company, i.e. what it does, whether it is doing it well, and possibly whether you consider it a good prospect.

- *Address, telephone, fax.* These are normally so widely available that you cannot miss them. Include as many as might be useful, for example, if the head office is in another country you might include the national office as well. If it is a small company its 'registered' office might be its accountant or lawyer's office. This is probably not of any use to you. You are more likely to need the address from which business is actually conducted.

- *Key subsidiaries.* These will be listed in the annual report or directories such as Dun & Bradstreet's *Who Owns Whom.* An alternative is to list brand names. These may well be more familiar than the company's overall name, and provide a hook on which to hang subsequent information.

- *Directors and key officers.* In most countries there are numerous publications which will supply these names. Hard-copy sources will inevitably be a little out of date, even when you first receive them. Online company databases are also prone to being out of date. It is therefore worth supplementing them with a search of the press.

Some online databases, notably Reuters *Textline*, have available a code for management changes. If you use this code (in conjunction with the company name or code) then you retrieve only those articles that cover management changes, which can be immensely useful when you are dealing with a well-known company that would otherwise throw up hundreds of references.

The directors and their responsibilities should be listed. Also mention whether they are non-executive (which in some books is indicated only by an asterisk). Executive directors are people with a 'hands-on' managerial role, while non-executives might turn up infrequently to oversee the general progress of the company and ensure that no obvious abuses are occurring. Non-executives are often highly respected business executives who hold key positions in other companies.

The executive/non-executive divide can in some ways be compared with the two-tier board system which is common in Germanic countries. The Germanic supervisory board possibly has rather more influence than the non-executive directors on a single board who generally serve with a strong chief executive. An exception is the non-executive chairman who might be a former chief executive and is likely to wield considerable influence. However board dynamics are very complex and each company will be different.

There are considerable differences in the role and power of executives in different countries who appear to share the same title. The problem is partly that titles do not translate directly from one language to another so a near fit is chosen. However it can also be a problem between countries that share the same language.

You might also like to note here whether you have any contacts with the directors, though it might be preferable to exclude some of these – see the section above on confidential information. You might, for example, state whether they are graduates of your university or friends of your charity.

## 4. General background

This contains points of note which do not fit under the other headings. This vagueness permits you to adjust to the varying requirements of very different companies. The following are examples of what might appear here:

- *Company history*. Was it until recently a private company (in which case there might be a strong family influence), or has it come from the public sector? Was it formed out of the amalgamation of two companies? Has it been subject to a hostile take-over which might mean simmering resentment?

- *Regional loyalty.* Some companies were founded and have retained their headquarters in a particular town. Although they operate nationally or internationally they are very conscious of their responsibility to their particular region.

- *Court cases.* Is the company currently or has it recently been involved in a court case? This information is more than just background knowledge: it could have a considerable effect on its giving capacity, e.g. it might have to pay compensation or be excluded from a particular market.

- *Corporate image.* Is it battling against complaints over pollution or un-ethical practices? Is it seen as a particularly enlightened employer? You might check a book such as *The 100 Best Companies to work for in America* from the Reference Press to gain an impression of what matters to the company.

- *Stability.* Does it steadily follow the same course, or is it about to have a major change in the boardroom? Is its board dominated by one key figure, and if so is this person young, popular or strong enough to retain that position? Are there large shareholders (other than pension funds) which threaten to alter the course of the company?

- *Family ties.* Are the directors related to each other? Such ties can be particularly important in a private company or a public one where the founder is still at the helm.

- *Control.* Are there any shareholders with stakes so major that they can affect the company? This might be the founding family, predators, or investors who might be persuaded to sell their stake. If there is a take-over battle looming this might not be a good time to launch an approach.

## 5. Activities

In the case of a large public company it is easiest to compile this section around two tables which can normally be found ready-made in the annual report. Numbers inside brackets are negative ones, such as losses. You can extract the figures and write an explanation of what lies behind each one using the narrative part of the annual report, press coverage, etc. It will show a contact that you know what you are talking about and enable the person who makes the approach to talk intelligently about the company and to pinpoint the directors' major concerns before a meeting.

- *Analysis by business segment.* What proportion of the company's turnover (sales) and pre-tax profit come from each aspect of its business? A large company will generally operate in various different markets and it is interesting to see which are the most important to it. This can be followed up with an analysis of each segment. What this covers depends on the type of company, but here are some questions you might ask: What exactly does it do in this area and what are its brand names? Who are its major customers? What is its market share? How are market forces affecting its competitive performance? Is demand depressed by the weather, or is it losing out to a more successful product? What are its plans for the future?

- *Geographical analysis.* Which countries provide the company's markets and where does it manufacture? How is each region performing? As more companies become truly international they can be severely affected by fluctuating exchange rates and political unrest.

## 6. Finances

This section covers the company's overall performance. If possible obtain figures going back for up to five years as they often fluctuate considerably and you need to pick out the trend. In the annual reports of large public companies there is often a table giving five years' performance.

The balance sheet and profit and loss account are the key tables to look for. The remainder of the annual report is likely to contain smaller tables and notes which explain how each figure in these key tables was derived. The profit and loss account is possibly more reliable than the balance sheet as the former is a record of the performance over the year while the latter is a snapshot on one day.

It is time-consuming to reproduce the entire profit and loss table and probably unnecessary, if it is required you can always append a copy, otherwise you can produce an abbreviate table. The key figures are normally turnover (or sales) and pre-tax profit. Many profit figures are given, but pre-tax profit is the one most commonly used because tax can have a considerable distorting effect. It might also be interesting to look at retained profit (i.e. level of investment as opposed to the money handed out to shareholders) or net cash or debt.

Occasionally you might be confused by the presence of two sets of balance sheets and profit and loss tables in a single annual report. One will probably be the parent company's own results (and the parent might be little more than a non-trading shell which takes money from shares in its subsidiaries), and the other the consolidated (i.e. joint) results for the parent company plus its subsidiaries.

Figures of companies in different countries should not be compared at face value as accounting practices vary so widely. Even within the same country there is room for considerable leeway in the presentation of accounts.

136

There are numerous calculations which can be done to obtain a measure of the company's performance. The most basic is a percentage change on last year's figures. In smaller companies this is all that is possible, but for larger ones that are forced into more disclosure you can analyse the figures in some detail. Financial mathematics is too complex a subject to be covered in any detail here. Some of the more popular and straightforward calculations are shown below. There are variations on them – e.g. profit after tax might be used instead of pre-tax profit – so check that the same figures are used when comparing ratios from different sources.

*Current ratio: current assets / current liabilities*

This is a basic check of short term liquidity. If assets exceed liabilities then a company can pay its debts, at least for the moment. It could be refined by deducting stock from assets as stock cannot be converted into cash at very short notice.

*Gearing: net debt / net assets x 100*

Measures of gearing are often encountered in the press. They show how high the debts are in relation to the company's ability to repay them. In the US a company with high gearing might be called highly leveraged. Debts are generally inevitable as they enable the company to invest or expand; however if the gearing is much higher than the industry average this is a sign of weakness. This is a particular problem when they are short term debts (current liabilities) as they have to be repaid sooner. However long term debt is also a problem as it can mean substantial interest charges.

*Profit margin: pre-tax profit / sales x 100.*

This is a standard measure of efficiency and profitability: the higher the percentage the better.

*Return on capital employed: pre-tax profit / capital employed x 100*

The decision whether or not to invest in the company is based on figures like this.

*PE ratio: Price per share / latest year's earnings per share*

This compares the share price with the amount of money that the company made per share. A high figure means the shares are much sought after. It is a measure of investor confidence in the firm, but could also mean that the company is considered to be a take-over target.

When doing these calculations it is important to remember that each industry has its own norms: a supermarket will operate on high turnover and tight margins, while a retailer of luxury goods will normally have higher profit margins. Service industries do not employ huge amounts of capital, while manufacturers must invest heavily in machinery. To find out whether your company is doing well you should compare it with the industry norms. These are available in book form, for example, Dun & Bradstreet's *Key Business Ratios* covers the UK. There are slight differences in the way that different books perform some of the calculations, but they should explain their procedures in the front of the book.

There are also various distorting factors which must be eliminated when considering the company's underlying trading performance, such as:

- *Disposals.* When a sector of the company is sold there is an influx of cash (generally listed separately from the normal trading income) but a reduction in turnover and profit (unless the sector was making losses). Money does not normally sit around unused (though the occasional company is notorious for its cash pile), so anticipate purchases of other businesses.

- *Restructuring.* When a company undertakes a restructuring programme so as to improve performance, it is likely that the initial result will actually appear to be a decline in performance. This is because of expenses such as redundancy payments and redesigning stores, as well as a decline in income caused by the reduction in the level of activity. It is not an indication that the policy has not worked.

- *Currency fluctuations.* Companies which make much of their money overseas can be very severely affected by this problem. They are likely to adopt tactics to minimise it, and some actually become adept at currency speculation. A company can appear to be badly hit by a currency change, even when trading remains buoyant; however this does not mean that in reality it has suffered. Currencies must be converted on paper for the purposes of the published accounts, even when in reality the money has not been touched. If the company reinvests in the same country or waits until exchange rates have improved it might not suffer a loss at all. The figures are thus illusory. There is generally no need to worry about looking for these problems as companies are eager to protect their share prices by explaining what has happened in their press releases. Some, though not all, newspapers will thus mention the fact.

- *Revaluation of assets.* Apart from the continuous devaluation of machinery, computers, etc., known as depreciation, there is the rather more unpredictable impact of land and buildings. Every few years the company will conduct a revaluation of these assets, which can have a considerable impact on the balance sheet. Properly presented accounts should contain a note explaining what has happened in the year of the change, but you might have to work back several years to discover when the last valuation was conducted and so decide whether the current valuation is fair and in line with other companies.

Such factors are generally treated as outside the normal range of activity and allowances are made. However in some cases they are part of the genuine trading activity. Some companies specialise in buying and splitting up others, the parts being worth more than the whole. Some make large profits from currency speculation, while retailers in particular often place a significant emphasis on acquiring prime-site stores for their property portfolios.

The overall state of the economy can have a major impact on many companies. Some are also affected by factors such as the weather (e.g. sales of ice-creams, insurance pay-outs). Some companies attempt to overcome these influences by diversifying into markets which are not affected by them, hoping that this will provide a degree of stability. It might instead mean that they are operating in markets which they do not fully understand and in which they are not best placed to compete. Factors such as these can be mentioned in this section.

## 7. Contacts

These might be any of the following:

- Directors, officers, members of the charities committee. The higher placed the better your chances of success and the higher you might set your sights.
- Business associates of the directors.
- Fellow members of other boards. Top directors frequently hold non-executive posts on the boards of several companies.
- Fellow trustees of other charities. Company directors often serve on these committees, but they may feel awkward about using links forged by another organisation.
- Alumni of your university who have been employed by the company. Even if you only know the number of new graduates recruited each year it can indicate the company's level of interest in your university.
- Previous and present research, training or other business contracts undertaken by your institution on behalf of the company.

- Charitable gifts to you from the company.
- Shareholders.
- Advisors, e.g. accountants, lawyers (listed in some company directories).

For each person you suggest you should also consider how strong are the links with both your organisation and the prospect, and whether there are any competing demands, such as membership of the fund-raising committee of another organisation.

## 8. Likelihood of success and possible projects

This is the most analytical part of the report. Rather than handing over bare facts the researcher should look at the information gathered and use it to make suggestions about the way forward.

This requires a sound understanding not only of the prospect company's motivations, but also of your own organisation's strengths and requirements. What can you offer that will meet the prospect's needs? See the chapter on marketing for a fuller discussion on this topic.

You must also investigate the company's charitable giving, sponsorship deals, activities in the local community, etc. These should be listed here or, if there is considerable detail, summarise them here and append a photocopy of the full list. Does it have a stated policy or aim? Does it belong to an organisation such as The Per Cent Club which encourages corporate philanthropy?

These facts might be mentioned in the annual report. There might be a bald figure, or, increasingly, there might be a whole section devoted to publicising the company's good works. Larger companies might produce guides for applicants or have a separate foundation. See the chapter on foundations for further details. In countries such as the UK and US there are also books which list the giving activities of the major companies. See the country chapters for their names.

An indication of your potential for success and the most hopeful areas might be obtained from any of the following:

- *Previous links* between your organisation and the prospect. Were they successful, and were they followed up rather than being allowed to lapse through lack of interest?
- The prospect's *existing or previous tie-ups* with your competitors.

- The prospect's *areas of strength*. The company will wish to maintain or extend its competitive advantage in its key markets and you might be able to help, perhaps through providing research and development skills or through a sponsorship deal which will promote its name amongst key groups of customers.

- *Areas of expansion*. These will be stated in a company's annual report. Even if the sector is currently quite small it is probably taking up a disproportionate amount of the directors' attention, and they will be looking for ways to ensure that their investment succeeds. Similarly if a sector has been a particular problem and there are signs that it will be disposed of then there is no point in constructing a proposal around it.

- *Record of charitable donations*. Larger amounts will probably be gained from the company's marketing, public relations or research budgets rather than the charities budget. However if all else fails you can fall back on this. There might be a statement on donations policy plus a list of recent grants. These might be published in the company's annual report, in the charity committee's guide for applicants, or in a general book on company donations (such as those published by the Directory of Social Change in the UK or the Foundation Center in the US). If they are already heavily involved with another charity then it might be wiser to try a different angle rather than compete in the same field. Many companies have only an integral charities budget distributed by the board or a sub-committee of the board; however others have a related foundation and some even have both. See the chapter on foundations for further explanation.

- *Interests of the directors*. Try to discover who the key people will be in the decision over your proposal. Perhaps there is a strong chief executive, or maybe one of the directors has a particular interest in your field. Do you have any previous contacts with them which might suggest that some of them might look particularly favourably on your approach? How do they occupy their leisure time? Do they have anything in common with the person who will make the approach, for example the same university or the same club? Do they sit on the boards of charities, or do they have any hobbies which would suggest a particular interest? Do they have pet projects within the business? Might they be particularly swayed by the type of reciprocation you can offer, for example, might they like to meet some of your supporters, or might they enjoy being the centre of attention at your institution? Decisions are not necessarily made purely on the basis of what is best for the company; directors like to follow their own inclinations from time to time. There is often room for interpretation of the company's interests.

### 9. Sources and appendices

Sources should be listed carefully. Dates are particularly important as company information dates very rapidly.

The decision as to whether your solicitation is successful is normally in the hands of the directors, unless you are looking for a small donation from the charities fund (in which case a full report is not necessarily worthwhile). Try to find a who's who entry for each of the directors and append these to the end of the report.

It is increasingly likely that a company's annual report will contain pictures of the directors. These should also be appended as they could provide some clues to the personalities of the directors and will at least help in distinguishing them at a first meeting.

You might also like to append the annual report or a copy of its major financial tables, as well as a list of its charitable donations if these are very detailed.

## Sample report on a company

To follow is a sample company report. The details are entirely fictitious and are not meant to represent any actual company.

A genuine report might be longer than this as there would be scope for precise details about products, markets, finances, etc. As it is not based on a full series of financial tables there are no ratios or calculations of performance. Information about trading conditions, in particular markets, becomes out of date so rapidly that only a basic impression can be given here.

This report starts with a separable section containing particularly sensitive information which should be seen by the requester only. This assumes that the main body of the report will be passed on to a contact who might well be a director of the company. The report begins with key data, which in A4 or foolscap format would ideally fit onto one page. You could, if you wished, precede it with a cover sheet for confidentiality or a more professional finish.

As a report must have a strong element of marketing, it is written for a fictitious institution called Dorchester University. Dorchester's needs and strengths will be very different from those of other institutions, but it will show what type of approach can be taken.

# CONFIDENTIAL NOTES
## MEGACORP PLC

| | |
|---|---|
| **REQUESTER:** | TIMOTHY SMITH |
| **RESEARCHER:** | VANESSA HACK |
| **DATE:** | 21 MAY 1996 |

## The state of the company

Megacorp currently has financial problems. Its gearing is very high in comparison with other retailers. There have been suggestions that the best solution might be to break the company up as its components are so different in style. As yet there does not appear to be any sign of a predator and it is possible that the new Chief Executive (CE) might be capable of turning it round by selling the loss-making home improvement sector.

This is therefore not the best time for an approach. However it cannot be entirely ruled out as it has such strong contacts with the Dorchester area and its giving is very locally oriented. The question should possibly be whether to approach it now for a relatively small gift, or start to build up a relationship with the hope of a large gift when the situation improves.

### Mr Patrick J Mole (former CE)

Unfortunately Mr Mole, who is a long-standing contact of the University, abruptly left his position at Megacorp last year with 18 months still to run on his contract. It is thought his resignation was influenced by the Jamesson family who are major shareholders. He was closely associated with the company's vigorous acquisition strategy of the 1980s which left it so heavily in debt. His replacement, Chris Lucas, is seen as much more cautious.

Although not himself a Dorchester graduate, Mr Mole was born and brought up in the town and has taken a considerable interest in the University. He has dined with the Vice-Chancellor on numerous occasions and was a guest at last year's performance of Handel's Water Music. He was awarded an honorary degree in 1992.

Mr Mole has been an active volunteer for the University, helping in the successful approaches to Manufacturecorp and Bigco. He was also responsible for Megacorp's 1993 gift of £25k for the new swimming pool. However great care should be taken in approaching him on this occasion as he may feel very resentful about his untimely departure from the company. Nevertheless, during his 10 years at the helm of Megacorp he appears to have been a popular and charismatic leader. He may well retain friendships and influence with some of his former colleagues. He might be able to arrange an introduction, and could at least advise on the chances of success of various approaches.

## Mrs Joanne J Brown

Mrs Brown is a graduate of Dorchester University but has not been approached so far because Mr Mole appeared a better contact. In 1991 she responded to a mailshot with a gift of £10 for library books.

RESEARCH REPORT – STRICTLY CONFIDENTIAL

MEGACORP PLC

| | |
|---|---|
| REQUESTER: | TIMOTHY SMITH |
| RESEARCHER: | VANESSA HACK |
| DATE: | 21 MAY 1996 |

## Summary[1]

Megacorp is one of the UK's leading retailers. Besides the well-known grocery shops it sells clothing, car parts and DIY/home improvement goods. It also has substantial property investments. The majority of its operations are within the UK, though its Megamarket grocery chain is very successful in Europe. Megacorp is an acquisitive company which has considerable debts as a result of rapid growth in the 1980s.

### Address[1]

Megacorp plc,
1 Megacorp Road,
Megaville,
Essex
ME21 1UX
Tel: 01111 11111
Fax: 01111 11112

### Principal subsidiaries[1]

Megamarket Ltd
Megamarket (US) Inc
Top-to-Toe Style Ltd
Carbits Ltd
Home Style Ltd

**Directors**[2,3]

| | |
|---|---|
| Sir Humphrey Popple, CBE | *Chairman* |
| Mr Christopher M Lucas | *Chief Executive* |
| Mrs Joanne J Brown | *Finance Director* |
| Mr James Featherly | *Managing Director, Property* |
| Sir Thomas LC Coe | *Non-executive* |
| Mr Ashley B Thomas, CBE | *Non-executive* |

Mrs Brown read Management Studies at Dorchester from 1979 to 1982.[4]

# General background[8]

Megacorp came into existence in 1985 with the acquisition of James Jamesson Ltd by Megastores. James Jamesson was a family firm founded in 1888 which specialised in ladies' fashions. Megastores, by contrast, was a dynamic young grocery retailer.

Megacorp grew rapidly during the 1980s, acquiring companies such as Carbits Ltd and Home Style Ltd. The architect of this strategy was the Chief Executive, Mr Patrick J Mole. Mr Mole's long reign came to an end last year with the appointment of Mr Lucas who has introduced a more cautious management style. Mr Lucas has declared that his main goal is to reduce the company's heavy burden of debt. Evidence of cost-cutting is already apparent and there are rumours of a major disposal (probably the loss-making Home Style).[5]

The largest shareholder in Megacorp is the Jamesson family trust which acquired 8.9% of the shares as part of the purchase price for James Jamesson Ltd. The next largest is the Investco pension fund with 3.4%. Both appear to be long-term investors. Although they do not generally appear to play an active role in the company, the Jamessons recently expressed their concern at its level of debt. They are thought to support the new CE, Mr Lucas.

# Activities

### Analysis by business segment[1,6,8]

| Year to 31 Dec | 1995 | | 1994 | |
|---|---|---|---|---|
| £m | Turnover | Pre-tax profit | Turnover | Pre-tax profit |
| Groceries | 4,021.2 | 350.5 | 4,793.0 | 361.2 |
| Clothing | 1,821.9 | 108.2 | 1,897.4 | 111.8 |
| Car parts | 350.2 | 15.3 | 347.5 | 14.2 |
| Home improvement | 220.7 | (33.9) | 231.9 | (19.8) |
| Property | 89.9 | 47.5 | 98.5 | 53.2 |
| TOTAL | 6,503.9 | 487.6 | 7,368.3 | 520.6 |

*Groceries*

This is the core activity with 108 Megamarkets in the UK and 67 in Continental Europe. Although groceries are traditionally resistant to fluctuations in the retail cycle, competition from foreign chains has led to a price war. Megamarket has responded by cutting the prices of a range of everyday items, but is still not performing as well as in previous years. Last month Mr Lucas announced plans to open a new range of low-price out of town superstores. However he might find it difficult to obtain planning permission given the shift in government policy towards revitalising city centres.[7]

## Clothing

Top-to-Toe Style Ltd is a traditional retailer whose customers tend to be older women. This section of the population is increasing in numbers and spending power, but this has encouraged competitors such as Hi-Fashion Ltd to enter the market. Although Top-to-Toe is not at the height of fashion it benefits from a respected brand name. The attempt to complement it with a Young Style range was generally considered to be a failure as younger buyers did not appreciate the connection with clothing bought by their grandmothers. An attempt to enter the US market has so far not been particularly successful.

## Car parts

This sector is one that has actually benefitted from the recession and the decline in consumer confidence. As the market for new cars has slumped consumers are holding on to their old cars for longer and undertaking more routine maintenance. Sales of rust remover have been particularly strong. Increased awareness of auto-theft has led to a boom in sales of security devices. Unfortunately this accounts for a relatively small part of Megacorp's overall turnover.

## Home improvement

The Home Style chain turned in a disastrous performance last year. Unless there is a decisive change in government policy on mortgage relief there seems no end in sight to the slump in the housing market. Shortly after his appointment Mr Lucas announced his intention to take this sector firmly in hand. Whether this means closures or sale is still not clear, but it is rumoured that a buyer is being sought.

## Property

In common with many retailers, Megacorp has a substantial property portfolio. This includes both out of town superstores and prime high street sites. Unfortunately it has been badly hit by the slump in property prices. It has not taken advantage of the low prices to acquire new properties.

**Analysis by geographical segment**[1,6]

| Year to 31 Dec | 1995 | | 1994 | |
|---|---|---|---|---|
| £m | Turnover | Pre-tax profit | Turnover | Pre-tax profit |
| UK | 5,166.5 | 428.6 | 5,951.6 | 460.0 |
| Rest of Europe | 1,034.2 | 48.3 | 1097.2 | 48.7 |
| Rest of World | 303.2 | 10.7 | 319.5 | 11.9 |
| TOTAL | 6,503.9 | 487.6 | 7,368.3 | 520.6 |

The majority of Megacorp's operations are in the UK, though Megamarkets has a sizeable presence in Continental Europe. Unfortunately the weakness of sterling has reduced the impact of contributions from overseas, despite a general improvement in performance.

**Finances**[1,6,8]

| Year to 31 Dec | 1995 | 1994 | 1993 | 1992 | 1991 |
|---|---|---|---|---|---|
| Turnover (£m) | 6,503.9 | 7,368.3 | 6,899.7 | 6,801.8 | 6,500.2 |
| Pre-tax profit | 487.6 | 520.6 | 498.9 | 492.6 | 485.3 |
| Retained profit | (49.7) | (23.3) | (18.6) | (16.4) | (2.1) |
| Dividend | 112.1 | 113.4 | 100.9 | 99.2 | 87.8 |

In 1995 turnover decreased by 11.7% and pre-tax profits by 6.3%. The extent of this decline is partly explained by the relatively strong performance in 1994; however the main reason was the decline in the performance of the core groceries sector, which had a major impact on the figures. The increased competition which lies behind this problem does not seem likely to be overcome in the near future.

Apart from the recent problems in the groceries sector, the overall trend in recent years has been towards a gradual increase in business rather than the marked expansion of the 1980s. The company continues to hand out relatively high dividends rather than reducing its debt problems. These are likely to be exacerbated in the short term by the promised restructuring exercise; however this should yield longer term benefits.

## Contacts

Our former contact, Mr Mole, has now left the company. Nevertheless we have a graduate on the board, the Finance Director Mrs Joanne Brown. Mrs Brown has not yet been invited to events at the University. We do not have any links with the other directors or with the Jamesson family. There is a precedent for generosity towards the University in the form of Megacorp's 1993 gift of £25k for the new swimming pool.[4]

Megacorp is one of the largest companies in the Dorchester area. It annually recruits in the region of 10 Dorchester graduates for retail management or head office roles such as sales and marketing. It has a special relationship with the University careers service, which arranges numerous work experience and 'sandwich' placements.

## Likelihood of success and possible projects

### Donation history[1,9,10,11]

1995: £1,459,000

1994: £1,071,000

1993: £1,205,000

Megacorp is generous to charity. The above amounts do not include other community contributions such as seconding employees to advise charities and supplying stock remainders to old people's homes. It is proud of the fact that its staff play active and prominent roles in their communities.

Megacorp is a major sponsor of the Local Enterprise Agency network which provides free help and advice to small businesses. In 1995 Megacorp sponsored 79 agencies at a cost of almost £60,000, in addition to time given by some of its managers.

Although Megacorp does give some money for overseas aid, national and international issues take up a relatively small part of its budget. Its prime interest is helping in the local community, for example it has recently funded coaches for handicapped children, drug prevention programmes and childcare facilities. See the appended list of the latest grants for full details.

## Likelihood of success

This is not a good time to ask for a very large gift as Megacorp is struggling to reduce its debt. A high profile gift at this point would probably not be appreciated by employees who were recently given a 0.5% pay rise, nor would it impress shareholders. However Megacorp is a relatively generous company and has previously considered the University worthy of a gift. There is no reason why Dorchester should not either ask for a small charitable gift now or, if considered feasible, lay the foundations of a strong relationship in preparation for a future large ask.

Megacorp likes to help in the communities where its customers live.[1] All sectors of its business have a sizeable presence in the Dorchester area so a gift to the University would fit in well with this policy.

A good opportunity to re-establish contact is now approaching. As Megacorp is a donor to the swimming pool it would be appropriate to invite a representative to the official opening ceremony. Sir Humphrey Popple or Mr Lucas might like to attend as senior representatives of the company though neither has any particular connection with the University. Mrs Brown, being a graduate, might respond favourably to an invitation. If possible the visit might be extended to include other aspects of the University.

## Possible projects

**Management Studies** is a prime candidate, being both the subject studied by Mrs Brown and a key concern of Mr Lucas. Megacorp has made a point of supporting advice networks for small businesses, appearing to feel that its leading position in the local community implies a responsibility to help others.[1] In building up the relationship Mr Lucas, himself a graduate of INSEAD, might be willing to give a lecture at the Management School. There might also be scope for encouraging Megacorp to send its junior managers on short courses at the

School. This is probably the area where a large donation is most likely as the post could be named after Megacorp and generate some useful publicity.

Collaboration in the field of **Computing** is another possibility. Our Information Science Department has produced some good work in the field of stock control and accounting. Megacorp might be interested in talking to the Department about its ideas, with the possibility of funding future research into areas which are of particular concern to the company.

Further donations in the field of **Sport** are a possibility, depending on the company's opinion of the success of the previous gift. Unfortunately Megacorp's £25k was eclipsed by the generosity of other donors; however the company's name does appear on the plaque in the foyer and it has been mentioned in press reports. It might be worth mentioning that as one of the earliest gifts it was vital in giving the scheme credibility and encouraging other donors to follow suit.

Other suggestions are **scholarships, access for disabled people, childcare** or a **hardship fund.** Any of these schemes could carry the company's name and might offer the widespread publicity and aura of community spirit which a food retailer might appreciate. Such a gift could be relatively large as it might be drawn from the marketing budget rather than the charity one.

Finally, should Sir Humphrey prove to be the most accessible board member, it might be worth suggesting funding for **Archaeology**. Sir Humphrey studied this subject at Cambridge and has retained a strong interest in Greek vases. The department's recent research into firing methods might be of particular interest to him.

# Sources

1. Megacorp annual reports 1994 and 1995

2. *The Corporate Register* March 1996

3. *Financial Times*, 01.04.96

4. Inhouse database

5. *Observer*, 20.03.96

6. *Investor's Chronicle*, 15.05.96

7. *Financial Times*, 12.05.96

8. *Independent on Sunday*, 24.04.96

9. *A Guide to Company Giving* 1996

10. *Hollis Sponsorship and Donations Yearbook* 1995

11. *The Guardian Guide to the UK's Top Companies* 1995

## No reference found

*Economist* index, 1995 & 1996 first quarter

## Appendices

Biographical entries for the directors.

Database print-out of Dorchester graduates known to be working for Megacorp.

List of grants made in 1995.

# 10. Foundations and Trusts

## Varieties of foundation

Not all foundations, trusts or charities are grant-making bodies. They might, for example, be tax-avoidance schemes or straightforward businesses. Each country has its own rules on what can or cannot be a charity or foundation, so be prepared for overseas organisations to behave in a totally different manner. The following are some major types of foundation which might be encountered.

### 1. Personal foundations

A wealthy person does not necessarily set up a foundation or trust simply to give money to charity. There are often considerable tax savings to be made from holding money in this way. Some trusts are means of passing money from one generation to the next without paying inheritance tax. However a genuine foundation could equally have been set up to take advantage of tax benefits for charitable giving, perhaps with the additional aim of ensuring that the creator's charitable intentions continue to be acted upon after her death.

Some might have been set up to deflect fund-raisers' attention: all communications are directed to the foundation so that its creator does not have to be troubled. This sort of foundation will generally have a very powerful administrator, who should possibly be solicited as well as – or occasionally instead of – the creator. Although this sort of foundation might be no more than a cynical public relations exercise, it is not necessarily as hard-hearted as it seems: a deluge of requests can cause great distress to someone who wishes to help, but cannot do everything.

The gifts of a personal foundation are likely to be heavily influenced by the creator or his relatives, who are normally trustees. It is worth checking the maiden names of female trustees to see whether they are related to the founder. Other trustees might well be respected family friends.

The administrator is often also a key person. Although he does not necessarily have the final say in granting a gift, the administrator can advise the fund-raiser on how to weight a proposal, will be responsible for sifting the applications, and might influence the trustees' ultimate choice. The trustees might occasionally fund projects which would otherwise not appeal to them, simply

154

to please a respected administrator. The administrator of a large foundation or trust might be a full time employee, but in a smaller one he is more likely to be the family's lawyer.

Some personal foundations can be difficult to distinguish from personal wealth. If it is little more than an alternative bank account then there might be no formal guidelines for applicants and it is less likely to be publicised in a directory of foundations. Rather than applying to the foundation it is more effective to treat it as an approach to a person, in other words researching and building up a relationship with the creator before asking for money. As with any personal donation, there can be an element of 'swapping donations'; if your volunteer asks someone to support his favourite charity then he might have to return the favour by supporting theirs.

## 2. Corporate trusts

Grant-giving bodies which take the name of a company may have been founded either by the company or by the family which originally owned the company. They are likely to remain quite closely tied with the company though there are exceptions, notably the Wellcome Trust whose willingness to sell its shares in order to expand its philanthropy caused dismay in the Wellcome company.

The trust's objectives might match the business interests of the company, the philanthropic interests of its founder, or might be designed to appeal to the employees or customers (e.g. health and welfare, local schools, etc.). The trustees are likely to be present or retired employees of the company, reinforcing its influence over what might theoretically be an independent body. It might have an independent income in the form of shares in the company (which it might subsequently have exchanged for better investments elsewhere) or it might be totally reliant on the company for injections of cash. Alternatively it might receive money from the employees' fund-raising efforts.

The existence of a company trust does not necessarily mean that the company itself does not also have a charitable budget. Donations from the latter are likely to be decided by the board or a subcommittee of it. If there is both a trust and a charitable budget then there are likely to be rules about what sort of application will be accepted by each, so make sure you apply to the appropriate one. The charitable arm of a company is not necessarily the best part to target. Larger sums can often be obtained from its marketing or research budgets, though you must make a good case for the benefits to the company before it will be prepared to invest.

In some countries (such as the UK) it is possible for companies to register themselves as charities. This does not mean that they are any more likely to be philanthropic than other companies, though their activities might be educational or public-spirited in some way.

## 3. Government foundations

In some countries the government might promote science, culture, international relations, etc., by setting up grant-making bodies. Japan is one example of a country where there are many foundations under the supervision of the government. Such foundations can be difficult to distinguish from the government itself. Sometimes they have boards composed of leading academics or businessmen who have the interests of their subject or country at heart.

The UK recently established a similar series of boards to distribute the proceeds of the National Lottery. They provide written guidelines for applicants, or you might be able to obtain a personal interview with one of the administrators to fine tune a major application. Since these funds are so large there are books and courses which explain how to approach them, notably those of the Directory of Social Change.

Although not exactly foundations, government bodies themselves often have funds to disburse and invite applications in the same way. Branches of the European Union are an area of growing interest. See the chapter on European sources for guides to the funds available.

## 4. Independent foundations

These might have been set up by a number of people, or might be so long-established that the influence of the founder has ceased to be a factor. Their objectives are in theory governed by the legal documents which created them. However there is frequently room for the wishes of the trustees to play a major part in the disposal of the money, either through interpreting the rules or deciding between competing requests.

## 5. Fund-raisers and non-grant-making charities

Not all registered charities will provide gifts. Some are fund-raisers in their own right (though this does not mean they will not give grants to other fund-raisers). In the UK universities, hospitals and even fee-paying schools are classed as charities. There is normally some straightforward justification, such as a public service being provided. However in some countries it is not impossible for it to be merely a means for a company or person to avoid paying so much tax.

# International comparisons

Many English-speaking countries enjoy a robust charitable sector. Foundations proliferate and are well publicised through directories. The US boasts a particularly large and well developed charitable sector and the UK also has a strong record. In such countries fund-raisers consider that regular approaches to these bodies are an essential part of their work. This is by no means the case in other countries. Although philanthropy exists everywhere, legal structures and tax rules did not necessarily encourage the creation of independent bodies. Instead help might be given directly by private individuals or the Church.

In some non-English speaking countries many of the major foundations were created post-1945. A combination of governmental encouragement and support from international organisations (such as the European Foundation Centre) has helped to expand their numbers. In the English-speaking countries many of the foundations are effectively independent because the founder is dead or they were set up by groups of people with a clear philanthropic vision, and many were founded with inherited money. Elsewhere there is a stronger tendency for foundations to be government-inspired or founded by a modern self-made industrialist whose wealth comes from a well known company.

In Continental Europe some of the following reasons might help explain the relatively low numbers of charitable foundations. In the UK church and state were united in the sixteenth century when the monarch was proclaimed head of the Anglican Church; however those governments whose people remained loyal to the Catholic Church often felt threatened by the presence of a 'foreign' power (i.e. Rome) in their midst. Charitable trusts were often linked with the Church and this ability to disburse money gave the Church power, hence the tendency of the state to discourage them.

A second reason is the more rigid nature of the Roman law system which prevailed in many parts of the Continent making it harder to create and run foundations. The UK's 'common law' (also inherited by the US) meant that funds need only conform to established practices, while on the Continent foundations were created and managed according to a rigorous set of rules and regulations. The division is not sharp: Scandinavia, the Netherlands, Ireland, Switzerland and Germany developed systems more closely aligned with the British pattern. Germany, for example, was well endowed with foundations until its political and financial difficulties in the first half of this century overwhelmed many of them. Countries which have been under the sway of colonial powers often show the influence of whichever pattern the relevant European country followed.

The situation is now changing in Continental Europe. One result of the European Union's attempt to formalise and harmonise european life is the creation of the European Foundation Centre (EFC). This was initially set up with the aim of helping foundations. It provides information, a forum for discussion, and a unified voice for its disparate members. More recently it has spawned an information service for fund-raisers; however this is as yet relatively new and still seen as subsidiary to its role in helping the foundations. It still has some way to go in matching its services and fees to the requirements of fund-raisers.

One aspect that might shock the unsuspecting fund-raiser is that it makes a point of telling foundations who has enquired about them. This can totally ruin a solicitation because the foundation might pre-judge the charity rather than let it prepare and present its own case. To illustrate this point, to an outsider Oxford University might conjure up images of well-fed dons passing the port, ruling out any chance of a donation; however its cancer research or refugee studies departments could well be in dire need of support, and it would be unfair to prevent them from presenting their case. The EFC is covered in more detail in the European sourcelist.

No serious attempt to harmonise the charitable sector has yet been made by the European Union. When it does address this problem there is likely to be disagreement over which types of activity should be classed as charitable. In the UK and the Netherlands, for example, the definition of charitable activity extends way beyond the basic relief of poverty and distress.

In Oriental countries there is a tendency for foundations to be seen less as a means of disbursing charitable gifts. The strong sense of the country pulling together to improve the lot of all its citizens is reflected in the aims of its foundations. In Japan, for example, the large foundations tend to have been created post-war by wealthy industrialists, large companies or the government. Their aims are often the economic or political furtherance of Japan, for example they might offer grants for education, scientific research, or the promotion of Japanese culture overseas. Japan has one of the more open charitable sectors from the point of view of foreign applicants. This is partly due to the desire for good public relations with trading partners. Japanese embassies, especially in the US, might be able to provide information on Japanese philanthropy.

Do not expect to be able to obtain support from every foreign foundation. A great many operate under geographical restrictions. These might be enshrined within their own constitutions or very occasionally there might be legal restrictions on exporting money from the country.

One major problem is that while domestic charitable gifts might be exempt from taxation, those sent overseas are quite likely to have to pay. Donors resent this devaluation of their money so much that they are often reluctant to consider foreign gifts. It might be possible to create a vehicle to get round this problem, such as a 501(c)(3) tax-exempt organisation in the US. Major charities or a taxation expert might be able to advise.

Another matter to consider is that in some countries there are restrictions on activities which might be considered to be political, the definition of which varies. In some countries it might include religion or human rights. While in the US it is acceptable to fund information campaigns on public policy issues such as the reform of the health system, in the UK this would probably be ruled too political.

There is also a psychological barrier: it seems unpatriotic to help foreign institutions when there are so many deserving causes in the home country. Even if the donor himself is willing to send the money, he might be swayed by the likely public reaction. This is particularly the case when a wealthy country or institution is asking for money from a generally poorer country. At first sight this might seem an unlikely situation, but in many poorer countries there are often huge inequalities in wealth, with an internationally-oriented élite capable of making huge donations. Although it might be felt that they ought to give money to the needy within their own country, they might not feel inclined to do so. A foreign institution, however, might offer sufficient prestige to persuade them to donate. This is not an 'either/or' situation: if the foreign institution had not approached them it is quite possible that nobody would have obtained a donation. One way round the taxation and psychological problems posed by foreign donations is to ensure that the gift benefits the donor's country as well as the recipient organisation, for example scholarships.

In every country there are trends in philanthropy. Recessions bring both greater needs, for example, the alleviation of poverty, and a lower level of wealth from which to meet them. Governments might contract their welfare provision, causing more pressure on the voluntary sector. In some countries hospitals, universities and schools are increasingly having to raise money that would formerly have been provided by the government. In the UK the creation of the National Lottery meant competition with charities in areas such as the sale of scratch cards. Events such as a famine in Africa or the opening up of Eastern Europe can also divert funds. If you wish to keep up to date with these issues there are various publications devoted to them. As well as the general charity magazines there are publications such as *Giving USA* (AAFRC Trust for Philanthropy) and the books of the British Charities Aid Foundation.

# Sources of information on foundations

This type of report can be either the easiest or the hardest to research, depending on the country. Foundations often want to give you the very information you need. However in many non-English speaking countries information can be very hard to find.

- *Directories.* See the source lists for details of publishers. They range from the well indexed US variety to the very basic list of names and addresses. In many countries they do not exist and where they do they are generally disappointing to someone used to the US or UK ones. There are a few international directories, e.g. from the European Foundation Centre and Europa. The latter's *International Foundation Directory* contains not only foundations but some of the overall bodies that might provide further information on others.

- *The foundation's own guide for applicants* (if one exists). This probably means informing the foundation of your interest.

- *A trustee or administrator.* If you are asking for a large amount of money they might be willing to talk to you, especially if you can find a contact. This might be partly to persuade them of the value of your application. However they can also offer advice which ensures that the application is tailored to meet the requirements of the foundation as closely as possible, which is in the foundation's interests as well as yours.

- *The national registry.* If you do not know where this is check a directory of foundations for that country (if one exists) or a yearbook, or ask a body such as the European Foundation Centre or the US Foundation Center, the country's embassy, a major charity in that country, or even a library. Not all countries have registries, and some are so small that some sources will deny they exist.

- *International bodies.* The European Foundation Centre is by no means a registry for all European foundations. It might be able to obtain information direct from the foundation (which means informing it of your interest) or it might point you in the direction of other sources. Although under the aegis of the EU it also has some information on Eastern Europe. There is no guarantee it will be able to help.

  For other regions you might try the international section of the US-based Foundation Center or the World Fundraising Council. They might be able to give details of organisations in the country of interest that can help you find sources.

-  *An online search.* If the foundation is difficult to track down and has an uncommon name it is probably best to check as wide a range of databases as possible – even the entire host if this can be done easily (e.g. *Dialog's Dialindex* file, 411). You might find something unexpected, such as the foundation's name being the name of a person or company, or you might find press reports about donations.
- *Contacts.* In some countries they are the best source of information due to the lack of anything else.

## Selecting the foundations to approach

In countries where there are directories and databases it is relatively simple to select your foundations. This should be done carefully on the basis of relevance. Directories often have indexes which place the entries within overall headings. However each entry should be checked to be sure it is really what you want. A foundation listed under the heading 'education' might fund nursery school places so would not meet the needs of a university. The foundation's rules might also place restrictions on geographical area covered. Sending an irrelevant application wastes everybody's time and money and can cause considerable annoyance.

You should also check how much money the foundation has to disburse. If it is very little then it is not worth your while writing a report on it. The larger the foundation the more care you should take in preparing a tailored application for it.

Countries which do not have these sources pose a very different problem. There are a few international sources, notably *The International Foundation Directory* (Europa), the European Foundation Centre, and the international section of the US-based Foundation Center; however their coverage is limited. In these areas contacts are very important.

Foundations of the US and UK style need publicity if they are to receive applications. In those countries where foundations are not publicised it is likely that either few sizeable ones exist or they are different in nature. They might restrict their coverage to the immediate locality, where they are already quite well known. Alternatively there might be personal foundations which disburse money on the whim of the founder rather than taking written applications. These will discourage applications by keeping their names out of directories and press reports. In this case you are likely to discover their existence through a contact and you should treat them as people rather than foundations.

# Writing a report on a foundation

The information required might be as follows:

- *Contact details*: address, telephone number, name of correspondent or administrator

- *Founder*: why founded, family background, career, still alive, etc. You must determine whether this is primarily a foundation or the philanthropic arm of a person or company. If the latter it might be preferable to write a personal or company report instead. If you think the foundation is a separate entity you might still consider it worth writing a lengthy profile of the person or company to append to this report.

- *Trustees*: relationship to founder (if any), biographical notes of interest.

- *Financial status*: how large are the assets? What is the annual income? What is the annual expenditure?

- *Grant-making policy*: what they give money to and why. You might find huge lists of previous grant recipients and pages on donation policy. If so summarise the key points (e.g. 'the majority of the gifts were to ecological projects, which were a strong interest of the founder'). The full details can be appended to the report in case anyone is interested. If a foundation sends out guidelines for applicants it is wise to read them thoroughly, but there is no reason why you should laboriously type them out. If it helps you can highlight the key points. Make sure you pay particular attention to restrictions on funding, which might be geographical or cover particular types of grant, e.g. no money for buildings.

- *Contacts*. Do you have any links with the founder or any of the trustees? Have you received any previous gifts?

- *Project possibilities* and likelihood of a gift. Which of your needs fit in with the policies of the foundation and what are the relative chances of success with each one?

- *Sources*

- *Appendices*: biographies of trustees, lists of sample grants, etc.

# 11. International Comparisons

Prospect researchers generally start off by looking at their own country. However as business becomes increasingly international and fund-raisers compete more aggressively researchers suddenly find themselves tackling a new region. In the absence of any other guidance they naturally fall back on past experience. This can be seriously misleading. No matter how similar the countries appear there are inevitably differences in the amount of information available, attitudes towards the disclosure of information, and cultural responses to approaches.

Unfortunately little has been written on prospect research techniques and sources, other than in the US. However unless you understand the kind of differences that can exist you might easily overestimate what can be achieved and find yourself totally bemused by the unexpected. This chapter is a first step in anticipating the problems. Later chapters on sources will help you negotiate them.

## Variations in the level of information

At one end of the spectrum are countries such as the US where the proliferation of sources can be overwhelming, while in the former Soviet Union it can be difficult to find anything at all. How do you know whether information is likely to be available before you invest time and money in trying to find it? To follow are various indicators which might suggest how likely you are to find useful information. They are by no means infallible, but useful as a general guide.

- *The political system.* Communist or non-democratic countries tend not to encourage the production of accurate information. Information has a political impact. In the former Soviet Union factories and farms had to be constantly increasing production, even when it was totally impossible for them to do so. There were effectively penalties for telling the truth. By contrast, in capitalist societies information is considered vital to investment decisions, so penalties exist for providing inadequate or inaccurate information.

163

There are also marked differences in the freedom of the press. There are many countries, including some which are economically advanced and nominally democracies, which impose such arduous restrictions on opposition parties that they are effectively one-party states. They are often capable of censoring or closing down newspapers which do not toe the party line. This can mean not only that the press says what the government wants to hear, but that there is little point in it saying very much at all. This sort of newspaper might read like a political manifesto, but if you only see a few articles in isolation, perhaps through an online search, you might not realise what sort of publication you are using.

Foreign news organisations, such as Reuters or the BBC World Service can be useful in this situation as they are independent, but they do not have the resources for extensive coverage and tend to focus on political events rather than businesses or individuals. There is a danger that lack of resources might mean they take their cue from the national press without questioning it. An alternative is to look for a regional journal published in a neighbouring free country, though even there the degree of independence might not meet your expectations.

• *The country's state of economic development.* The more developed the country, the better the level of information is likely to be. Information is not uppermost in the minds of subsistence farmers, nor is it of much interest to outsiders if companies are all very small and making limited profits (unless, as in Central Europe, there is a sudden influx of foreign investment). Governments see publicly accessible banks of information as unnecessary and costly to maintain, unless there is some clear benefit such as increased investment in the economy. However less developed countries will often have a government-sponsored almanac or yearbook, possibly as a way of asserting national pride.

• *The degree of equality of wealth.* Some of the wealthiest people in the world live in generally poor countries. It is unlikely that these people will figure in a who's who, perhaps because everyone who is anyone already knows them, or because the country contains so few people with the money or interest to buy such a book that it is not worth publishing it.

• *The influence of the stock market.* Some highly developed countries, such as Germany, have a strong (though declining) tradition of privacy because of the predominance of private companies and investment by local banks. Countries with a high proportion of public companies tend to be more open. Outside investors demand a great deal of reliable information before they will chance their money, and as there are so many countries where they could invest each has a powerful incentive to improve standards. Once the habit of openness becomes established it tends to spread, hopefully to the press and to publishers.

- *Privacy.* Some countries have a freedom of information ethic (e.g. the US), while others lean more towards protecting the privacy of the individual (e.g. France). Closely linked with this are libel laws which place the burden of proof on the author. It has been suggested that one reason why the media tycoon Robert Maxwell received relatively little bad press until his death was his declared intention of suing at every opportunity.

Besides the legal structure, there is the pervasive culture which determines how much people are willing to divulge about their personal affairs and how much their friends and acquaintances consider it reasonable to say. Outside the US who's whos are rarely indexed by charitable affiliation, alma mater, etc., indeed some publishers pride themselves on not making their books accessible in this way as that would make it easier for salesmen or fund-raisers to pull out a mailing list of likely targets and pester them.

Privacy can extend to personal benefactions. In some countries few people would feel totally at ease providing a full list of their benefactions as this would seem like bragging. People who inherited wealth are possibly more likely to keep their gifts quiet, as are certain religious groups such as Quakers. In the UK, for example, the only indication of philanthropy that will appear in a biographical directory is a (possibly abbreviated) list of trusteeships. This means you have to rely on contacts to mention it or trawl through the press in the hope that gifts have been reported. Local papers will often publicise gifts, but you will probably need to travel to their head offices or a local library to look at back issues. The 'quality' national press, which is easily accessible online, is not unduly anxious to publicise donations. In fact it can seem that the British papers only pick up on a story when they can criticise or highlight disagreements. In the US, by contrast, it is much more acceptable to publicise donations.

- *Data protection legislation.* This is closely allied with the previous point. In wealthy countries such as the US there are companies which specialise in building up huge databases of personal information containing everything from date of birth to shopping preferences. Financial institutions and direct marketing companies make particular use of this information. It might be possible for the prospect researcher to purchase access to it, perhaps arriving at a list of wealthy people or cross-matching it to improve the quality of his own database. However the public is often unhappy at so much personal information being so widely available, and many countries have passed legislation to restrict the number of holders and type of information. In the UK, for example, anyone who wishes to collect personal information on an electronic database should register with the Data Protection Registrar stating precisely what they intend to hold and justifying why they need it. It is not possible to pass it on to a third party without the permission of the people covered.

• *Security*. Politicians, judges and military officials can be subjected to terrorist threats. For this reason it is common for them to issue only a business address. Even when the press knows a home address it might well decide not to divulge it, not least because readers would disapprove. There are many other reasons why people might wish their home addresses to be kept secret, for example those involved in abortion or animal experimentation might be worried about attacks. Corporate executives might not wish angry shareholders or potential blackmailers to know where their families live. In some countries very wealthy people feel themselves to be constantly in danger of robbery or kidnap attempts. The level of threat and public attitudes towards it varies from country to country.

• *The number of prospect researchers in the same field*. In the US information suppliers are conscious of the buying power of an army of prospect researchers and produce books or online services which are geared specifically to their needs. Thus you can buy books which contain ready-made profiles of the wealthiest people, and others which cross-index company directors by education and philanthropic affiliations. Once the prospect researcher knows and has access to these sources, the tasks of finding new prospects and compiling reports are relatively easy.

However this is one of the easiest countries in which to conduct research. In many other parts of the world the researcher has to work hard to cobble together information from a variety of sources which were normally designed for a totally different purpose. Outside the English-speaking world the researcher might have to rely on an unindexed who's who and the occasional newspaper article for personal information.

## Culture and attitudes

Unless you understand something of the culture of the prospects you run a serious risk of puzzling, embarrassing, annoying or appalling them. This is not a good negotiating position. Here are some examples of differences in culture causing problems.

- *Religious and political convictions.* Americans often declare these in their biographical entries, and define themselves in relation to them. By contrast it is unusual to see anything other than an indirect reference in a British directory. To some people it can seem that in labelling someone as different they are being singled out in an offensive manner. They might believe that religion is irrelevant to the person's value as a prospect. This is by no means always the case, but people can be uneasy about it.

  There is thus a tendency to assume that unless someone is obviously different (e.g. they have an unusual name), or they have specifically said otherwise, they will fit in with the norms of British culture, that is they will drink alcohol, eat all meats (unless they are vegetarian), and observe the same public holidays. However in the US a person who proudly proclaims his heritage might be offended that it is not recognised. It could be considered foolish to expect to arrange meetings in New York without regard to Jewish holidays or offensive to ask people for their 'christian' names.

- *Racial sensitivities.* Some apparently harmonious communities might be very sharply divided under the surface. You should be careful about simply approaching the wealthiest or most powerful people without regard for their race. In some countries a racial minority holds considerable economic influence but limited political power (an example being the Chinese in some Oriental countries). There might be statutory or unspoken rules about ensuring a good mix rather than dealing only with one group. Although you might prefer simply to find the best prospects you should not forget to consider whether you are likely to lose the goodwill of the government or of other sections of the community.

- *Getting to know people.* You must understand how much work it will take to win the prospect round. In some countries the prospect will anticipate what you want from the meeting and be prepared to say yes or no straight away. In others prospects will expect a great deal more polite manoeuvring before they make a decision and might not even understand what it is that you want. As an example, Americans are accustomed to attending fund-raising events for their colleges and will be puzzled if they are not asked to reach for their cheque books. In Continental Europe it is still possible to arrange an event and find that the guests expect nothing more than a jolly get-together and resent being asked for a donation. In Japan there is an expectation of a long-term partnership so the build up is slow and cautious.

- *Women.* There is no doubt that women have a harder job than men in some parts of the world. In some Oriental countries, for example, women are not expected to be in the workplace once they are married, which means that they do not have the opportunity to reach senior levels. Although some allowances will be made for Westerners, there is still a tendency to assume that a woman must be a secretary and to exclude her from dinner invitations. In such countries status is likely to be very important, so the woman's apparent lack of status (even if this is denied) might persuade them that you are not particularly committed to the relationship. If you refuse to acknowledge this you are starting from a disadvantage in a society where you might already have to fight hard for acceptance.

- *Status.* Similar to the previous point. In some societies 'important' people only meet those who are on the same level as themselves. If you are only the envoy of the top person you might find meetings difficult to arrange and politeness rather less in evidence. Remember that job titles do not mean the same thing in every country so check up on relative rank. Your status will also depend on what institution you represent. Larger and more prominent companies are likely to have higher status than smaller ones.

- *Political influence.* Researchers in the UK or US are likely to consider motivation in personal or economic terms. However at the international level political considerations are often significant. International links are particularly likely to attract government attention as they have an impact on political and economic relations with other countries. In many countries there is value in currying favour with the government, perhaps because of its influence over regulation or the disposal of contracts. If a political leader supports a project it is more likely to be successful. Another factor is public approval: some nationalities set great store by being seen to be advancing the good of the country as a whole.

## Which country?

Countries will generally suggest themselves very strongly so researchers do not often face this question. However if it does come up here are some points to consider:

- *Where are your constituencies?* Do you have a pool of alumni or members, or do you operate branches or overseas programmes in a particular country? Are your projects particularly relevant or appealing to a specific nationality? A country might value educational opportunities, research, political acceptability, etc.

- *Experience of the person who will handle the operation.* Ideally you should recruit someone after choosing the country as you need someone who has some knowledge of the country and language. If a person is already in post and has no useful knowledge then you might consider looking at countries which seem relatively similar to your own, for example someone in the US might look at English-speaking parts of Canada as a possibility.

- *Historical links.* Although colonial empires have disintegrated their influence remains in language, legal systems, education, imported television programmes, etc. An English speaker might target countries of the former British Empire as the language and culture might be a little less foreign to him.

- *Proximity.* It is easier and cheaper to control a foreign operation which is not too far away. It is also likely that you will have a greater understanding of the country. Even if you aim to establish an office there it is likely that top ranking people will wish to visit, and their time is valuable.

- *Costs.* Either of travel there or of maintaining an office. Living costs and office space in a city such as Tokyo are astronomical. One way round this is to persuade a large company to provide you with space in its offices free of charge or at a reduced rate.

- *Government restrictions.* You might be debarred from operating in certain countries without a government permit. This applies even to fundraisers. Once you have obtained a permit, you might find that if you do not conform very rigidly to what the government wants you might have it revoked, so losing your investment in that country.

- *Ease of operation.* Some countries are more receptive than others. The US might seem a good target for a foreign fund-raiser because it has so much wealth and a strong culture of philanthropy. However there is also more competition, so if you have strengths in other areas do not neglect them.

- *Taxation on gifts.* Each country has its own way of taxing (or not) charitable donations. In the US it is possible to list donations to charity, admission to museums, etc., as deductions on the income tax form, which means the overall tax bill is reduced. This means the individual gets a personal incentive to donate to charity. In many other countries it is harder to reclaim tax, and it might be impossible if the recipient is an overseas charity. You might be able to set up a legal vehicle to handle the transactions. If not, what is the relative cost of taxation on local and foreign gifts? The greater the gap the greater the incentive to give to a local cause.

- *Exchange restrictions.* Very occasionally you will find a country does not permit large sums of money to cross its borders. This is not a widespread problem, but where it does exist it might be circumvented if the prospect has businesses overseas which can provide the money, though he might prefer to retain this valuable foreign cash for investment.

- *Trading links.* You might have a better chance of success if there is a long history of partnership between your two countries. Alternatively, you might find that a country wishing to establish new links takes more interest in you.

- *Competition from local projects.* It is difficult for a prospect to justify giving money overseas if his home country is in dire need. It can also cause bad publicity for a charity if it is thought to be taking money out of a country where children are starving.

Ultimately, the question might be irrelevant. Some of the wealthiest people and companies are international. Rather than focus on a particular country it might be easier to follow your contacts wherever they lead. It is quite possible that such people think nothing of travelling to another country, especially if they already had a business trip planned; indeed they might feel that their privacy is being invaded if you pursue them to their home. Although it is courteous to be willing to go to them, if it makes no difference then there is no point.

# 12. A Report on a New Country

The prospect of researching a new, unknown country is a daunting one. Ideally the researcher should have a good knowledge of each country researched; however this is not always practical, especially if a small team has to cover the whole world. However small your knowledge of the country, you should be able to provide useful information.

This chapter shows how you might put together a list of prospects in a new country. The following chapter deals in general terms with the types of sources that you might use, while subsequent ones list specific sources for each geographical area.

## General background

Before launching into a report it is useful to do some background work. If there is enough lead-in time and the country will continue to be an important part of your work in the future you might consider learning the language. Even more important, especially if your colleagues have no knowledge of the country, is to investigate its culture.

### Languages

A foreign language often seems the most difficult problem to overcome. Ideally you should be able to understand it, but if you don't there is no need to despair. Fortunately for English speakers this language is widely spoken throughout the world. The British Empire carried it far and wide, and the present economic strength of English-speaking nations ensures that it is often spoken as a second language. Reference books, such as who's whos, are often written in English, either because they are published in the UK or US, or because they are expected to achieve greater sales by appealing to the international market.

However don't restrict yourself entirely to English books. Reference works tend to follow a standard format, and once you have acquired a dictionary and translated basic words such as 'born' and 'educated' you will find that it is not too much of a problem. What you lose are the nuances, especially in job descriptions. Unless you have a large dictionary you will end up trying to compare the word with similar ones which might have been derived from the same root, but whose meanings have diverged. Even so, locally produced directories are more likely to have a representative coverage and accurate information than those produced by an international publisher in another country.

Upgrading your language skills is probably a good career move, but which language you choose must depend on your particular needs. Useful international languages include Spanish (in Latin America), French (in Europe and possibly Africa), German (in Europe), and Japanese (Japan is economically powerful in its own right and is particularly obscure to foreigners with no experience of it). Chinese might also be tempting as the Chinese are economically powerful in many Oriental countries. However, they have a multiplicity of dialects and often speak English. It is no use learning Mandarin if you wish to focus on Hong Kong, as they tend to speak Cantonese or English there.

## Culture

If you do not know the language, the least you can do is find out about the culture. English-speaking nations tend to be relatively informal, and must work hard not to appear rude or boorish in countries where status and rituals are more important.

Gifts might be important but some types are considered ill omens. Some religions forbid the consumption of alcohol or certain types of meat. It might be offensive to blow your nose in public. The Japanese expect you to present and accept a business card in a particular manner: the way you treat the card reflects your respect for its owner.

Although some allowances will be made for foreigners, it will impress the prospect if an attempt is made to fit in with local practice. Thus, unless your report will be read by someone who understands the culture well, it is important to provide some guidance. The researcher should speak to people who know and understand the country and obtain background books. These might be standard travel guides or books for people who are emigrating or doing business there, such as the *Culture Shock* series (Kuperard/Graphic Arts). A weightier international guide is *International Business Communication* (HarperCollins). Embassies might be able to help out with information or reading lists, or they might even be prepared to advise on arranging a reception for your prospects. If you work for a university ask members of the faculty for advice.

If you intend to show your report to contacts who are nationals of the foreign country be particularly careful that there is nothing in it which might cause annoyance. Your sense of humour might not be understood. Pointing out the human side of government ministers or undemocratic tendencies might offend someone who takes a great deal of pride in his country. Even criticising your own government might be misunderstood by someone who does not routinely look at his own in that way. It is best to be respectful about everyone and everything until you know your contact well enough to be open.

## Different views on fund-raising

Cultural differences also extend to fund-raising. In the US it is ubiquitous and profitable. In many European countries there is a tendency to expect that the state should pay for certain services, such as education and healthcare. This means that fund-raisers can be met with puzzlement or even outrage, though the climate is changing, particularly in the UK, as government cut-backs bite. In Asia there is possibly more of a tendency to concentrate philanthropy in areas which will benefit members of the family or clan (particularly under the influence of Confucianism), or please the government.

There are also political limitations on the type of projects which can be supported. Anything which could be seen as questioning the current political system, even on a social level, would find it difficult to win support in certain countries. Fund-raisers from liberal western backgrounds might not realise how controversial their projects appear unless they have contacts who know the society well and are willing to speak openly. This latter point is important as in some societies it is even dangerous to explain the political realities to someone whom you do not know well. This can be the case in what are apparently free and democratic societies. Similarly, if a project is seen to be in line with government policy it can be in a business person's interests to support it so as to win favour (e.g. in the awarding of construction contracts). It is worth considering approaching the government first as political approval can have a major influence on the amount of support you win.

In some countries it would be pointless sending a professional fund-raiser because such a person would not have the prestige to obtain introductions or win donations. Where status is very important it might have to be either a local person of high academic, political or financial standing, or the head of your institution.

There are also differences in the amount of time which must be spent bringing people to the point of giving. Some expect a long drawn-out solicitation while others simply do not understand what is expected of them. Do not assume that everyone who is invited to a dinner is coming prepared to sign a cheque. Similarly, some nationalities expect more reciprocation and information about the application of their donation.

It is often easier to solicit large donations from individuals and foundations than from companies, which might not feel they have a duty to support the community in the way that they do in the US. However the reverse might be true in Japan. Equally, different projects will appeal to different parts of the world, and there will be alternative motivations for giving, e.g. in Taiwan you might emphasise national benefit rather than personal recognition.

### Information on the country

You might also include information on the historical, economic, social or geographic background of the country. This information could come from a yearbook (e.g. *The Europa World Yearbook*). It might, for example, be useful to provide a map. You could point out the areas where there are heavier concentrations of prospects as these might make good bases or useful locations for large-scale entertaining. You might also explain the ethnic make-up of the country and give the exchange rate.

It is also essential, as with any other prospect, to be aware of the potential for bad publicity. If your organisation is linked with a regime whose record on the environment or human rights is poor it might be damaged. Similarly there might be no regulations to prevent companies from being exploitative and polluting. Each prospect must be viewed on its own merits, but it might be possible to pick out a trend before committing too many resources to the country.

### Names

It is very important that you understand the correct way of addressing people. You must know which is the given name and which the family name. A further problem is how to separate title from name. Who's whos sometimes have a section explaining the more common titles, as do travel books. If you are still unable to work it out ask an embassy or specialist library for help. If you are dealing with top-level people such as royalty or diplomats you might try *Protocol: The Complete Handbook of Diplomatic, Official and Social Usage* (Devon Publishing).

### Activities of competitors in the country

Have others got there first? If so, what are their strengths and weaknesses and where are they focusing their attention?

## The prospects

Although an inside contact can offer good advice, it is still useful to go to the meeting fully briefed with a research report. You might wish to impress your contacts with your commitment to a project, or ensure that they do not overlook important prospects. Unless they know your work well they might find it difficult to choose appropriate prospects.

You might find prospects from amongst the following: the government, royalty, the wealthiest people in the country, the largest companies, those companies with the strongest links with your own country, those companies in your own line of business, grant-giving foundations, or your contacts with the country. As usual you should also suggest those projects which would be of particular interest to the prospects.

As this is an overview of the possibilities within the country it is impossible to present a full report on everyone mentioned. A list of the top names is not very informative, but a few lines to summarise each should be a feasible solution. This overview should enable the reader to pick out the better targets, at which point you can produce a limited number of full reports.

### The government of the country

The government is sometimes the best starting point in overseas ventures. In some countries it can have considerable influence over the success of your approaches by signalling that you have official backing. It might also have its own funds to disburse or might suggest the best ways of achieving your goal.

You need to understand how the government operates before you approach it. The most democratic of them can sometimes be swayed by lobbying when deciding how to disburse funds or exert their substantial influence. A company might buy a gift for the president in the hope that he or she will grant it lucrative defence or infrastructure contracts. A government might offer an aid package in return for trading contracts. However any suggestion of bribery and corruption could embarrass even the most illiberal of governments. Mainstream country reference books will steer clear of mentioning such arrangements. Newspapers occasionally uncover scandalous stories, though even they can be subjected to pressure from both the foreign government and their own government. The latter might be embarrassed at its own part in the scandal, or worried about the costly impact on trading or diplomatic relations.

Confidential discussions are often the best way of understanding the environment. If you try talking to a local contact you must clearly be circumspect in your approach, as the suggestion that corruption is rife in the country can be very offensive. Alternatively you can talk to your country's foreign office, business people who work in the region or academics.

Information on the government is clearly important for a company, but it is no less so for a fund-raiser. It is not unusual for companies (local or foreign) to put money into charitable causes which they believe are close to the government's heart in order to improve their chances of winning contracts. An individual might do the same in the hope of a knighthood. If a charity can win over the government it might find that much more patronage follows. The government is often acting in the national interest, for example promoting overseas scholarships to improve its workforce, research into environmental degradation, or new treatments for endemic diseases. It is therefore important for the fund-raiser to understand the country's needs and demonstrate how it can meet them.

It is also important to know who actually holds the power and how secure they are. Some governments are repeatedly re-elected because they make life very difficult for opposition parties. They are not necessarily corrupt or oppressive, they might genuinely believe that they are acting in the national interest by suppressing disruptive elements, and their policies might be immensely beneficial to the country. This sort of country might effectively be ruled by one person whose authority has gone largely unchallenged for decades, and it is that person who you must consider to be your prospect. Alternatively there might be two factions within the ruling party and you must decide which to back. If one person has already supported a project similar to your own it might be worth looking to the other who might wish to get even.

Alternatively, you might view the government as a series of ministries. Your activities might fall under the remit of more than one, as well as the prime minister's office. You should be aware of their interests and what they are trying to achieve before deciding who to approach and with what aim.

Numerous books will provide lists of ministers, e.g. *The Europa World Year Book* and *The Statesman's Year Book*. However governments change so frequently that you might wish to check the information, either by contacting the embassy (which can be a slow and time-consuming process) or searching online. A reliable and timely list of ministers for virtually any country can be obtained from the Reuters *Textline* database which has a separate section specifically for government lists. A new, complete list is entered each time there is a change of any sort; you simply enter the country name and choose the most recent date. Unfortunately the completeness of this service varies from host to host. Some hosts unintentionally miss out some of the more recent lists altogether, though in all other respects *Textline* appears to be the same. Unfortunately not only might their helpdesks be unaware that it is incomplete, but they possibly might not know it even exists. Knight-Ridder's *Data-Star* is one host which appears to have a complete set of lists.

Finally, you should check when the government came to power and when it next faces election. Is there any real chance of defeat? Some countries are effectively one-party states while in others governments collapse with monotonous regularity. It can take a long time to build up a relationship and you would not want to be associated too strongly with an outgoing party.

## Royalty

Even where the royal family no longer wields political power it generally retains influence. If you can arrange a meeting it will at least ensure that people notice you, probably enhance your social standing, and if it is a social gathering possibly provide you with useful contacts. It is also possible that the royal family has major business interests or great wealth of its own. Beware that in some countries the nobility has lost its traditional status. While some might still respect it, self-made business people might despise it as living off inherited wealth.

## Wealthy people

Many countries have their own 'rich lists'. These estimate the wealth of what appear to be the richest people, and give brief details of their background. They are inevitably rough estimates, as so much wealth is held in private and rarely sold that its value can only be guessed at. It is normal to borrow against one asset in order to acquire another, which means that the real owner, should anything go wrong, is the bank. See the chapter on finding the prospects for details of how to find rich lists. Having acquired the names, do some basic research into who these people are, how wealthy they are, their business interests, their philanthropic record, and whether you have any contacts with them.

One point worth remembering is the impact of the culture on the ownership of wealth. In the West we tend to be more individualistic: a business empire might pass intact to the eldest child, leaving relatively little for the other children or cousins who might squabble and tear it apart. However, amongst the Chinese, for example, the family tends to be more important, and though disagreements can occur there is a stronger sense of everyone joining in for the good of the group. This sense of community even extends to helping people who came from the same village or region.

You should also attempt to gain some notion of the relative status of the prospects. Ideally you should approach the most important prospect first, since if you are successful this will cause others to view you more favourably. If your first successful contact is with a lower-status prospect you might find that your own standing declines and higher-status prospects do not wish to stoop to your level. In Japan, for example, status is crucial. There might be less clarity about the status of a newly-arrived foreigner, so aim as high as your own status and contacts will permit, because the first few contacts really count.

177

Thus you can provide a list of the top people with a few lines about their business empires, family, contacts with your organisation, etc. In some countries it is particularly important to note whether they are allies or opponents of the ruling party.

**Top companies**

As with rich lists, there are ready-made lists of the top companies in various countries. Examples include *The Times 1000* (from the UK newspaper *The Times*, though it covers numerous countries), *The European Business Top 500* (Ingerstedt Publishing), and *European Business Rankings* (Gale). Company directories for specific countries might also include a listing of the top companies or one might be obtained (slowly) from the embassy.

Alternatively you can produce your own by manipulating an online database on a host such as *Dialog* (Knight-Ridder) which enables you to rank entries and print out specific elements (e.g. name of company, area of business, address, name of Chairman). This can be an expensive process so check on the cost before starting. Assuming you are ranking by turnover, you might proceed as follows:

- Choose a database with good coverage of the country. If the documentation does not say how many companies are covered try a quick search for all companies based in that country. You might also like to check how many of them have a turnover figure greater than zero as the field might be empty in some cases. Also check whether it covers private companies as well as public.

- If the database covers several countries then select only those companies based in the appropriate one.

- If there are a lot of companies then ranking them is a slow process. Reduce the numbers by selecting those with a turnover over a certain amount. Do this repeatedly until you arrive at a manageable number (perhaps up to 50).

- Rank them in descending order.

- Print out your chosen elements of information in a table of the top x companies.

Company lists are more accurate than rich lists as companies are more likely to have to provide details of turnover, profit, etc. However there will still be discrepancies between them, as publishers take different approaches to the raw data. In any country the accounts can be massaged slightly to make them suit the requirements of the moment, and transient conditions might alter their ranking quite markedly.

A company might make provisions against future losses. International businesses can find the performance of subsidiaries badly affected by fluctuations in exchange rates. The sale of a subsidiary will reduce the level of turnover, though it might rise again shortly afterwards when a new subsidiary is purchased.

Some publishers amend the figures, especially when they are covering different countries. Levels of turnover, profit, etc., can never be directly compared between countries as accounting practices vary so widely, but publishers sometimes attempt to reduce the differences by recalculating the figures. Fluctuating exchange rates also affect international rankings, regardless of the performance of the companies. As financial year ends can occur at any time you might find that two lists agree on some figures, but disagree on others because one list came out a few months after the other.

Finally, check which figures are used for the ranking: are they, for example, turnover, pre-tax profit, or number of employees? A highly mechanised factory will have fewer employees but not necessarily lower profits than an old-fashioned labour-intensive one. Supermarkets operate on higher turnover yet lower profit margins than retailers of luxury goods. It is therefore impossible to find a totally fair method of comparison across industries.

It is important to discover who owns the companies. In the USA or UK they are largely publicly quoted companies owned by a mass of small shareholders. In this case control is probably in the hands of the directors. However in many countries the largest companies are private. Although the directors can have influence and be useful contacts, the company is effectively part of a person's wealth, and it might be that person (or family) whom you should approach rather than the company.

As well as naming the owners or top directors of companies you could write a few lines on their activities and any link with your country. Addresses and telephone numbers might also be useful. You must be particularly careful to look for contacts as these can make a major difference.

You should also be conscious of the possibility of links between apparently separate business empires; US or UK companies tend to operate as individuals, but in many other countries there is more of a community spirit. This might be visible as cross-shareholdings, but information on more obscure links (such as loyalty between families that originated from neighbouring villages) might only be obtained from a well-informed contact. This sort of information is important if you upset or fail to impress a prospect, since you might then be wasting your time trying to cultivate links with friends.

If you have a large network of contacts or represent a university which has alumni in that country it is worth looking for links into the companies. You might check the names of the directors to see whether they are known to you, or interrogate your database for anyone who claims to work for that company.

## Companies with business interests in both the target country and your own

These might be foreign companies with good links with your country, or vice versa. Either might be more likely to take an interest in you than a company which has little interest in your country. You might be able to offer a foreign company useful contacts or prestige in a new country. Alternatively you might be able to help a compatriot gain recognition overseas, for example if they pay you to provide scholarships, research, services, etc., which are of value to the foreign country.

You might be lucky enough to find a ready-made list. Jordan's produces a book of the top foreign-owned companies in the UK, though this requires a little work to extricate the entries for a specific country. You might persuade the foreign country's embassy (easily tracked down via the telephone directory for your capital city) to provide you with a list of its top exporters to your country. If you take this route be prepared to wait for a couple of weeks for the reply.

Alternatively you can use an online database. This is a relatively complicated and inaccurate search to perform. You must first find a database which gives not only details of a company, but also the name and country of its ultimate parent. If you are looking for foreign subsidiaries in the UK or US there is not too much of a problem. Performing the search the other way round, i.e. foreign subsidiaries of British or US companies, is another matter. The information from the foreign country is likely to be scanty, and even if the database claims to have the appropriate fields, there is no guarantee that these fields actually contain much data. Many may simply have been left blank. It is best to check for blank fields before spending money on the search.

As this is rather a complicated and expensive search it is safer to write out your strategy beforehand. There will be similar information for both parent and subsidiary, and it is very easy to confuse the fields. The first stage is to find all the variants on your country's name. This is not necessarily as straightforward as it might sound. The UK is particularly troublesome in this respect as it might be described as: 'Britain', 'UK – Scotland', 'UK – Wales', 'England', etc., plus all the typing mistakes that inevitably occur with large-scale data input. Having combined all the variants on both countries' names, select those records which contain them in the appropriate fields. If there are very many companies, you will probably wish to select only those companies above a certain turnover, altering the figure until you get a manageable number. This could well exclude a number of large companies whose turnover figure is not available. The next step is to sort the results by turnover to find the largest ones. There may be no indication of which year each figure comes from, so it is not necessarily a very fair comparison. Finally, you can print out a table of the results containing the appropriate fields, such as subsidiary name, parent name, chief executive's name, and turnover.

Alternatively several business information companies would be capable of producing a customised print-out for you. You could ask for quotes from the major corporate databases. You must first decide exactly what information you want (e.g. address, telephone number), what you want to rank it by (e.g. sales or pre-tax profit), and whether you want the next parent in the hierarchy (there might be several tiers) or the ultimate parent. This is likely to be costly. It also runs the risk of being misleading because you must trust that the database does not have large numbers of blank fields and that the searcher understands how the information is arranged.

The search described above will be useful for large industrial companies, but excludes partnerships such as lawyers or accountants, which often operate internationally. Although smaller scale they can be very lucrative for the individuals concerned. Details of these can be found in their professional directories, e.g. *The Martindale-Hubbell Law Directory International Edition* (Reed Elsevier).

### Grant-giving foundations

See chapter 10 on foundations.

### Contacts

What contacts do you already have with the country? Has your institution made visits or received visitors in the past? If you have a database which includes country codes you could pull out all those people with addresses in that country. Do you have any donors for projects related to the region, as they might be a source of information, contacts, or initial funding for a new project.

If you are working for a university, is there any favourite subject studied by alumni from that country? This might reflect the preferences of the government if it provides financial support. Do any academics have particular interests in the region, are they collaborating on a research project, or have they taught or studied there? Do any of your alumni or current students look interesting?

# 13. General Sources for a New Country

Later chapters provide details of books, online services, etc., for specific countries. However there are various other sources of information which you might also like to consider, especially if you are not doing enough work on a country to justify obtaining an expensive library of your own. Examples are listed below.

## Contacts

When researching a new country contacts who know it can be invaluable. They can suggest whom you should meet and maybe provide introductions. They can advise on the culture and help you avoid religious festivals. If relevant, overseas subscribers, internal overseas experts or alumni associations might be able to help.

## Foreign embassies

To find information on a foreign country it is sometimes worth contacting its embassy in your own country and asking the information officers whether they can help. They might, for example, be able to provide a list of the top companies doing business in your country. Ask what books they stock for answering queries: they might be able to give you a publisher's address, particularly for business books or a yearbook. If they have not heard of, for example, a who's who or foundation registry, this does not mean that it does not exist. Alternatively they might point you in the direction of an overseas trade organisation or a specialist book shop.

## Home government departments

Your country's foreign office will have a range of information sources for servicing its own needs. You might contact the department which specialises in your area of interest or there might be an enquiry service. If the local staff cannot help they might be willing to contact their embassy overseas for you (this is also something you can do direct).

This is possible for both companies and fund-raisers, both of which aim to attract money to their country. Universities might be able to obtain help from an institution such as the British Council which aims to promote British education overseas.

Alternatively the trade department might help with information on companies or the business environment in a specific country. Thus in the UK both the Foreign Office and the DTI produce relatively cheap booklets such as country profiles and sector studies, and have country desks that might give free advice.

## Chambers of commerce

Chambers of commerce are bodies which represent the interests of groups of companies. They might be companies operating in the same locality, in a foreign country, or owned by people of the same ethnic background. They vary widely in their usefulness but can be very helpful though sometimes expensive.

In some countries (e.g. Germany) they are valuable repositories of information on local companies. For information on international links you might approach your own country's chamber overseas, or the foreign country's chamber in your country. It might sell a directory of its members, though there is no guarantee that this information will be publicly available. If not it might give you the names of the president and top officials. Alternatively it might provide a list of its country's top exporters which you can then check out in directories. You will not find one in every country, though if there is a lot of trade you can be reasonably hopeful.

You can obtain contact details from a telephone directory, your national chamber of commerce (probably located in the capital) or from the foreign office or embassy. Some addresses can be found through *The Europa World Year Book* or its regional equivalents, though they are not comprehensive. CBD publications also provide some addresses.

## Universities

If you are researching a foreign country a university can often help. Its library might hold useful directories and its librarians or academic staff (if they do not mind answering your questions) can provide valuable background information. The best universities to contact can be found through directories of information sources such as the ones mentioned in the various country sections below. If you yourself work for a university you should be particularly well placed to obtain help from faculty, student groups and parents.

## Libraries

If you can visit a large research library it is worth checking its shelves, both for useful information, and for books that you might like to add to your own collection. In London, for example, the British Library's Science Reference and Information Service (SRIS) is very well stocked with business reference books covering much of the world.

If you do not wish to visit the capital then public libraries in county towns often have very good business reference sections too. If they do not hold the books you want they might be willing to buy them provided they are not too obscure.

It might be worth ringing regional libraries for help with their particular locality. There are often obscure sources that you would not otherwise find, but which they know well. Local business information, local newspapers, and even electoral registers might be available, though you should ring to check, especially as the smaller branches might have restricted opening hours. They might even be willing to chat about a local celebrity, though their knowledge should not be relied upon and there is always a danger they might mention your interest to the prospect.

Many libraries operate enquiry desks; however the better known ones, such as the New York Public Library's service, are so popular that it can be difficult to get through. The British Library's central Enquiry Point can also be very useful (Tel +44 (0) 171 323 7676). It also has subdivisions such as the SRIS Business Information Service (Tel +44 (0) 171 323 7457) and the Japanese Information Service (Tel +44 (0) 171 323 7924) which will search the major online databases for you. These can be quite costly. Even regional libraries may now offer an online searching facility, though if they do not have much practice they might not be as efficient.

In order to find the best library for your needs you might like to invest in a guide to information services. They are mentioned at the start of individual country sections below. Check those for your own country, the target country, and the international ones.

## Membership organisations for researchers or fund-raisers

These might run courses, hold speaker meetings, or be a way of meeting other people in the same field who can share their experiences. Groups are listed under the appropriate countries below. The list is not exhaustive so if you are not sure whether one exists in your country try asking a major charity or the World Fundraising Council.

## The telephone directory

Try looking in the directory for the capital or other major cities. Look under the name of the country, or possibly a religious grouping if there is one strongly connected with the country. You might find social organisations for expats, newspapers, trade organisations, book shops, or nothing at all, but it is generally worth looking.

## Book shops

Specialist book retailers in your own country or major book shops in the foreign country can often suggest books that you did not know existed. Unfortunately they might know less about directories as these are often sold direct by the publishers, but it is worth asking. They also have the advantage of being a single source for ordering various books, might speak your language, and sometimes do not charge you the overseas postage. Shops might be found through the embassy's information department, a specialist library, or the telephone directory.

## Catalogues of books in print

These are available in book form on the shelves of libraries (e.g. from KG Saur, part of Reed Elsevier), on online databases such as Knight-Ridder's *Dialog* file 470, as CD-ROMs, or free over the Internet.

Some major libraries have put their catalogues onto the Internet (though others cannot afford to computerise the whole catalogue), so you should have quite a choice. Trial and error will show which is the best (and quickest!) catalogue to use. There are various American college libraries on the Internet though they tend to be quite popular. The most comprehensive collections of UK books are held at the copyright libraries which obtain them free of charge as of right. Examples are the British Library and Oxford's Bodleian Library. Unfortunately there is no guarantee that the publisher remembered to send a particular book or that a reader has not stolen it. If you are looking for foreign books then these libraries, like any other, are constrained by budget and shelf space.

Although a directory of international books in print might be more comprehensive, an electronic index has the advantage that you need only enter part of the title, or a subject area.

## The press

If you are studying a particular country in depth it is worth reading its press, possibly both business and social. Books on information sources can generally give you the names of the major newspapers. Alternatively there are names and addresses in the *Europa World Year Book*, or the country's embassy can suggest which best suit your needs. Several major papers have a weekly international version in English so do not despair if you do not understand the language. Alternatively you could use a source such as the BBC's *Summary of World Broadcasts* or an online service such as *Textline*.

## Online databases

The major hosts are building up collections of international press and company information, but there is generally much less information for countries outside the host's home country (other than the US). This means that you have to adopt different strategies for searching for foreign information.

Firstly you should be aware that foreign information might be more expensive than domestic sources. Secondly, as the information is scarcer, you might have to conduct much broader searches. Thirdly, if you are searching for a foreign name it is safest not to be too specific as it might appear in a different order, it might have alternative spellings in translation, or part of it might be mistyped by someone who saw it as nothing more than a peculiar assortment of letters; try searching for parts of the name or for variants on it.

Unless you are looking for a well known person or company you might find that there is no point in selecting your databases very carefully. It is time-consuming to work out the relative merits of databases, and you run the risk of excluding what little information there is. It is quickest and safest simply to search large bundles of files, or even the entire host. This is not particularly expensive and might throw up files in places you would not think to check. If there turn out to be a lot of hits you can print out some contexts to see whether they refer to something else then narrow down your search.

As an example, rather than picking specific newspapers to search as you might in the US you might choose the whole *Textline* group, or *Dialog's Dialindex* file (411) or *INTLCO* group. *Dialog* (Knight-Ridder) also has a useful company name finder file.

The drawback with this technique is that often you find the same article in several different databases and duplicate removal procedures often fail to solve the problem. It might be easiest to print out all the hits in brief context form as this is often very quick and cheap and enables you to rule out the duplicates yourself before you do your final print out.

## The Internet

Sources change too rapidly to be included in detail. A few are listed in later chapters, but if you have access to the Internet it is worth checking what resources are available for your country of interest. This can be done via your own Internet search tools.

## Major international stock exchanges

Rather than tackle a complicated overseas search for company information it is sometimes possible to find the information more easily closer to home. Since the US and UK both have major international stock exchanges they tend to draw foreign companies looking for investors. There are three major US stock exchanges competing to attract foreign companies to list on them: the New York Stock Exchange, Nasdaq, and the American Stock Exchange. Try the US's SEC form 20-F filings which are for foreign companies operating in America. SEC filings can be found online, e.g. through Knight-Ridder's *Dialog*. The *Financial Times* carries details of the London stock exchange. Alternatively you could ring the company's US or UK sales office to ask for an annual report as it might send a detailed English language one specially designed for that country.

## The source lists in the following chapters

The remainder of this book provides some basic suggestions to help you create your own research library. It is arranged geographically so that you can focus on a particular country in depth if you wish to do so. However do not neglect the international sections which precede it as they contain not only books which cover the whole region but also country-specific sources (such as those produced by Dun & Bradstreet or Kompass) which are so similar and universal that it is not worth repeating their details in every section.

If you intend to study a country in great depth then good initial purchases are a national almanac or yearbook (e.g. *Whitaker's Almanack* in the UK) and a business telephone directory for the country's capital. *The Europa World Yearbook* describes each country's history and a summary of its major businesses. It also provides useful addresses for the press, publishers, chambers of commerce, major banks, etc. You might also wish to obtain the country's biographical, foundation and business directories, where these exist. If they are being ordered from overseas this will take a considerable time (possibly a couple of months) so try to anticipate needs wherever possible. Ideally you should also read the local or regional press and build up country files covering the overall economic or political situation, major companies, profiles of wealthy people, etc.

There is insufficient room here to list all of the overseas distributors for each publisher, so you might like to check whether there is one for your country. A closer supplier has the advantages of being cheaper to contact, speaking your language, and charging less for postage. However you might be able to negotiate a larger discount with the publisher itself and you might find that the distributor does not sell all of the publisher's titles (or even if it does it might not know their contents, publication dates or prices very well).

Large international publishers, however, might be even harder to deal with than distributors. The various parts of the empire might have a very hazy idea of what the others are doing, even when they operate within the same country. They can give you totally wrong information and deny that a book exists when you know that it does. Although there can be discounts for buying in bulk you might prefer to deal with the individual branches as they will have a better knowledge of the books. Occasionally an overseas branch can offer you a wider range of books than your local one because it acts as a distributor for other publishers in the country.

It is impossible in the space available to cover every country or provide a complete list of the sources available. An attempt has been made to cover many of the major economies of the world, but it is inevitably only a start. For those who wish to look further, directories of sources are listed at the beginning of many of the sections.

Descriptions of contents given below are meant only as an indication. There is no guarantee that they have not totally changed from one edition to the next. Before you buy a book always ask the publisher to send some publicity material so that you can be sure it is what you want.

# 14. Specific International Resources

Later sections will elaborate on the sources which are specific to each country or region, but there are a few which are so international that it is worth mentioning them here. International books often have a bias towards certain countries, perhaps because it is the publisher's own country or because information is more readily available there. Either way, the bias is often towards the US.

## Information sources

*How to Find Information about Foreign Firms – Washington Researchers*

Sources of information on non-US firms including country experts, international associations, government agencies, publications and databases. Written from a US perspective, i.e. many of the sources are American. If you are interested in particular regions it might be worth buying one of its more detailed sister publications instead. Washington Researchers also produces a monthly newsletter, price $160, on new information sources, and is willing to conduct tailored research.

*Directory of Special Libraries and Information Centres – Gale*

This is a very comprehensive series which provides information on holdings, services and personnel of information centres throughout the world organised under subject heading. The complete set would cost in the region of £1000 and include much that is not directly relevant to the prospect researcher. You might prefer to confine yourself to volume 1 or look for it in a public library.

*World Guide to Libraries – KG Saur (part of Reed)*

This ranges from the major national libraries to university, governmental, religious and business ones. It covers 167 countries, giving contact details and information on holdings. Sister volumes are *World Guide to Special Libraries* and *Directory of Special Collections in Western Europe*. Another Reed imprint, Bowker-Saur, produces a series which includes *Information Sources in Finance and Banking* and *Information Sources in Patents*.

*World Directory of Business Information Libraries – Euromonitor*

Detailed information on subjects covered, sources available, and services offered. Indexed by special interests.

*The International Directory of Business Information Sources and Services – Europa*

Coverage of about 4500 organisations in about 50 countries. They include chambers of commerce, trade-promotion organisations, governmental organisations, and business libraries. For each entry there are contact details and details of information available and activities.

*Emerging World Markets Reports – Effective Technology Marketing Ltd*

Reports on key business information services, both in hard-copy and electronic form. The countries selected are from the more difficult areas for the information specialist to deal with: Africa, the Middle East, Eastern Europe, Latin America, India and Asia.

# Background information on countries

*Year books*

Many countries produce relatively inexpensive annual collections of international facts, examples being the UK's *Whitaker's Almanack* and *The Statesman's Year-book* (Macmillan). Gale's range includes several similar books, such as *Countries of the World and Their Leaders Yearbook* and *Handbook of the Nations*. More detailed (and expensive) coverage can be found in the Europa range, either *The Europa World Year Book* or the more comprehensive regional volumes. These books provide information such as historical and geographical background, population, languages and religion, members of the government, and trade statistics. The Europa books provide much more detail including lists of major companies in industry, banking and the media, and the largest chambers of commerce and industrial organisations. An alternative is *The World of Information Reviews* from Kogan Page.

*Analysts' reports*

Country reports are readily available but likely to be expensive. One source is *The Economist Intelligence Unit* (also available on CD-ROM from Knight-Ridder). *Dun & Bradstreet* can also provide reports on the political situation, guides for exporters and risk assessments. *Euromoney* produces country profiles with a more financial slant for the serious investor. *Business Monitor Inter-*

*national* is another business and political service. Others can be found through online databases. A daily service from a network of scholars and specialists is provided by *Oxford Analytica*. Check what proportion is devoted to political and macroeconomic coverage as opposed to business.

## How to do business in ....

Some of the major firms of accountants produce booklets on doing business in specific countries. They hope to follow these up with paid advice, but the booklets themselves are free. The Confederation of British Industry produces similar handbooks though it charges for them. These can provide useful addresses and background, though if you are not planning to set up in business much of the detail on legislation, taxation, etc. is irrelevant.

## International Company Filing Requirements – Informed Business Services

Information on types of company and where to find official registries in various of the world's major economies. It is useful for working out what letters like 'plc' and 'GmbH' in company names actually mean, where to find information on these companies, and what sort of information you can hope to find. Informed also provides research services.

# People

## Rich lists

Notable international rich lists are published annually by the US business magazines *Forbes* and *Fortune*.

## The International Who's Who – Europa

This is a long-established, respected publication containing 20,000 biographies, most of which are very full. It covers most countries of the world, though as some are easier to research than others the entries are predominantly northern European, northern American and Japanese. It includes not only politicians and business leaders, but also notable people from the cultural sphere. It claims to replace single-nation directories, but if you are particularly interested in a specific country you would probably need the national who's who as well (if one exists). There is a useful section on reigning royal families, but unfortunately no indexes. Even so it is an indispensable book with an impressive coverage.

## Who's Who in the World – Marquis

A collection of people from many different countries, notably the US. A sister volume is *Who's Who of Women in World Politics*.

### Biographical Archives – Bowker-Saur, part of Reed Elsevier

This series provides biographies of key people in each of several countries. They span several centuries, not quite reaching the present day. These sources are far too expensive for most researchers and their information generally too historical. However if a public library has acquired them they can be of use in building up information on your prospect's famous antecedents.

### Who's Who in International Organizations – KG Saur, part of Reed Elsevier

This three-volume set covers 12,000 people, though many entries give relatively little information. It is particularly useful for tracking down names and contact information for people who would not appear in standard who's whos, though it is not updated annually.

### Worldwide Government Directory – Gale

This provides names and addresses for officials and government agencies throughout the world. More comprehensive than most other publications, e.g. yearbooks. However less frequently updated than Reuter's online Government Lists service (available as part of *Textline* through some hosts, e.g. Knight-Ridder's *Data-Star*).

### Who's Who in International Banking – Bowker-Saur, part of Reed Elsevier

A truly international book, though not all entries are totally comprehensive. Each of the more than 4000 biographies provides a contact address. The second section is a country by country directory of around 1,500 of the world's largest banks, though currently not up to date.

### Who's Who in Finance and Industry – Marquis, part of Reed Elsevier

This is a major work containing around 25,000 biographies. Although it claims to be international there is a strong bias towards the US.

### Who's Who in World Oil and Gas – Cartermill

Brief profiles and contact details for senior personnel in these industries. Indexed by name, company name and company location. Published under the name of the reputable UK newspaper *The Financial Times*. A companion volume goes into more detail on the companies.

### The Arts and Sciences

Numerous publishers produce international directories of authors, musicians, scientists etc. Gale has a particularly wide range including designers, architects, and the fashion world. The International Biographical Centre produces books on authors and musicians. KG Saur (part of Reed Elsevier) has built up a databank of artists, but this is probably too specialised and expensive for most libraries. Reed's wide range also includes *Who's Who in Entertainment* and *Who's Who in American Art*. St James Press has a series which includes *Contemporary Artists, Composers, Dramatists*, etc., while Cartermill produces various industry-specific who's whos, e.g. *Energy and Nuclear Sciences International Who's Who* and *Agricultural and Veterinary Sciences International Who's Who*.

## *Contemporary Black Biography – Gale*

Pictures, biographies and sources of further reading on notable black men and women. They cover the entire spectrum from politics to sport, science and literature. This is a cumulative series with about 70 profiles in each book.

# Business

### *The Spicer and Oppenheim Guide to Financial Statements Around the World – John Wiley & Sons*

Although this title has been out of print since 1993, it is still a very useful country by country overview of accounting and reporting practices. It gives the form and content of a company's financial statement, filing requirements, audit requirements, etc.

### *The Times 1000 – The Times Newspaper/The Reference Press*

A valuable book of lists. The core is an authoritative summary of the top UK and European companies, ranked in order of turnover. It also includes exports, profits, number of employees, net assets, names of two key directors, addresses and telephone numbers. There are also lists of the world's top industrial companies, Europe's top banks, and top companies in several countries, notably the Far East. A relatively cheap yet very useful source.

### *Company directories*

The big names in company information operate on a truly international level and in various media. Examples are *Dun & Bradstreet, Graham & Whiteside* and *Kompass* (Reed Information Services) which often produce directories for individual countries as well as overarching international or regional ones. *Kompass* directories can overlap because they are produced by several different national publishers, using the name and format to market their books as a single series. Alternatively, *ELC* produces broader directories of the largest public and private companies in Europe and Asia, though only naming the top director. In general, the broader the geographical coverage the less detail they contain. These books tend to follow standard formats, though do not take this for

193

granted as some stray quite far from the norm. As well as books they might provide information online, on CD-ROMs, or as bespoke searches.

*Extel* is another specialist in company information, though it offers a slightly different format. If you do not want to spend time compiling your own library of annual reports and press cuttings you might prefer to subscribe to one of its card services, which cover several countries. This means you receive a 'card' index containing a comprehensive sheet for each company. Extel also produces various handbooks, news summaries and more specific services dedicated to taxation, new issues, etc., and is expanding its electronic services. Specific research requests can also be met.

Their products can look confusingly alike. In choosing between publishers you might consider: price (including the possibility of a discount), number of companies covered, whether private companies are included, whether all or just the top directors are named, how much financial information is available (and do you want it all), whether activities are described or merely given as standard categories, what indexes there are (e.g. directors, activities, geographical, brand names) and whether there are standard lists of facts or editorial coverage of recent events, prospects, etc. There are also less obvious differences which will only become apparent over time, such as accuracy and timeliness of information (the publisher might update the financials without troubling too much about the names of directors), or whether subsidiaries are listed as companies in their own right alongside or instead of the parents.

A rather different range is available from *Gale*. It often has a slightly different slant from the standardised facts and figures provided by other publishers. One example is its *Encyclopaedia of Global Industries* which gives overviews and outlooks for entire industries. *World Market Share Reporter* provides rankings and details of participants and their market shares for numerous industries. Its *Trade Shows Worldwide* might also be of interest: perhaps you might wish to attend to view the competition, or in a country where business information is scarce you might try to obtain the programme to see which companies are advertising.

## Hoover's Handbook of World Business – The Reference Press

While the directories above give small amounts of information about a very large number of countries, this is the opposite end of the spectrum. It provides profiles of over 225 public, private and state-owned companies which are based outside the US. They come from all parts of the world, though the larger economies of Europe and Japan inevitably predominate. A useful feature is the profiles of 65 different countries.

*International Brands and their Companies – Gale*

This is one of a series on brands and the companies associated with them. They are rather too specialised for many users, but if you want to look up obscure brands and find which company produces them or look up a company and obtain a long listing of its brands then these are the books for you.

*International Directory of Company Histories – Gale (St James Press)*

This comprehensive series contains the histories of the world's major companies, industry by industry. It does not attempt to remain totally up to date. However the wealth of background information can be fascinating and can easily be supplemented by annual reports and press coverage. If you cannot afford to buy it for your own library it is the sort of book that often appeals to public libraries.

*Who Owns Whom – Dun & Bradstreet*

There are four parts to this series: Australasia & the Far East, North America, UK & the Republic of Ireland, and Continental Europe. This is an expensive set of books and provides quite basic information, but it is very comprehensive and can prove invaluable. It is used simply for researching corporate structures: you can look up a company and discover the name of its parent or else obtain a listing of its subsidiaries. The top company of each corporate family is accompanied by address, telephone number, and category of activity. The information is unexciting but very comprehensive. It is also available online. Alternatives, containing more text, are available from Reed Elsevier, e.g. *Directory of Corporate Affiliations/International.*

*Britain's Top Foreign Companies – Jordan's*

This allows you to select, for example, the top US-owned companies operating in Britain. However it is a laborious process as the company information is listed in order of size and must be cross-referenced with the geographical index in order to pull out companies from the relevant country. Volume 1 covers the top 1250 companies, and volume 2 the next 1250. For each company there is a three year summary of financial performance, together with details of ownership, activities, directors and registered address and telephone number. There are also rankings of the top companies by various measures, such as pre-tax profit. Some online databases can provide the same information, though it would be a relatively complicated and expensive search. Alternatively Jordan's can do bespoke searches for you.

### *The Bankers' Almanac – Reed Information Services*

Covering the world's major international banks in alphabetical order, giving contact details, names of directors and senior officials, ownership, brief finances, and some information on branches. It is also indexed geographically and is available online and on CD-ROM. Other Reed products include a world ranking of banks. Banks do not generally provide the same sort of figures as standard companies. Asset values are likely to replace the turnover figure.

### *Assecuranz Compass – Assecuranz Compass*

International insurance year book. Provides contact details, names of directors, etc., for insurance companies in 181 countries. Written in English and four other languages depending on the country concerned. An alternative is Cartermill's *Financial Times World Insurance*.

### *The Martindale-Hubbell Law Directory International Edition – Reed Elsevier*

Details of 4000 law firms and 100,000 lawyers in 130 countries worldwide. American lawyers are excluded except where they have international interests, so see the full Martindale-Hubbell for the entire American legal profession. Arranged geographically and indexed by name, firm and field. Details include education, specialisms and languages.

### *The press*

Most serious business papers have international sections, but they are generally heavily biassed towards their own country. The UK's *Financial Times* has reasonable international coverage. There are also specially produced international editions of papers such as *The International Herald Tribune* and *The Wall Street Journal*. However these are again biassed towards the areas where they are sold, i.e. the European edition will contain a larger percentage of European stories than the Asian one, though the core remains the same. You can obtain the foreign editions, but they are slower and more expensive. There are also international business magazines, e.g. *Business Week International*, though they tend to focus on America. If you are interested in a particular area the ideal is to obtain publications specifically devoted to it. These might be published in the region, though overseas ones might be capable of providing a more independent view and are more likely to use English.

If you want to find journals for a particular industry you can check a press guide in a library. Alternatively there are services which provide contents summaries, e.g. HW Wilson's *Business Periodicals Index* and Predicasts databases either of which might be found in a library or online.

# Foundations

*The International Foundation Directory – Europa*

Outside the English-speaking world foundations can be quite difficult to track down, often because there are far fewer of them. Although no substitute for a national directory (if one exists), this book is a great help. Unfortunately, in trying to find entries for as many countries as possible, it has occasionally picked up bodies which are more academic than grant-making; however it is still a very useful source. It gives clear explanations, in English, of what each body does, who are its trustees, and how to contact it. There is also an index of interests in the back, which should narrow down the field a little. Greenwood Press has also produced an *International Encyclopaedia of Foundations* though it is now a little old.

# Electronic information

Most hosts have a bias towards their country of origin, but they are rapidly acquiring foreign databases in a scramble to compete for overseas markets. When choosing a host don't look only at your national ones: the large international hosts might have a very good coverage of your country and might even offer gateways to other hosts you were considering using. See the earlier chapter on online information for ideas on how to choose the right host. Some of the larger international ones are covered here, but there are many more.

One of the giants of international electronic information is the Knight-Ridder team of *Data-Star* and *Dialog*. *Data-Star* is predominantly European while *Dialog* is very American though with a reasonable coverage of UK and Canadian databases as well as some Asia/Pacific and international ones. Together they can offer everything from the Bible and an encyclopaedia to scientific papers and patents. From the point of view of the prospect researcher their main strength is their coverage of business, the US regional and national press, and even some who's whos and US foundation information. *Dialog's* huge coverage and powerful indexes (notably 411, *Dialindex*) mean that it is an ideal place to search for obscure people anywhere in the world. It is also widely available outside America. Its traditional query language is being replaced by a more user-friendly system which will lead to the fusion of the two services.

Other major international hosts are *Lexis/Nexis* and *Dow Jones* (*The Wall Street Journal*). *Maid* is an example of a very business oriented service. It contains expensive market research information, country briefings and stockmarket quotes as well as company information and the latest news.

A less US-oriented host is *FT-Profile* which is owned by the publisher of the *Financial Times*, the UK's premier business newspaper. Needless to say it offers the *FT*, whose availability is restricted on other hosts. It is very strong on the British press, and has taken the unusual step of including one or two tabloids. However its international range is also very strong including European and Asian (especially Japanese) news and business sources, plus expensive market reports and analysis. It has many of the standard international business sources such as Investext, Dun & Bradstreet, Reedbase Kompass and Extel. Its InfoPlus format allows you to search through user-friendly menus. *FT-Profile* is itself available via other hosts, such as *New Prestel* and *BT Business Information*.

*CompuServe* is one of the international giants, but is slightly different. It is a combination of the databases you might find via a host like Knight-Ridder and the more popular services of the Internet. It provides discussion groups, email, general interest information like flight times and the chance to shop electronically as well as a link to the Internet. Despite the more frivolous offerings it also has a wide range of business and press information. Although *CompuServe* was the first to become international there are many similar services. They include *Delphi* (containing *News International*'s services), *Europe Online*, and the US-based *America Online* and *Prodigy*.

The UK-based *New Prestel* is another service which provides information on holidays, weather, etc. It also provides access to both the British *FT-Profile* and the French *Minitel* as well as British and French telephone directories, credit databases, and a comparatively limited amount of company information. Its geographical range is relatively narrow and several of its services are in French; however its gateways give it good access to the press.

Individual databases are often available on several hosts. One example is the Reuters press database *Textline* whose hosts include *FT-Profile*, *Dialog* and *Data-Star* though it takes on a different language and format in each one. If you find online information intimidating and want to focus on just one database then this might be the one. It is a good source for world news, though especially strong on the UK. Besides an extensive range of national newspapers from all over the world it offers BBC Monitoring Service and Reuters news agency reports. It is also very well coded. Similar groupings with more of a business orientation are available from *IAC/Predicasts* (e.g. *Promt* and *Globalbase*) and *McCarthy*.

Internet users might be interested in the following guides to business information: Sheila Webber's list is at *http://www.dis.strath.ac.uk/business/index.html.* Yahoo is at *http://www.yahoo.com/Business/Electronic_Commerce/*. Another business resources list can be found at *gopher://refmac.kent.edu/*.

There are also Internet discussion lists for researchers and fund-raisers, though they are inevitably dominated by Americans. A major Internet discussion group for prospect researchers is the *PRSPCT-L*. This is a free mailing list which enables all members of the group to receive the same messages. It is based at the University of California, Irvine. You can join it by sending an email command to *listserv@uci.edu* as follows: subscribe prspct-l firstname lastname (for firstname and lastname you type your own name). To remove yourself from the list: unsubscribe prspct-l.

A web page devoted to research with links to useful sources is: *http:// weber.u.washington.edu/~dlamb/research.html.* For international research try *Intfund*: email the message 'subscribe intfund' to *listserv@vm1.mcgill.ca.* One useful site pointing to net worth information is: *http://networth.galt.com/www/ home/netiic.html.* Genealogy is covered on *roots-l*: send the message subscribe roots-l firstname lastname to *listserv@vm1.nodak.edu.*

Fund-raisers might find *The NonProfit Times* of use. This is at *http:// haven.ios.com/~nptimes/index.html.* It contains a databank of articles on the entire spectrum of fund-raising. You can also email it at *nptimes@haven.ios.com.* For a weekly summary of articles on philanthropy in the media, try the Foundation Center's *Philanthropy News Digest* at *http://fdncenter.org/aboutp/ philmain.html.* Alternatively try *http://asa.ugl.lib.umich.edu/chdocs/nonprofits/ nonprofits.html. Fundlist* is a discussion group for university fund-raisers: send the message subscribe fundlist firstname lastname to *listserv@jhuvm.hcf.jhu.edu.* Alternatively try *USNonProfit-L*: send the message subscribe usnonprofit-l to *majordomo@coyote.rain.org.* A useful web page is: *http://web.city.ac.uk/~bh543/ fundraising.html.* A newsgroup can be found at *soc.org.nonprofit.*

For further sources try *The Internet Prospector* at *http://plains.uwyo.edu/~prospect/.*

# Membership organisations

National organisations are beginning to branch out overseas, e.g. CASE (education), APRA (prospect research) and NSFRE (fund-raising), all of which can be found in the US section. One group that is specifically international is *The International Fund Raising Group* which can also provide information on an international fund-raising workshop.

# 15. The United Kingdom

Although the terms UK, Britain and England are often used interchangeably (not least by the English), strictly speaking they mean different things. To describe a Welsh person as English might lose you a great deal of goodwill. The United Kingdom is composed of England, Wales, Scotland and Northern Ireland (this last is sometimes referred to as 'Ulster'). Southern Ireland ('Eire') left the UK in 1921 and is now a totally separate country. (For resources for Northern Ireland see also the European section as books often overlap both countries.) 'Britain' means the mainland, i.e. England, Wales and Scotland. England tends to dominate in terms of language, economics and politics, but the other countries have their own sense of national identity and languages, Welsh being particularly strong.

The jurisdiction of the UK does not extend to some of the small islands dotted around its coast, such as the Channel Islands (e.g. Jersey, Guernsey) and the Isle of Man which are dependencies of the Crown with their own legislative and taxation systems. They have taken advantage of this independence to become tax havens for the wealthy. For practical purposes they are often included in British directories, so they are covered in this section. However be aware that information on prospects based there is not necessarily held in British registries such as the Charity Commission. You will have to approach the registry on the appropriate island, if one exists. Each island has its own rules and any information which is publicly available is likely to be less detailed than on the mainland.

Even within the four nations of the UK there are considerable variations in culture, outlook and wealth. The south-east of England is particularly prosperous and metropolitan, with London as its focus. There is also a great deal of wealth in parts of Scotland, notably Edinburgh and Aberdeen, which boast a strong financial sector and wealth from the offshore oil industry.

## Information sources

*Current British Directories – CBD Research Ltd*

A guide to sources of information. It covers directories of every type, including many devoted to specific industries and associations which publish lists of members. A good way of finding contact details for publishers or books you didn't know existed (from the subject index), though liable to date quite rapidly. Includes the UK, the Channel Islands and the Republic of Ireland.

*Aslib Directory of Information Sources in the United Kingdom – Aslib*

This is not a directory of directories. It provides contact details and subject coverage for a wide range of libraries, museums, societies, companies, charities, etc., which might be able to provide specialist information on your particular area of interest. Whether this is hymnology, rubella, Cuba or integrated circuits the index will guide you to an expert.

*Croner's A-Z of Business Information Sources – Croner Publications Ltd*

This is a loose-leaf information service on sources within the UK. Though relatively small in comparison with the above it is cheaper and constantly updated.

*Guide to Directories at the Science Reference and Information Service- The British Library*

This might be useful as a way of planning your search before a visit as it has a subject index which cross-references countries or business sectors with the main body of the book; however as it gives little more than title, publisher and shelfmark you might feel frustrated at not knowing what each book contains. Alternatively it might be used as a way of finding new publications for your own library, though as it does not tell you how to contact publishers or what the book contains it might be easier to go to the library and look at the books.

*Guide to Libraries and Information Units: In Government Departments and Other Organisations – The British Library*

This guide will direct you towards information sources for any subject from ballistics to raspberries. Although the information providers are all in the UK, they include foreign agencies such as the United States Information Service. Excluded are most academic, public and commercial libraries.

*Guide to Libraries in Key UK Companies – The British Library*

Details of over 200 specialist libraries which are willing to take enquiries.

# People

### Private addresses and telephone numbers

The more exclusive the publication's circulation the more private the information you might find there. *People of Today*, because of Debrett's reputation as the publisher of the aristocracy, is possibly marginally more likely to be given home address than *Who's Who*. Many otherwise confidential addresses are available in *The City of London Directory and Livery Companies Guide*. If your prospect is a director of a registered company then apply to Companies House for the records and you should find that a home address is given in the return of directors.

British Telecom produces telephone directories, CD-ROMs and an online service, any of which might be available in a public library. It is no longer a monopoly, a notable competitor being Mercury. Unfortunately a sizeable proportion of the British population is 'ex-directory', i.e. their telephone numbers are strictly private and should not be published anywhere nor available through Directory Enquiries. Whether ex-directory or not, Directory Enquiries will not give you an address, even if it is printed in the telephone directory. Speaking nicely to the operator or saying you are not sure which is the right number will often elicit a small amount of information. You might even get him to confirm an ex-directory address belongs to your prospect, or give you the postal area of an ex-directory person. Data collection agencies might provide numbers if you wish to buy in bulk.

### Titles

If you are interested in titled people it is essential to address them correctly if you do not wish to irritate them. *Correct Form* (Debrett's) or *Titles and Forms of Address* (A&C Black) will guide you, explaining such niceties as the distinction between the name written on the envelope and the one used in the letter. They will explain how to address each rank of the nobility, and help you understand that 'Lady Jane Smith' implies something quite different from 'Jane, Lady Smith'. However if you have *People of Today* (not *Who's Who*) it is worth noting that at the end of each entry there is a heading 'style' which gives the person's preferred mode of address (which might be different from the one which is strictly correct).

It might also be worth checking in recent honours lists – which are published twice a year in the major national papers – in case any new distinction has been awarded recently. Full-text newspaper databases (such as *Dialog's* 710 and 711) will reproduce these lists. The distinctions are of different degrees of importance and if a person has several they must be listed in the right order. British people frequently make technical errors with other people's honours, though they can be sensitive about their own, so (apart from the official awards lists) do not trust newspapers to give the correct version.

## Wealth

Annual reports of public companies will show all holdings which amount to 3% or more of the shares. This is a large amount of money, and generally only institutional investors, such as pension funds, can reach this size. Alternatively, Companies House returns contain registers of shareholders and the size of their holdings (though for the very largest companies these might be too long to be reproduced if you wish them to be sent to you). The *Financial Times* or its sister journal *Investors Chronicle* will tell you how shares are performing. However there is no way of finding the full list of companies in which your prospect holds shares: the only clue is a directorship.

Unfortunately the land registry is not of much use. You cannot search for a person, only look up a particular address to find out who owns it. Even then if the property has not changed hands for some time it might not be registered.

If you have the person's job title you can obtain an idea of his salary by looking at the IDS pay directory. This gives standard pay scales for various jobs, though you could probably have guessed at them anyway. Alternatively if he is a judge, top civil servant, etc., you can find his salary scale in *Whitaker's Almanack*. For directors of quoted companies check their annual reports, which will list at least the salaries of the chairman and highest paid director (who might be the same person but is more likely to be the chief executive).

## Business career

Both current directorships and a chronological list of the prospect's previous business career can be taken from biographical directories. Indexes of directorships are also useful: in book form, e.g. *Directory of Directors*, *The Corporate Register* or the index of Dun & Bradstreet's *Key British Enterprises*, or on electronic company databases such as those of ICC, Dun & Bradstreet or Reedbase Kompass (available on various hosts).

*Textline* is also of use; not only does it contain the stock exchange's Regulatory News Service and the major UK dailies, but you can search it using the special code for management changes which is a great help in narrowing down the volume of articles.

However most sources do not include the smallest companies, which form part of the private wealth of many prospects. If you know the name of at least one of these companies then ask Companies House for a copy of its documents. In the return of directors' names, addresses, etc., there should also be a listing of other British companies in which each person holds a directorship. Records of these companies can then also be obtained from Companies House.

Alternatively, it is possible to look up a director's name on the Companies House database. This will list all companies where a person of that name holds a directorship. This only works with relatively unusual names as otherwise you have no way of knowing which of the many entries is the correct person short of checking each company's record. There are also commercial databases which present similar information in a more detailed and user-friendly form, but these are generally very expensive.

Using the press (e.g. *Investor's Chronicle*) or an online news database such as *Textline* you can build up a picture of how each company owned or managed by your prospect is performing. This affects not only the prospect's wealth, but also issues like how successful he feels and how much spare time he has (a hostile predator is of more importance than a fund-raiser), and it is also impressive if the solicitation staff sound interested and informed about the prospect's own concerns.

### Rich lists

UK lists are available annually in *The Sunday Times* (a standard newspaper) and *BusinessAge* magazine. As Philip Beresford, the compiler of the *Sunday Times* rich list, works freelance his lists occasionally appear in other magazines, as well as in the occasional book version of the *Sunday Times* list (Penguin). More recently the Directory of Social Change brought out an informative and cheap book called *The Millionaire Givers*.

The *Corporate Register* (Hemmington Scott) regularly produces a list of the highest paid UK directors. Many are nameless because companies are not required to specify which director receives what; however generally it is the chief executive who is paid most. The Labour Research Department occasionally produces similar lists (which are often picked up by the press), and *Tatler* also comes up with occasional lists of top benefactors or party-givers.

Alternatively mass mailing lists can be bought, e.g. Dudley Jenkins has lists of directors, professionals, etc. These are generally designed for selling rather than fund-raising so check direct marketing magazines for advertisements.

### National biographical directories

*Who's Who* (A&C Black) is well known and respected. First published in 1849 it now contains more than 29,000 biographies. However its more recent competitor, *People of Today* (Debrett's Peerage), is very similar and possibly more useful.

They both aim to cover those with distinction and influence, whether inherited or earned, political, economic, scientific, or artistic. They are the 'top people' at the national level: businessmen and politicians rather than teachers or employees of town councils. Those who have received some sort of national honour, such as an OBE or knighthood, are very likely to be included. There is no question of a financial motive for inclusion, though *Who's Who* has been criticised for being unduly secretive in its selection methods.

It must be remembered that people cannot be forced to be included (though many consider it an honour), nor can they be forced to divulge information which they wish to keep secret, such as home address or parents' names. There are often slight discrepancies in dates between them as they depend on the biographees' possibly faulty memories; however as each year the biographee gets the chance to correct the entry it should be reasonably accurate.

Most entries cover the complete range of biographical data; however the British are more reticent than Americans about disclosing their charitable and political interests. Unlike American directories British ones are generally not indexed or available online.

*Who's Who* has the disadvantage that once a person is in she stays in until death (except for a few foreign people who can no longer be traced) even if her subsequent career is insignificant or disreputable. This means that the selection panel is often reluctant to include people who have not proved themselves sufficiently reliable.

*People of Today* is more willing to take risks and more responsive to transient popular culture. *People of Today* is also slightly larger and has a few advantages derived from the fact that its publisher is a chronicler of the UK nobility: it is more likely to give family information (famous antecedents, names of children, etc.) and it always gives a person's 'style' (i.e. preferred title – Mr, Sir, etc.). The latter is a great help as titles are by no means easy to work out, and occasionally depend on personal preference.

After the first few editions it decided to develop a more populist approach, the result being that it is possibly slightly more likely than *Who's Who* to contain both obscure members of the nobility and pop stars. Both books contain top businessmen, their coverage being slightly different but neither having a particular advantage. In both it is reasonable to hope that the chairman, chief executive and possibly non-executive directors of the largest companies might appear, together with any other directors who have been honoured with OBEs etc.

Note that unlike *People of Today*, *Who's Who* does not put the entries into strict alphabetical order: titled people are placed before others with the same surname, so Lord (Peter) Smith will appear before Mr Albert Smith. As in many who's whos, members of the royal family are listed separately at the front.

A new competitor is *Burke's Register* (Burke's Peerage). Entries are again chosen by merit rather than willingness to pay. Like *People of Today* it is prepared to abandon existing biographies in favour of more interesting new ones; however unlike both of its competitors it sells advertising space in order to give copies away free to biographees, advertisers, public libraries, and selected others, so guaranteeing a large print run. It aims to retain an upmarket aura and high standard of editorial, which will be essential if it is to succeed in selling its remaining copies at the comparatively high price of £120 each. It has been subject to numerous delays, but if it does eventually appear it will be interesting to see what effect it has on a limited market.

## Who Was Who – A&C Black

This series is drawn from old editions of *Who's Who* dating back to 1897. Each volume contains the biographies of those people who *died* within the time span it covers. There is also an index volume which spans the set, though it contains only names, not biographies. The entries are as they appeared in the original volumes, which means that the early ones are less informative than their modern counterparts.

To fill the gap between the latest volume and the present *Who's Who* you might like to buy *The Times Lives Remembered* series (Blewbury Press). These are collections of obituaries taken from *The Times*, one of the UK's more respected newspapers. It covers the most interesting 10% or so of those obituaries which appeared in each year, i.e. a relatively small number of people. If you have access to online databases you might prefer to use those as they have a broader coverage; however many newspaper databases do not bother with the obituaries. Look for a 'full-text' database, such as *The Times* and *The Independent* (710 and 711) on Knight-Ridder's *Dialog*. Alternatively some larger libraries have newspaper indexes in book form.

## Debrett's Peerage and Baronetage – Macmillan

This is a detailed genealogical work covering the nobility. They no longer enjoy the degree of political and economic influence that they once wielded; many are struggling to maintain crumbling castles in the face of crippling inheritance taxes. However they are still of considerable social importance.

This book provides a wealth of information on family links, down to the names, addresses and children of distant cousins. It now includes illegitimate and adopted children though on request only. The only people who receive the full biographical treatment are the current holders of titles (who are almost exclusively male due to the rules on inheritance). Their antecedents are listed, together with brief details of their careers.

The book is divided into two sections: barons and above, and the lower ranking baronets. In between are two very useful indexes: one of surnames, and the other of courtesy titles (held by relatives of the key noble), both of which can be different from the main title. There is also information on precedence, principal foreign and commonwealth orders, forms of address, the royal family, etc.

Debrett's illustrious competitor, *Burke's Peerage*, is no longer published. Its last completely new edition was published in 1972, with a partial update in 1980. Burke's does not have copies, so you must go to book search agencies if you wish to obtain it.

### Who's Who in the City – Macmillan

Biographies of eminent people in the 'City', i.e. London's financial community, as opposed to industry or other services. It also includes people in regional financial centres, and has an extensive index of institutions in the back, followed by a sector index. Some of the entries are full and informative, but there are several that are no more than name and institution. This should not put you off buying the book as it has no real competitors, especially after it absorbed *Becket's Directory*.

### Dictionary of Twentieth Century British Business Leaders – Bowker-Saur, part of Reed Elsevier

Of the 750 people included, around 200 are still living. As well as biographical information there is a bibliography.

### Who's Who in the Channel Islands – Mr Alastair Layzell

The Channel Islands are regarded as tax havens, so contain more than their fair share of wealthy people, 'offshore' companies and financial advisers. Although under the sovereignty of the British monarch they are actually located off the northern coast of France and thus are heavily influenced by the French. They are quite independent in their tax and legal systems. Jersey in particular has a buoyant economy heavily reliant on tourism and finance.

Unfortunately plans to update the 1987 edition of this book seem to have fallen through, but the area is so wealthy that even a book of this age is still worthwhile. It is a small book, divided into separate sections for individual islands. There are interesting pieces on the history and government of the various islands, as well as full biographies; however an important point to note is that there are no addresses or telephone numbers. You must obtain these either from a telephone book (from British Telecom) or a local volunteer. As many people who move to the Channel Islands guard their privacy closely it cannot be assumed that this Who's Who is comprehensive.

### *Who's Who in Scotland – Carrick Media*

A standard who's who listing around 5000 people currently living in Scotland. As the number of people in Scotland is relatively small this book includes many people who might not be considered prestigious enough to appear in the overall UK *Who's Who*.

### Regional who's whos

Local newspapers sometimes produce a who's who covering their own area which contains people who would not be found in other publications. One example is *Northern People* from *The Northern Echo* in Darlington. *The Birmingham Post and Mail* also produces a local guide. Find out about these by asking newspaper publishers and local libraries.

### Alternative who's whos

Occasionally you might come across a cheap, chatty paperback which provides the author's personal views on the rich and famous. These are generally one offs, for example Compton Miller's *Who's Really Who* (Sphere 1983) and *Nigel Dempster's Address Book* (Pan 1992), both of which are probably now unobtainable. Look out for similar publications in popular bookshops. They can provide an interesting angle unobtainable elsewhere, but beware of relying too heavily on their accuracy.

### *Asian Who's Who International – Asian Observer*

A thorough, up to date paperback providing biographies and information on the Asian community including a business directory. There are also small sections covering Asians living outside the UK. Asians are overall possibly better educated and more wealthy than other communities.

If you are particularly interested in ethnic minorities *Indians in Britain – Who's Who* (Computers & Geotechnics) is another possibility. This is sold as a sideline by an engineering consultancy. It is now rather old, but possibly still of interest as most of its biographees will not appear elsewhere. It includes anyone of Indian origin rather than those specifically from India. Although they did not have to pay for entry, the low response to the editors' questionnaire probably means this is not a particularly representative sample.

### *Third World Impact – Hansib*

A who's who makes up a small proportion of this book. The remainder is devoted to articles on jazz, black children in school, Asian film makers in Britain, etc. There are also listings of relevant organisations. Its bias is more towards West Indians rather than Asians. The same publisher also produces two newspapers: *Asian Times* and *Caribbean Times*, which might include profiles of leading members of the communities.

## *Dod's Parliamentary Companion – Dod's Parliamentary Companion*

A well known biographical directory of the members of both houses of the UK government plus UK MEPs (members of the European Parliament). Standard who's who entries including many photographs and indexed by members' interests. Also a background to UK and European political institutions and a directory of key people in the various ministries.

Alternatively you might like to consider the publications of Parliamentary Profile Services Ltd which provide more detailed profiles and information on the MPs' parliamentary activities. You can also obtain regular updates of the *Register of Members' Interests* from HMSO. MPs are forced to declare their outside interests at regular intervals so that any conflict with their political duties is evident.

## *The Whitehall Companion – DPR Publishing Ltd*

Full biographies (often with photographs) of top civil servants and key Whitehall officials. Also how the various departments are structured and who is responsible for what. The UK civil service is increasingly being moved into the private sector, and this directory includes the 'next step executive agencies' as well as selected regulatory organisations and public bodies.

## *City of London Directory and Livery Companies Guide – City Press*

At first sight this is a rather unhelpful book, but like many books designed for a limited audience it is pleasingly free with private addresses. It is essentially a set of lists of the members of livery companies, which are prestigious social and charitable groups to which many notable people belong. An index of names in the back points you in the direction of a specific company where each person's private address is given. In most cases that is the only information available, but there are a few fuller biographies towards the back. It also contains details of various City institutions: insurers, banks, markets, courts, schools, etc.

The livery companies are the descendants of the medieval guilds which governed the various crafts and professions, the best known of which is the Masons. At the head is the annually-elected Lord Mayor of London. Although they sound archaic, membership still confers social status and new companies continue to be formed, e.g. there is now a Company of Information Technologists. Nowadays members frequently have nothing to do with the original craft, and women are beginning to appear. They are social and charitable organisations, capable of making donations in their own right.

Although these companies are based in London members come from all over the country, and even occasionally from overseas. They are likely to be drawn from the social and business élite, sons following fathers into the same company, as membership generally depends on nomination by existing members. It should not be assumed that the members of a company all know each other very well, as the full livery is seldom, if ever, gathered together, but a link might be worth following up especially if your contact held office within the company.

## Homes and gardens

The wealthy and the nobility tend to have impressive homes and gardens which they occasionally open to the public. There are various guides which will give some indication of what they are like. There might be information on the history and architecture of the house, art collections, or simply the planting of the garden (which is likely to be of great interest to the owner). They might provide an address, a clue to wealth or a talking point when meeting the prospect.

*Gardens of England and Wales* (The National Gardens Scheme) is one example of such a guide. The National Trust publishes guides to its properties (though the families who live in them no longer own them), and there are also guides to stately homes produced by organisations like the Automobile Association. They can often be found in Tourist Information Centres or popular bookshops.

An alternative source of addresses for lynchpins of the local community are *Diocesan Year Books*. If your prospect is a church warden, treasurer, etc., of the local church then provided you know roughly what area he lives in you might be able to find his address. These are published by the relevant church diocese but might also be available in local libraries.

## Wills

UK wills become available to the public between a few months and a few years after death. Not everybody makes a will, but wealthier people are more likely to do so. They vary considerably, but you can hope to find a value for the estate and details of members of the family who will obtain bequests. There may also be various more personal details and descriptions of property. Remember that the value shown is gross and might be subject to tax, settlement of debts, etc. An associated document is 'probate', which declares that a court accepts the will as valid.

English and Welsh wills are relatively easy to access as far back as 1858. Postal requests for those proved at the Principal Probate Registry in London should be sent to the York Probate Registry enclosing full name, place and date of death, and a small search fee, though this will take two or three weeks. Alternatively you can visit Somerset House in London and order the will there. Some larger libraries also have a microfilm copy of parts of the index. Irish and Scottish wills are generally kept at their respective principal registries.

# Business

## Companies House

The British Government insists on quite a high level of disclosure from companies registered in the UK. This information is made available to anyone who wishes to consult the records. Not all businesses need to disclose information: you are likely to be disappointed if searching for a consultancy or partnership. Those which use the words 'Limited', 'Ltd' or 'PLC' as part of their name are registered. Most (though not all) PLCs are also quoted on the Stock Exchange.

In order to cut back on 'red tape' for smaller companies there are different levels of disclosure for different sizes of companies. Officially they are classed as small, medium or large, and must file information accordingly. The information filed by a PLC will be quite similar to that provided in its glossy annual report; it is therefore normally easier to ask the company for its (free) annual report rather than pay Companies House for its rather less user-friendly version. The *Financial Times* operates a service for supplying annual reports, details of which are on its share price pages. Where Companies House comes into its own is for smaller or private companies.

One advantage that Companies House returns have over the printed annual report and most directories is that directors must list other British companies in which they hold a directorship, many of which will be small and will not appear in biographical entries. The Companies House return also gives personal details such as address, nationality and date of birth for the directors, though not for the secretary. The company secretary is not a clerical officer, but has important financial and legal responsibilities. The person who runs the company might occasionally hide behind the secretaryship so as not to divulge too much personal information.

One route to Companies House information is a personal visit. The major offices are in London and Cardiff (which each have English and Welsh records) and Edinburgh (for Scottish companies), with satellites in Birmingham, Manchester, Leeds and Glasgow. If you are visiting a lesser office check in advance that it has the records you wish to see.

The search room contains terminals from which you can choose your company, though for a simple system it is remarkably easy to be misled by it. It places companies into strict alphabetical order, ignoring standard words like 'limited'. In most cases this works well, but from time to time there are problems, notably with companies whose names are initials. It is also disappointing that you can only search for the first word of the name. Alternatively you can search for a director and see which companies he is involved with. However so little information is given on the screen that if the name is John Smith you might have to pay to look at rather a lot of records before you find the right one.

Alternatively you can post a request or ring the search room and the staff will use the terminals to find your company for you (provided you have a reasonably precise name or preferably a company number). Although they have plenty of experience in using the system there is no guarantee that they will be able to find your company. They are likely to be fooled by the same indexing problems as you.

Once the staff have identified the correct company they will arrange for you to be sent a copy of the records, in either paper or microfiche format. Microfiche records are relatively cheap and easy to store, but they can be difficult to scan quickly or to read for any length of time without feeling queasy. In the case of the largest companies you might not be sent the complete record as the lists of shareholders are so huge. Before you receive a copy of the record you will have to make a cash deposit as credit is not allowed.

Another method is to use a company search agent, such as ICC or Jordans, if you really must have the information on the same day. This is rather more expensive. You could also access services which contain the same information, such as Extel Financial, ICC or Dun & Bradstreet.

The official Companies House online service is available through Mercury's *Companies House Direct* service. This effectively means that you have your own Companies House terminal on your desk. You do not have to travel to the office or rely on the staff's accuracy. Unfortunately there is not a huge amount available on this system. It enables you to find the company and order a copy of the records, but does not itself contain the full details. However it does contain directors' names, home addresses, dates of birth, etc. This system is improving but is still primitive in comparison with fully fledged online databases. At present it is only available within the UK. It should ultimately become part of a network of online European company registries, due to the encouragement of the European Union. There are no plans to make it available outside Europe.

When you finally see the full record it can seem very confusing. It consists of endless repetitious forms. In fact they are in date order showing the finances, directors, shareholders, etc., year by year. They are grouped in major sequences, e.g. accounts. After a little practice you soon become proficient at finding what you want. At the beginning of the sequence will be information on the formation of the company. It might well have had a different name, different directors, and the declared intention of doing anything and everything. This might be an 'off the shelf' company created by company formation agents so that it is instantly ready for whoever wanted to buy it. Do not be misled by a long list of activities as many companies apparently claim to do far more than they actually do. It is simply a standard way of drawing up these documents to permit as much leeway as possible.

*The Times 1000 – The Times Newspaper/The Reference Press*

A valuable book of lists. The core is an authoritative summary of the top UK and European companies, ranked in order of turnover. It also includes exports, profits, number of employees, net assets, names of two key directors, addresses and telephone numbers. There are also lists of the world's top industrial companies, Europe's top banks, top companies in several countries, etc.

*The (Price Waterhouse) Corporate Register – Hemmington Scott*

This covers only stockmarket companies (i.e. generally the largest ones, though it does miss out some major private companies). Under each company is listed activities, directors, contact details, major shareholders, very basic financial information, and names of advisers such as bankers, brokers, auditors, solicitors. Some companies take out advertisements which provide even more information.

It is very similar to the *Company Guide* (below), but gives less financial information, concentrating instead on the directors. It gives their shareholdings, the salaries of the chairman and highest paid director, and sometimes the names of non-directors such as the personnel officer. The second section is a directory of directors, listing the stockmarket companies of which each person is a director and in some instances providing biographical information as well. The entries are also indexed by adviser (i.e. there are lists of auditors, solicitors, etc. and their clients) which is very useful for finding contacts. There are also articles, including a regular table of the highest paid directors.

*Directory of Directors – Reed Information Services*

One volume enables you to look up directors and discover which companies they are associated with, though there is generally little biographical information. The other volume enables you to look up the companies, providing contact details, directors' names, finances. It covers the top 14,000 British companies so comes mid-way between *Key British Enterprises* and *The Corporate Register*. It is particularly useful for listing a person's directorships of small or private companies which would be too obscure for other publications.

## The (Hambro) Company Guide – Hemmington Scott

Four paperbacks a year provide comprehensive and up to date information on stockmarket companies. What distinguishes it from the *Corporate Register* is that instead of information on the directors (other than names and positions) it gives a table of finances over the past five years, together with information on shares and dates of regular financial announcements. There are also useful articles and tables such as the top auditors, new issues, or a focus on regional companies. Finally, there are lists of advisers (solicitors, stockbrokers, etc.) and their clients.

## Key British Enterprises – Dun & Bradstreet

If you want basic information on a very wide range of companies then this six-volume set can provide it. It provides basic financial information for the top 50,000 British companies (including private ones) plus contact details, names of all directors, names of corporate parents, export markets, bankers, etc. Activities are given as codes (e.g. SIC – standard industrial classification codes). These are listed elsewhere in the set, but remember they are broad headings rather than specific descriptions of the firm's activities. These volumes are very well indexed by activity, location, export markets, trade names, directors, etc., and there are also rankings. As with any publication, D&B books will become out of date and should be checked against other sources. If the finances seem up to date the directors might not be.

D&B produces a range of other business directories for Britain and the rest of the world. If you want further financial detail you might supplement KBE with *Corporate Financial Performance*, though if you are only looking at a few companies the Companies House records will be cheaper. It also produces a series of *Regional Directories*. These include a wider range of companies over a smaller geographical area, for example they include partnerships, companies with turnovers under £1m, and local authorities which don't have turnovers.

If you wish to compare a company's performance with its competitors you might consider *Key Business Ratios* which provides ratios and average turnover, profit, etc. for each of a wide range of industries. This will tell you whether your prospect is performing well or badly in comparison with similar companies, though if the company has diversified into several activities this does not work so well.

The *Who Owns Whom* series is one you might consider, despite its price and the limited nature of its information. Its main purpose is to enable you to look up the parent, subsidiary, and complete family tree of any given company. This can also be done via online databases but you might find you use the book sufficiently to justify the expense.

*Macmillan's Unquoted Companies and The Macmillan Stock Exchange Yearbook – Macmillan*

The former covers the top 20,000 privately-owned UK companies and the latter the 3700 public companies on the London and Dublin stock exchanges, including USM companies. They contain the standard details of directors, financials, etc. *Unquoted Companies* provides league tables, and product, sector and geographical indexes. *Stock Exchange Yearbook* has longer entries including principal subsidiaries, major shareholders and company histories, giving it the edge over *Key British Enterprises'* much briefer entries. However KBE covers more companies.

There are numerous other producers of business directories, each with their own advantages. Jordan's range includes *Britain's Top Privately Owned Companies*. Jordan's is a specialist in the UK and produces a range of industry-specific directories as well as doing bespoke searches.

ELC produces *The UK's 10,000 Largest Companies*. This provides basic company information such as contact details, activities, sales and profit, parent. Where it loses out to other books, such as *Key British Enterprises*, is that it only names the top director; however if you want a cheaper source for a more limited range of companies it might be of use.

*The Guardian Guide to the UK's Top Companies – Fourth Estate/The Reference Press*

An accessible directory with its own angle on the corporate world. It includes in-depth profiles of 150 of the most prominent UK companies, including representatives from a variety of industries. As well as basic facts like contact details, directors, subsidiaries and finances, there is a sizeable piece of text on each company's history, policies and outlook. As befits the link with *The Guardian* newspaper, one of the more notable features of this book is its analysis of each company's social conscience, including political and charitable donations.

*Crawford's Directory of City Connections – Miller Freeman*

Lists of companies, their addresses and directors, together with the names of their stockbrokers, financial advisers, auditors, solicitors, etc. It then turns this round and lists the advisers, the major partners, and their clients. An alternative to the Hemmington Scott books. Their coverage of companies and connections is much more limited but might be adequate for your needs.

### Hollis Press & Public Relations Annual – Hollis

A book of contacts for public relations professionals: news, industrial, official information sources, public relations consultancies, sponsorship consultants, parliamentary consultants, etc.

### The Media Guide – Fourth Estate

A useful paperback both about and for the media. It provides contact details and information on newspapers, magazines and broadcasting as well as sections on media sources and outside contacts such as government and hospitals. It also includes lists of the top consumer and business magazines, ownership rules for the media, etc.

## Legal directories

*The Legal 500* (Legalease) is designed for people who are trying to choose a law firm. It covers the leading ones in England, Wales and Scotland, plus foreign ones in London. There are substantial profiles of some of the more important firms and guides to the best firms in specific areas. There are also biographical details of the lawyers themselves. Many entries are little more than name and firm, but there are numerous fuller profiles. The lawyers are also indexed by firm. Fuller biographical entries are to be found in Legalease's *Who's Who in the Law*, though as the 1991 first edition was also the last few bookshops now stock it.

*Chambers & Partners' Directory of the Legal Profession* (Chambers & Partners) is very similar to *The Legal 500* though cheaper. It covers the top 1000 UK law firms and all barristers' chambers, giving the leaders in each town, region, and area of law. It gives profiles of each firm, details of overseas connections and foreign firms in the UK, and an index of lawyers. It even includes biographical profiles of the leaders in each field of law sometimes including their education but not full home addresses.

Alternatively there are straightforward listings of practices and partners. The information is more comprehensive but lacks the narrative and evaluative aspects of the books above. These books are useful for providing addresses for lawyers who might be anywhere in the country. They can also provide listings of fellow partners which you can check for contacts. They are so different from the books above that it is worth obtaining at least one of each type.

There are three competing listings directories, none of which is perfect and all around the same price. Waterlow's and Butterworth's (Reed Elsevier) obtain their information from questionnaires so rely on them being filled in accurately and quickly. The Law Society needs only to list its members, but again has a problem with accuracy and timeliness so sends out questionnaires too. The Law Society also produces a range of cheaper regional directories.

When you compare the lists of partners you will find numerous discrepancies. Everyone has their own strong opinion on which is the best, but they all have their flaws. The final decision might come down to whether you can get a pre-publication discount on one of them, whether you find any of their extra pieces of information of use (e.g. judges, coroners, categories of work) and how easily you can find your way about them. This last point should not be overlooked: there are endless lists of solicitors and barristers in London, outside London, in other countries, etc., and it is very easy to become confused and look in the wrong list.

*The Directory of Management Consultants in the UK – AP Information Services*

An alphabetical listing of over 2750 consultancies including directors and senior consultants with their qualifications and responsibilities. There is also information on the consultancy's size and revenue, major clients, parent/branches, activities, etc.

### Miscellaneous professionals

Accountants, surveyors, etc., do not generally appear in standard who's whos, but they tend to be moderately wealthy so may be of interest. You can often find a directory by asking the relevant professional body (check in the London phone book or in a directory such as Gale's *Trade Associations and Professional Bodies of the UK*). In the case of accountants there are several bodies, each producing its own directory which might or might not include members of other bodies. Macmillan produces some directories, for example for valuers and auctioneers, chartered accountants, and chartered surveyors.

Professional directories are not particularly informative. They will tend to give the person's name and business address and the firm's area of specialisation but little else; however they can be useful for finding contacts as the partners probably know each other very well. Some give place and date of educational qualification, career and a few biographical details. *Crockford's Clerical Directory* (Church House Publishing) and *The Medical Directory* (Cartermill) are examples of this, though they are still disappointing by normal who's who standards.

*A Guide to Company Giving – The Directory of Social Change*

The charitable donations and community contributions of over 1400 British companies. It aims for breadth of coverage rather than a great deal of detail. As well as basic information on donations it provides contact details, a list of the top corporate donors, advice on subjects such as sponsorship, and useful contacts such as Business in the Community and ABSA. Unfortunately it is not indexed.

For more detailed information try its sister volume *The Major Companies Guide.* This explores the charitable giving of the top 400 UK companies, listing financial details, charitable giving policy and practice, types of grants made, and contact details. Again there is no index, though it does break entries down by area of activity. The same publisher also produces a quarterly journal on corporate philanthropy called *Corporate Citizen.* It is well worth looking through its entire catalogue.

*Hollis Sponsorship & Donations Yearbook – Hollis Directories Ltd*

This contains an A-Z of sponsoring and donating companies. It is only one part of a book which is primarily to do with sponsorship opportunities, so is possibly not as useful or cost-effective as the Directory of Social Change publications; however if you want all the information you can get then this can be worthwhile. Also useful is *Hollis Sponsorship Newsletter* which provides the latest news on who is sponsoring what plus comment and case histories.

*Community Affairs Briefing – Community Affairs Briefing*

Brief articles on company philanthropy and sponsorship with the occasional more detailed profile. Also information on publications and events. Quite expensive for what it is, but together with its index it is a useful way of building up a picture of corporate donations. An alternative is *Sponsorship News* from Charterhouse.

## The Press

*The Financial Times* is the major financial daily, containing details of stock exchange prices. Its sister publication, *Investors Chronicle*, provides weekly comment on company performance including latest financial announcements. *The Evening Standard*, a London paper, also has a highly regarded business section. *The Economist* is noted for its political and economic news coverage and analysis, but business and personalities are only a small aspect of it. The monthly *BusinessAge* (VNU Business Publications) claims to be Britain's biggest selling business magazine (and includes an annual rich list). *Management Today* also offers business coverage. To look north of the border try *Scottish Business Insider*.

# Foundations

## Statutory disclosure

If the administrator cannot provide sufficient information or you do not want to speak to him before your proposal is better prepared you might be tempted to approach the official body responsible for collecting information on charities. This might provide valuable information, but is time-consuming if you visit in person and slow if you have it sent by post. Unless you are looking for small or new charities (which might not be worth this much trouble) or ones that do not want their details published it might be easier simply to purchase one of the books of major charities described below. However it is often worthwhile checking the registered details of obscure foundations that are linked with wealthy people because their potential is rather larger than their size.

In the UK many different types of organisation can have charitable status. Besides fund-raisers there are grant-making bodies (foundations and trusts), some companies, private schools and public sector bodies such as universities. A few charities, such as universities, are specifically exempted from the requirement to register, however most other types have to send annual returns to one of the following bodies.

The *Charity Commission (CC)* is the repository for information on charities registered in England and Wales. This is based in central London with local offices in Liverpool (files for Wales and the North) and Taunton (the South West). Check on coverage at these offices before visiting. Scottish-registered charities are monitored by the *Inland Revenue* in Edinburgh, telephone +44 (0) 131 551 8127. Those in Northern Ireland are under the care of the *Department of Finance and Personnel – Charities Unit*, telephone +44 (0) 1232 484567. Those in the Channel Islands might be totally inaccessible, though you might notice that they are administered by or have a trustee from a firm of solicitors or accountants. The majority of important foundations are registered in England, though some might deliberately register in other parts of the UK so as to attract less attention.

The CC now has a computer database which is available in all three offices, but the majority of the information is still in manual files. In London the files are located in a different building from the search room. Whether you ring for information or visit the office yourself you will have to wait a few days for the files to be ordered and sent over from their repository.

The only information that is instantly available, to visitors and staff alike, is what is on the computer system. You can discover the registration number, date of registration (or removal), date of last amendment, parent and subsidiaries, a correspondent's name, address and telephone number (this is possibly just the administrator, though if it is a notable trustee it might be interesting to check whether this is a home address), a description of its objects (i.e. purposes), what documents are registered there, basic details of income and expenditure, and when the last accounts were received. The computer does not yet give a full list of trustees, though it is hoped that it will do soon.

If you ring, the staff will look up a named (or numbered) charity for you, but might be unwilling to do much more than that. There is no need for an appointment if you wish to visit, but you might find all the terminals are in use. You can look up a charity by its location or aims, or use the keyword system whereby you can enter one or more parts of the charity's name and the computer will pull up a list of all those which match. You can also get printed reports using a combination of search terms, such as high income charities with an interest in education.

If you want further details of a charity you can either visit the office and see the file for yourself (provided it has been ordered in advance) or ring and ask the staff to send you photocopies. They will expect you to know precisely what you want copied. Without seeing the file the easiest thing to request is the latest annual return, which gives information such as names of trustees and finances at the year end. Check that it is reasonably up to date before ordering it as recent returns might not have been received. This method will probably take two or three weeks, though it occasionally takes much longer. The cost depends on the number of pages but will be no more than a few pounds.

You might be disappointed by the contents of the files. The disclosure required of charities is not great. The main demand is that they submit regular but basic details of their finances. You might also find the document which established the foundation, details of its purposes, and possibly a list of trustees, but do not expect much information on actual donations.

You cannot guarantee that even this limited amount of information will be available because it is only recently that the Charity Commission has been given extra powers to demand information and it struggles to find the manpower to do this. If a foundation chooses to ignore its routine circulars it is quite likely to do nothing about it. Even when you ask the staff to pursue it they might be reluctant to do so unless you insist, and if the foundation does not readily comply you might get nowhere.

*Directory of Grant-Making Trusts – Charities Aid Foundation*

This contains details of over 3000 grant-making charitable trusts and foundations. They are primarily English, but there are quite a few Scottish and Welsh ones plus occasional ones from overseas. The information is quite basic, e.g. address, names of trustees, category of support, and total figures for income, assets and grants, though no details of individual gifts. It is well indexed by type of project funded and geographical location (of both foundation and area supported).

*A Guide to the Major Trusts – 2 vols – The Directory of Social Change*

A more recent competitor to the *Directory of Grant-Making Trusts*, this covers fewer charities but in much more depth. Again the majority are in England, though there are some Welsh, Scottish and Northern Irish trusts. Volume 1 covers 300 major trusts, all making grants of over £150,000 a year. Volume 2 covers a further 700, each making grants of at least £40,000. Entries in both volumes give details of trusts' background, interests and priorities. Both volumes are indexed alphabetically and by size of trust, however the geographical and subject index is only in volume 2. There is also a useful section on sources of advice on applying to trusts giving addresses for Charities Information Bureaux, etc. The same publisher also produces *Trust Monitor*, a journal providing news on existing trusts, information on new trusts, articles, etc.

*Directory of Charitable Trustees – CHM Consultants Ltd*

Unfortunately UK directories of foundations and trusts have not yet seen fit to provide indexes to trustees and administrators. This publication fills that gap, and so is invaluable when researching individuals. Unfortunately it gives no more than the person's name and the name and address of the foundation, so it must be used in conjunction with a directory of foundations such as the ones mentioned above.

*FunderFinder – FunderFinder Ltd*

A database containing all the trusts listed in the two major UK directories (above). It matches your needs with the sources available, ranking them in best match order and referring you to directories for further details. Some local agencies make it available free. It is only available to not for profit organisations.

*Directory of Scottish Grant Making Trusts – SCVO*

The larger foundations tend to be registered in England, but it has been suggested that a few deliberately locate in Scotland or Northern Ireland so as to escape the notice of directories and the mass of fund-raisers.

Scottish foundations are regulated separately from English and Welsh ones, but there are several included in the CAF and DSC directories (above). The SCVO directory, though small, has several times more entries; however it is less detailed. It provides contact details and a description of the trust's field of activity, but not full listings of trustees and not necessarily size of donations. It does provide geographical and subject indexes, and includes a few English trusts willing to donate to Scottish causes. Much of the information comes from the records kept by the Inland Revenue in Edinburgh. Although its records have been publicly accessible since 1990, the detail is still quite disappointing as there is little pressure to comply.

The SCVO also produces two fortnightly publications for the voluntary sector: *Third Force News* and *Inform*.

### The Scottish Grants Guide – The Directory of Social Change

Another guide to trust funding in Scotland. It contains details of hundreds of trusts, together with grants and procedures for application.

### Funding for Voluntary Action (A Guide to Local Trusts for Northern Ireland) – The Northern Ireland Voluntary Trust

A free guide to sources of funds for groups in Northern Ireland. It is small, including only those trusts which have a substantial presence in the province, plus semi-governmental organisations. It also gives advice on finding further sources. A foundation directory for Northern Ireland is available from the NICVO in Belfast.

### The Arts Funding Guide – The Directory of Social Change

This is one of a range of books for specific needs. They span company and foundation giving as well as government bodies. It is worth getting the publisher's catalogue as there are so many useful yet cheap books available. Also of use is the *Arts Funding System Pack* from the Arts Council, especially as this is free. It also has many cheap companion volumes, such as *Capital Grants for the Arts*.

### A Guide to the National Lottery – The Directory of Social Change

How to apply for funding from the national lottery. It covers all five funds: arts, sports, heritage, charities, and the Millennium fund. This publisher also runs courses on the same subject.

### The (Henderson) Top 2000 Charities – Hemmington Scott

This book is rather different. It contains primarily fund-raising charities, though there are a few grant-givers as well. It might be used for checking whether contacts are trustees, board members, etc., of charities, though as it is not indexed by person this is not very easy.

It neglects most non-registered charities (e.g. universities) and relies on entrants to produce their own figures, so its analyses might not be entirely representative of the sector as a whole. There are tables of the top 50 charities by various criteria, the top advisers and auditors, and the top corporate donors. There are articles on charity issues, an index by field of activity, lists of advisers and their clients, and a small section on stockmarket companies and the size of their charitable giving.

There are numerous smaller alternatives, e.g. *Charity Choice* and *Scottish Charity Choice* (Abercorn Hill Associates). Some are given out free of charge to lawyers. These are paid for by advertisements from the charities and intended to inform people who wish to include charitable bequests in their wills.

## Charity Trends – Charities Aid Foundation

Similar in some ways to the *Top 2000 Charities*, though smaller and with a different layout. It ranks the top 500 fund-raising charities, providing details of their finances. Similarly it ranks the top 500 corporate donors and top 500 grant-making trusts, providing a few figures for each. In a later section it also gives addresses and telephone numbers. There are various articles on the statistics and trends, but no information on specific donations. CAF also publishes a series of books analysing giving and volunteering in different countries and organises conferences.

## Unspecified legacies

Large sums of money are left in wills for unspecified charities. To help the executors decide which charities should benefit, fund-raisers often send in proposals, rather as they would to a foundation. Smee & Ford can provide a service notifying you of such wills.

## Fund-raising magazines

*Charity* (Charities Aid Foundation), *Professional Fundraising* (Brainstorm Publishing) and *Third Sector* give news, advice and case studies for not for profits. *Charities Management* (Mitre House Publishing) has longer articles on similar subjects though with more of a bias towards technical advice. All are useful for finding advertisements for events, services and new products. *Funding Digest* gives up to date details of regional, national and European funding sources and how to apply. They include Community Enterprise Awards, Rural Challenge, etc., rather than straightforward lists of foundations. Alternatively you could try Chapter One Group's *Charity Press Digest* or *Donor Digest* which summarise press stories. This is costly and you could read the press for yourself, however a small organisation might not have the manpower to do this. For information on computers in fund-raising try *Donors*.

### Other help for fund-raisers

There is a series of *Charities Information Bureaux* located throughout the country which can help new fund-raisers and those looking for small, local sources of money. Some Directory of Social Change publications contain the full list of addresses. There are also regional Councils for Voluntary Service and Rural Community Councils, which vary in the amount of help they can offer.

## Electronic information

Various international hosts cover the UK, for example *Dialog* (Knight-Ridder) carries the *Times* and *Independent* in full text as well as *Textline*, plus *ICC* and *Reedbase Kompass* UK business directories. *Lexis/Nexis* is also available in the UK. A more UK-oriented host is *FT-Profile* which is very strong on the British press. It is also available via other hosts. *New Prestel* is also UK-oriented, carrying *FT-Profile*, *Phonebase* for telephone numbers, and some useful credit databases. Another UK-based service is *Mercury Business Intelligence* which carries a relatively small number of databases covering British company information but has the advantage of including the official Companies House service.

Two Internet discussion groups for UK information professionals are LIS-IIS and LIS-LINK. To subscribe send the message: subscribe LIS-IIS (or LIS-LINK) firstname lastname (i.e. your name) to *mailbase@mailbase.ac.uk*.

The major national newspaper the *Daily Telegraph* can be found in reduced form on the Internet at *http://www.telegraph.co.uk/*. A small amount of the *Financial Times* can be found at *http://www.ft.com/*. The *Scottish Herald* is at *http://fleet.britain.eu.net/cims/herald_html/home*.

## Membership and training organisations

### Aslib (The Association for Information Management)

Besides books (such as this one) Aslib provides numerous training courses in various aspects of information management. These range from copyright to presentation skills, sources of business information to advanced online searching strategies. It also arranges conferences, can provide consultancy and recruitment services, and will do online searches for you. If you are considering buying CD-ROMs you can view various alternatives from its library before committing yourself to buying them. There are different types of membership, some of which entitle you to discounts on publications and training courses, and special interest groups for subjects like business information and computers. Aslib has a growing presence in Continental Europe including an office in Brussels.

## CASE (Council for Advancement and Support of Education)

For fund-raisers in the field of education. It originated in the US and is still very much US-centred, but it recently opened a European office in London and claims members in 25 countries around the world. It holds conferences and training courses, publishes a newsletter, books and membership directory, and provides fund-raising information and services. European membership charges are quite high especially as its presence is not so firmly established as in the US.

## Directory of Social Change

Courses on various aspects of fund-raising including the national lottery. Also standard charity managerial courses, finance, law, communication, etc.

## ICFM (Institute of Charity Fundraising Managers)

Professional body for fund-raisers. It runs courses on many aspects of fund-raising including a certification programme.

## IIS (Institute of Information Scientists)

Membership body which runs training courses relating to all aspects of information work. It also produces newsletters and circulates job vacancies. It has various special interest groups including the *City Information Group* which has its own newsletter and meetings.

## The Library Association

A professional association for qualified librarians which also runs courses.

## Researchers In Fundraising Network

This group encompasses both market researchers and prospect researchers. It is a relatively new group but has already established a pattern of regular speaker meetings including authors of rich lists and a database expert. London-based charities take it in turn to host the meetings. The atmosphere is friendly and there is plenty of time to chat to other researchers. At the time of writing it is in the process of affiliating to the ICFM (qv).

## SCVO (Scottish Council for Voluntary Organisations)

Training courses for voluntary organisations in Scotland.

## TFPL Ltd

This company offers services to the information sector in the fields of training, recruitment, publishing and consultancy. It is not a membership organisation. Its courses range from the basic to the more advanced, including finding information, British company law, project management, company accounts, etc. It also organises an annual European Business Information Conference.

## Women in Fundraising Development

A small group useful for networking and sharing experiences and skills non-competitively. Regular meetings in London plus a fundraising advice shop at the annual Charityfair.

# 16. Western Europe and Scandinavia

The attention given to the European Union (EU) might persuade a non-European that a new federal entity, similar to the United States, has emerged. This is far from the case. Although the politicians talk of monetary and political union, there is no unity of culture or language. Although some areas are moving closer together, for example in the disclosure of company information, for the moment each country must be approached as a totally separate entity. Availability of information varies widely, the UK being one of the better countries; however nothing matches the amount published in the US.

## Regional variations

The countries of Europe, and even the regions within those countries, have very strong individual characters. They are divided by language, culture, and centuries of mutual distrust. Wars have been common and have resulted in the frequent redrawing of boundaries.

Not only are there different time zones, but also different holidays and working hours (for example, the southern regions take afternoon siestas, while even in a major city like Paris many businesses are closed during August). You cannot guarantee that people will still be at their desks at the end of the afternoon, especially on Fridays, or that there will be anyone available over major holidays like Christmas, Easter or the summer vacation period.

## Languages

Outside the UK and Ireland English is not the first language, though many nationalities speak it as a second or third language. If you speak only English you might prefer to concentrate on countries such as Denmark, Sweden, Norway and the Netherlands whose languages are spoken by few other nationalities and whose people often speak very good English.

In countries with more dominant languages, such as France and Germany, you would be expected at least to attempt the local language. Whether you are purchasing a book or asking for help there are frequently occasions when you receive a rather better response if you try to speak the appropriate language. The most useful languages to learn are possibly French and German followed by Italian as these are spoken in the most economically powerful countries.

However if English is all you know then don't be put off – you can get by. It might, however, be better to communicate by fax rather than by telephone as this will give the recipient more time to decipher what you are trying to say (or find someone else who can) and will avoid the embarrassment that many people feel when trying to speak a foreign language.

With different languages come variations in the alphabet. This affects the order of alphabetical entries, for example accented letters might appear separately at the end. It is also possible that when the typeface does not easily lend itself to a particular accent one letter might be replaced by two, e.g. the German 'ü' might be replaced by 'ue' in an attempt to replicate the sound.

### Legal and accounting frameworks

Legal frameworks are based on totally different principles. Under the Continental or Roman law system there is a rulebook to cover all aspects of life. By contrast the UK has a strong Common Law tradition which gives more weight to precedents, in other words it follows the patterns set by common practice and earlier court judgements.

In practical terms this means that a continental company's accounts have traditionally conformed to a precise set of rules, while a British company's accounts can encompass more individual interpretation and must be checked by an independent auditor who gives his personal opinion of whether they represent a 'true and fair view' of the company's finances. This 'true and fair view' can increasingly be found in the annual reports of Continental companies due to pressure from the EU and the internationalisation of finance.

### Types of company

Each country has its own rules and structures for business enterprises. Different forms of ownership can be distinguished by letters such as PLC, GmbH, Ltd, AG, etc. A book such as *International Company Filing Requirements* (Informed Business Services) will explain these.

The mix of public and private companies varies quite widely. In the UK there is a major stock market and it is common to find large, publicly quoted companies. In Germany there is a strong 'Mittelstand' of smaller, family-owned companies backed by investment from the banks. In some countries there are also the remnants of state-owned enterprises, which were formerly particularly predominant in areas such as the utilities, transport, communications and defence. Many were sold into the private sector in the 1980s, and some are in transition.

Private companies are more prevalent in Continental Europe than they are in the UK. They might be sole traders, small family businesses, or very large private operations. This means that publicly accessible information is severely limited. Profits will tend to be depressed, both because of reinvestment and for tax reasons. When a private company is about to be sold it can appear to have a surge in profitability as it is then in the interests of the owners to make it look more appealing. These companies often use the family name, though they might also retain it after sale. Many were set up after 1945 and as the founders retire there is a tendency for them to be sold off or handed over to professional managers. They are often very conscious of their importance to their locality and duty to help the local population.

One noticeable feature of larger companies in Austria, Germany, Switzerland and Scandinavia is the two tier board. There is often an executive board for the day to day running of the company and a supervisory board of non-executives who provide an overview.

### Company information

The European Union has sent out various directives aimed at harmonising the public disclosure of company information. However standards still vary widely. The UK remains one of the better countries, both because of the quantity of information available, even on private companies, and because its records are relatively centralised and easily accessible. Obtaining information elsewhere can be difficult.

As a result of the efforts of the EU each country has company registries to maintain publicly accessible information, though the number and geographical range of offices varies from country to country. Germany, Italy, Spain and Switzerland have largely decentralised systems. Details of registries can be found in books such as *International Company Filing Requirements* (Informed Business Services) or *European Companies* (CBD).

The EU aims to have registry information available online, though as yet coverage is far from complete. Again the UK is one of the better countries (via *Mercury*), while Italy and France also have reasonable systems. However they are independent of each other rather than forming a unified service.

To follow are some general sources for Europe followed by a closer look at some of the larger or more affluent countries.

## Europe-wide

*Croner's European Business Information Sources — Croner Publications Ltd*

A country by country survey of information sources in the various countries of Europe. It provides a general round-up of the country, its employment and immigration laws (only for some countries), contact details for chambers of commerce, sources for various industries, relevant directories, newspapers and electronic sources. The list of sources is not as comprehensive as in some other books (see below), but it has the advantage of being continually enhanced with loose leaf updates. There is also *Croner's Europe* for legal and business developments within the EU.

### European Companies – CBD Research Ltd/The Reference Press

A guide to sources of information rather than to companies. Very comprehensive but liable to date rapidly. It covers all the countries of East and West Europe. For each it provides details of the official registry, stock exchanges, credit reporting services, company directories, electronic sources, newspapers and periodicals, etc. It also has a useful section translating business and accounting terms from various languages into English.

### Current European Directories – CBD Research Ltd

Similar to *European Companies* (above), but restricted to directories. It covers a much wider range of subjects, including many directories for specific industries and associations which publish lists of members.

### European Markets: A Guide to Company and Industry Information Sources – Washington Researchers

Sources of information on European companies. Written from a US perspective but including international sources. An alternative is the *Macmillan Directory of EC Industry Information Sources.*

### Guide to Libraries in Western Europe – The British Library

If you need information from a foreign country and are not sure how to locate it this book will give you contact details for libraries that might be able to help. It covers libraries in government departments and 'official' ones with a national role, e.g. patent offices. If you are not able to visit the library then you will often find it is willing to answer telephone or postal enquiries. Services might be free or fee-paying, and they might range from telling you where to look to conducting a substantial search on your behalf. The amount of trouble they take is often down to their own discretion, so be nice to them. Often these services are very popular and you might find it difficult to get through. There is no guarantee that the librarians will speak English, but many do.

### European Business and Industry (Who's Who Edition) – Who's Who Edition

Biographies of senior managers in European enterprises as well as profiles of the companies they work for (though beware that these are effectively adverts). It now includes some Eastern European entries, though these are still in the minority. This is one of the rare who's whos which is also available electronically. The CD-ROM is actually cheaper than the book though it lacks the company adverts; alternatively you might prefer to access it online (on Knight-Ridder's *Data-Star*, *Genios*, or *Lexis/Nexis*). The electronic versions offer more flexibility, for example instead of merely looking up a person by name you could search for all graduates of a particular university, those under 45, field of business, etc.

*Who's Who in European Institutions and Enterprises (Sutter's International Red Series) – Eurospan*

An English language who's who together with surveys of each country's history, government, diplomatic representation, media, universities, associations, religions, etc., as well as profiles of the major companies.

*Who's Who in European Politics – Bowker-Saur, part of Reed Elsevier*

This covers East and West Europe including all the former Soviet Republics. As well as biographies it offers a directory of key people and a glossary of terms and institutions.

*Who's Who in European Business and Directory of European Business – Bowker-Saur, part of Reed Elsevier*

The Who's Who gives biographical profiles of many of the senior executives from 4000 leading business and related organisations across 35 countries of East and West Europe. Many of the entries are no more than contact details, probably because the editors have undertaken a particularly ambitious project which they have found hard to achieve in the first edition. Many of the people covered will never before have been asked for biographical details, and it will take a while to persuade them that they should hand anything over. There are useful indexes by country and by company.

The Directory also covers 35 countries of East and West Europe as well as the major pan-European organisations. It is rather like a gazetteer of Europe and is particularly useful for its coverage of the smaller service companies such as accountants and lawyers. The largest companies do feature in it, but there is room for relatively few of them. If it is those you want, see the books below. There is a two or three-page introduction to each country: its political system, overall performance, business culture, legal system, etc. This is followed by useful details of service companies (accountants, banks, law firms, etc.) which would be considered too small to feature in most directories. There is a section on the major companies, and others on newspapers, ministries, foreign embassies, etc. Company information is rather variable but generally quite basic, e.g. contact details, senior personnel, income, number of staff.

### *Who's Who in European Commerce and Industry – Intercontinental Book Publishing Co*

Primarily a directory of companies giving contact details, one director, and activities. The biographical section is relatively small and heavily germanic, and the entries are not particularly long. Not as informative as some other directories.

### *European accoun ting*

Pitman publishes a range of *Financial Times* guides to understanding accounting practices in individual countries of Europe. They include lists of useful terms with their English translations.

### *Dun's Europa – Dun & Bradstreet Ltd*

Europa is a major four-volume directory containing the 60,000 plus largest companies in Europe. Although Europa's information is basic (contact details, directors, year started, principal activities, parent company, nominal capital, sales, number of employees, and bankers) it is sufficiently well established to be fairly consistent and comprehensive. It covers the EU and EFTA countries, but not Eastern Europe. The indexes enable you to find the largest companies, or those in a particular business sector (it uses the SIC numerical business classification, which is not as incomprehensible as it looks since there is an alphabetical index). Unfortunately there is no directory of directors. Entries are arranged by country, which is rather more confusing than it sounds as country names are rendered in their own languages (e.g. Germany is under DE for Deutschland).

If you do not think you will use it very often you might prefer to obtain access to Dun and Bradstreet information (or alternatives) through online services, e.g. Knight-Ridder's *Data-Star*. Alternatively, if you intend to cover some of the countries in depth you might look at D&B's range of national directories. These provide similar information to Europa but over a wider range of companies. For some countries there are also publications which list debt defaulters and bankruptcies.

Alternatives to the Dun & Bradstreet range are produced by Kompass and Graham & Whiteside. There is also *Europe's 15,000 Largest Companies* (ELC) which covers the top public and privately owned companies in Western Europe (including Scandinavia). It gives basic facts, but unfortunately not the full list of directors. Extel Financial produces *European Handbook*. This two-volume paperback set gives contact details, three years' financials, several directors, activities, and major shareholders. It also includes lists of the top companies in the region, in each country, and in various industries. Extel also produces a European 'card' service. These cards are an alternative to building up a library of corporate annual reports and press cuttings.

Finally, if you want to focus on the largest companies there is *Hoover's MasterList of Major European Companies* (Reference Press). This provides 3000 profiles of the largest public and private companies, including all those on the major European stock exchanges. Coverage is of Western Europe including Greece and Turkey. Information is basic: contact details, key officers, industry descriptions, sales and employment data.

If you do not speak the language of the country you might prefer to restrict yourself to the Europe-wide directory producers as these can generally be ordered easily in English. However company directories generally follow a fairly standard format, which means that with the aid of a dictionary you can rapidly work out roughly what foreign words mean. One problem is in understanding job titles as roles are different in other countries; however English language directories might not translate the full nuances of the job, which if you do not see it in the original you might not realise.

### The European Business Top 500 – Ingerstedt/Cedar Tree

Although relatively expensive this book of company rankings proves immensely useful when you need to find a list of top companies. It is possible to create many of the rankings yourself by using electronic databases, but that is complex and costly. As well as the overall top 500 it gives rankings and financial information for the top companies in various industries and countries, e.g. top 50 banks, Belgian top 20. It also gives contact details and some directors for the companies mentioned. A cheaper alternative is Gale's *European Business Rankings* which lists the biggest in advertising, insurance, law, etc.

### Nordic Stock Guide – The Reference Press

This covers all public companies in Denmark, Finland, Norway and Sweden. It gives eight years of financial information plus overviews of the companies' activities, contact details, and names of chairpersons and major shareholders.

### Law firms in Europe – Legalease

This informative guide provides commentary on firms (including partners' specialisms) and recommends those with the best reputations in specific fields. It also gives an overview of each country's legal market.

*Hollis Europe – Hollis*

Public relations consultancies in Europe. It includes country profiles, trends and recent developments for 33 European countries, and contact details for public relations decision makers in leading companies.

*The European Directory of Management Consultants – AP Information Services*

Alphabetical list of over 3250 consultancy firms in Western and Eastern Europe covering such information as managing directors and principal consultants, turnover, major clients, services offered and professional bodies. There are indexes of specialisations, industries and location.

## European Foundation Centre

The EFC was set up under the aegis of the European Union with the primary aim of uniting and assisting grant-giving bodies in the member countries. It even takes an interest in Central and Eastern Europe. More recently it extended its activities to helping fund-raisers (from anywhere in the world) via the Orpheus programme; however it is not as user-friendly as the US's Foundation Center. Annual subscriptions are quite costly so be sure that you understand what it will and will not do for you before paying.

You can use the Centre's library, which has foundation directories for individual countries, books on fund-raising, as well as company and foundation annual reports and guides for applicants. However this is not much help for people who do not visit Brussels. You might find it easier and cheaper to obtain its publications list and get the books for yourself (though language might be a barrier). You can also use the regional EFC networking centres, though their information is more local. Possibly more usefully, you can also ask the EFC to recommend a list of grant-givers in your field, though this service is limited by the number of foundations it knows.

The EFC will also send reports on particular foundations. This takes anything up to a few weeks. It is useful to have an English-language report containing information that might be basic but would have been difficult to obtain by other means. European foundations are often so difficult to research that even an address is impossible.

However it might startle fund-raisers to learn that the EFC is likely to tell the foundation of your interest in it, which can bias the outcome of an approach even before it gets underway. There is also no guarantee that it will be able to find the information. There is no legislation forcing foundations to co-operate with the EFC, and no reason why the EFC should know of every European foundation's existence. It gives assistance rather than having a regulatory role. If you plan to make heavy use of the EFC's services check that it will not object as staff time is limited.

However, the EFC's publications are useful. They include (limited) directories of foundations and a list of books in the library. The subscription also includes notices of competitions for funded programmes. The EFC is working on developing online access to funding sources in partnership with the EU's Aries network.

*More Bread and Circuses: Who does what for the arts in Europe – The Arts Council of England.*

A guide to the funding policies and potential of supra-national and intergovernmental agencies and pan-European foundations, e.g. the European Commission, Council of Europe and UNESCO. Designed for fund-seekers in all aspects of the arts, from the performing arts to museums.

### The press

Europe sees itself as too diverse to produce many Europe-wide publications. This is hardly surprising given the size of the population and the number of languages spoken. However there are a few, notably the English language weeklies *The European* and *European Voice* (from The Economist Group). The major national papers will have some European coverage; however to cover the region in any depth it is necessary to read papers from different countries. Examples are listed below.

### Electronic information

The best known pan-European database is Knight-Ridder's *Data-Star*. Many countries have their own specific online hosts, but *Data-Star* is one that aims at a coverage of the whole of Europe. It has two specialisations: business and science (i.e. biology, chemistry, pharmaceuticals). Although its European business coverage is impressive, if you are more interested in the press check that it provides sufficient databases in languages you understand.

## Institutions of the European Union

The EU evolved out of the EEC (European Economic Community, subsequently shortened to EC). It is constantly expanding, for example it recently admitted several members of another Western European grouping, EFTA (the European Free Trade Association), which means it now encompasses virtually the whole region. Central and Eastern Europe are still excluded and are dealt with in the next chapter (apart from the former DDR which is now part of the united Germany).

In some ways the EU might be looked at as a state within a state. It has the institutions of a state: parliament, council of ministers, commission and judiciary. As yet their influence is not as strong as that of their national counterparts, though the EU's directives are binding and its courts can overrule national ones. However it has a great deal of money to disburse.

There is no 'capital' but the main business is conducted in Strasbourg, Luxembourg and Brussels. The EU should not be confused with the Council of Europe, which is a separate institution.

*The European Companion – DPR Publishing Ltd*

Biographies, many with photos, of the leading politicians and senior civil servants in the EU. Also an explanation of the various institutions of the EU together with a glossary of terms and listings of who is responsible for what within each branch. Much cheaper is *The Times Guide to the European Parliament* from HarperCollins. This comes out every five years after the elections. It contains biographies and photos of the MEPs and analyses the election results and the prospects for Europe.

*Euro Who's Who – Who's Who in the European Community and other European Organizations*

*Yearbook of the European Communities and of the other European Organizations – Editions Delta/Cedar Tree*

The former gives biographies of MEPs, civil servants, etc. The latter explains the institutions and bodies of the EU and associated groups, e.g. the parliament, council, commission, courts of justice, European Investment Bank, Economic & Social Committee. It explains the structure and activities of these bodies, and lists employees (though there is no biographical detail). It also lists official EU publications.

*A Practical Guide to the EEC Labyrinth – Editions Apogée/Cedar Tree*

A basic paperback explanation of the structures of the European Community. It is clear and well organised and written in English, though growing a little old. For more detailed and more up to date information see Cartermill's books on *The Council of the European Union, The European Parliament*, and *The European Commission*, or Europa's *The European Union Encyclopedia and Directory*. Alternatively, try Kogan Page's *The European Community Fact Book* which is in question and answer format.

### EUR-OP NEWS – EUR-OP

Free newsletter published by the EU covering all aspects of EU published information. It is supplemented by the online database *Eurobases*.

### Grants from Europe – NCVO and Directory of Social Change

A basic guide to securing money from the European Union. It explains what the EU is, works through options for categories such as disabilities, human rights, etc., and even helps you find your way around Brussels. The Economist Intelligence Unit has written a rather more expensive report on obtaining financial assistance from the EU, entitled *Euro-Grants*.

### Networking in Europe – NCVO

A basic paperback guide to the EU including the institutions and various programmes, foundations and networks (refugees, poverty, etc.). Also how to find further information on Europe.

### European Information Centres

A network of local centres has been set up throughout the EU. They are intended to provide information to small and medium-sized enterprises, but can provide more general information as well. They can advise on legislation, grants and loans, or even European markets. If they do not have the details they can communicate with other members of the network. The closest one can be located through your public library, chamber of commerce or telephone directory.

### Electronic information

There are many online databases produced by and about the EU, though most are rather dry details of laws and the implementation of directives. *RAPID* might be of interest as it gives daily press information. Several hosts carry EU databases, e.g. *FT-Profile* and *Data-Star* (Knight-Ridder). These include *Celex*, *Euroscope, Spicers Centre for Europe*, and *Spearhead*. The *Cordis* database gives up to date information on EU-funded research.

# Denmark

### Kraks Blå Bog – Kraks Forlag AS

Written in Danish, this who's who covers Denmark, the Faroe Islands and Greenland. Although geographically quite far apart, the Faroes and Greenland both became Danish colonies.

*Green's-Børsens Handbog om Dansk Erhvervsliv – A/S Forlaget Børsen*

A rather costly company directory; however it does incorporate a directory of about 12,000 directors and shareholders of over 10%. Written in Danish.

*Trade Directory for Denmark – Danish Foreign Trade Information Office*

English-language directory of companies grouped by industry. Little more than contact details, including one name, and area of activity; however it is free to libraries and those wishing to trade with Denmark.

*Danish Foundations – Nyt Nordisk Forlag, Arnold Busck A/S*

An English-language book particularly strong on the histories of foundations and their creators. As it is only published intermittently it does not attempt to keep up with the latest awards, but it does give an indication of the type of projects supported. Attractively presented with numerous photographs.

*Kraks Fonds- & Legatvejviser – Kraks Forlag AS*

Danish-language information on funding and grants.

*Denmark Review – Danish Ministry of Foreign Affairs*

English language business magazine.

# Finland

A relatively easy way to buy Finnish books is through *Akateeminen Kirjakauppa*. This is a huge academic book shop which can recommend or supply whatever you need using the medium of English. Unfortunately the books themselves are likely to be in Finnish.

*Kuka kukin on – Otava Kustannus Oy*

A who's who written in Finnish with two pages of English explanation.

*Suomen Yrityshenkilöt – Suomen Asiakastieto Oy*

A directory of directors written in Finnish.

*Sininen kirja Talouselämän suurhakemisto – Startel Oy*

Business directory written in Finnish. Covers 100,000 organisations though not in great depth.

*Listed Companies in Finland – Kauppakaari-yhtymä Oy*

This useful English-language publication provides comprehensive information on each listed company as well as the most actively traded OTC and Brokers' List companies. Details include names of directors and major shareholders as well as detailed financial history. Also general sector charts and stock market statistics.

*Finnish Business Report – Oy Novomedia Ltd*

A monthly English language business newspaper.

# France

*Who's Who in France – Editions Jacques Lafitte*

Despite its English title this is written in French. It is a large, well-established work containing over 20,000 biographies. The largest group are industrial executives, followed by government officials and diplomats, and a wide variety of other notables. The biographies are full, and there is also information about France and its government. A sister publication is *International Who's Who in Wine.*

*Le Bottin Mondain – Société du Bottin Mondain*

A guide to the upper reaches of French society. Information is basic but can be difficult to locate elsewhere. The central part is an alphabetical listing of people, giving their address, telephone number, and the names of their spouse and children. Also facts such as clubs, wine-makers, foreign embassies.

*Le Guide de Pouvoir – Editions Jean-François Doumic*

French language guide to the country's politicians. Biographies (including photos) and organograms covering people at national and local level and even the political press. This is one of a series which includes, for example, people in human resources and in communications.

In France there is a circle of powerful people who move between politics, business and the civil service in a manner quite different from career patterns in the UK. They have often been educated for this role at one of the élite grandes écoles, such as the Ecole Nationale d'Administration.

*Qui Décide – Bottin SA*

Large three-volume directory of 350,000 directors of the leading 100,000 companies in France. Written in French. The volumes are also available individually.

*French Company Handbook – International Business Development*

Profiles of the companies of the SBF 120 Index plus nine more. Information includes names of CEO and Investor Relations Officers, company background and major activities, recent business developments, subsidiaries, major shareholders, and finances. There are also articles on French industries and the economy. Written in English.

The French stock exchange is much smaller than the UK and US ones. State involvement is relatively large and there are many private companies which makes accounts harder to obtain.

### *Guide Annuaire des Fondations et des Associations – Groupe Juris Service*

Provides address, telephone number, name of contact, etc. for French foundations. Written in French. Beware that some so-called foundations are in fact grant-seeking rather than grant-giving. Of particular interest is the Fondation de France which channels personal and corporate donations from many different foundations towards appropriate non-profits and which produces its own directory of 31 foundations (*Portrait de trente et une Fondations*).

### *France: A Journalists' Guide – French Embassy*

All the basic information on France you could possibly want, including addresses for government, political, cultural bodies, etc., plus sources of further information. Immensely useful, especially as it is free and in English. Strictly speaking it is only for journalists, but others might be able to obtain a copy too.

### The press

The major business papers are *Les Echos* and *La Tribune de L'Economie*. Popular French dailies *Le Figaro* and *Le Monde* contain company sections and listings of Paris Stock Exchange quotations. There are numerous business publications available, notably *L'Expansion* (Groupe Expansion Magazines SA) which includes an annual list of the top 1000 companies. An English language overview of the main political, macroeconomic, financial and sectoral developments can be found in *French Business Trends* from Europrospects.

### Electronic information

*New Prestel* is quite a good British route into French information. French hosts include: *L'Européenne de Données* (also on Knight-Ridder's *Data-Star* and *Minitel*), *Minitel* (also on *New Prestel*), *Questel* and *OR-Télématique* (on *FT-Profile*, which in turn is on *New Prestel*).

With government encouragement *Minitel* has long been available in many ordinary homes and it remains dominant in the French market, despite being a little slow. It is rather closer to the Internet, carrying services such as home shopping and lonely hearts as well as online information. It can also help you contact people if you know their name and have a rough idea where they live. France Telecom can advise on overseas access to the service.

Notable databases include *Delphes* (company articles – on *Data-Star, Dialog* and *L'Européenne de Données*), *Telefirm* (produced by the French Chambers of Commerce and Industry and available as FRCO on *Data-Star*) and the *Diane* CD-ROM of company accounts. For press articles (in French) try *Agence France Presse*, the French press agency, which again is available on other major hosts.

# Germany

The reunification of Germany is still quite recent, and the East is still relatively backward and poor, though receiving substantial investment from the West. The quality of information is also not quite so good in the East, though it is rapidly improving. The capital of West Germany was Bonn but since reunification Berlin has taken over. This means headquarters might be in either city.

Germany's statutory company records are dispersed throughout the country. Companies must register on the Handelsregister at their local court and join their local Chamber of Commerce. The information available depends, as in the UK, on whether the company is classed as small, medium or large. Rather than go to the Chamber of Commerce, you can look for financial statements of AGs and large GmbHs in the Federal Gazette (Bundesanzeiger). Basic information from this is available online (e.g. on Knight-Ridder's *Data-Star*) which will point you towards the registry where each company files. Quoted companies must also publish their statements in at least one newspaper.

While large companies must deposit a great deal of information, medium and small ones are a problem as the disclosure laws are not always enforced. Partnerships are exempt from filing requirements, making a large swathe of German business inaccessible. Germany has a tradition of direct investment by banks in industry, which means they do not need to go public to obtain more money. There are also many cross-holdings of big firms in one another. This fosters corporate stability and long-termism, but means information is difficult to obtain. As banks are such large investors in German industry it is not uncommon for them to have a representative on the board.

The German postal service is attempting to insist that all mail has a postcode, so use one if possible. There are three distinct types of postcode. If you have a choice then use the corporate or PO Box code. If you don't have either of these then use the street code. Another source of puzzlement is that the German language is in the process of changing. It has been announced that spellings will alter over the next few years so do not be confused at finding variants.

If you do not wish to deal with publishers in German there are English speaking distributors – such as *Otto Harrassowitz* – that will sell you books without extra charge. Unfortunately the books themselves are likely to be in German.

### Wer ist Wer (Who's Who) – Schmidt Römhild

A straightforward who's who written in German. It lists almost 40,000 prominent Germans, nearly 2000 of whom are accompanied by a photo. It is still predominantly West German, but top officials from the East are also included. It also has a section on members of the national and state governments. Unusually it chooses to index its biographees by their birthdays (though the entries themselves are in alphabetical order). It is also available on CD-ROM and online via *Genios-Datenbank*.

### Who's Who in Germany (Sutter's International Red Series) – Eurospan

An English language who's who. It also contains surveys of German history, government, diplomatic representation, media, universities, associations, religions, etc., as well as profiles of the major companies.

### Who is Who in der Bundesrepublik Deutschland (The Blue Series) – Who is Who, Verlag für Prominentenenzyklopädien AG.

A comprehensive who's who written in German. Lists of politicians and diplomats, occasional photos, and a brief directory of companies. It has a sister publication for Austria and South Tirol, *Who is Who in Österreich und Südtirol*.

### Leitende Männer und Frauen der Wirtschaft – Hoppenstedt

Directory of directors giving their postal addresses and directorships, though not personal details. Written in German, but with abbreviations in English as well. A companion volume, *Wer Leitet – Das Middlemanagement der Deutschen Wirtschaft* – provides information on the next tier down of German management.

Hoppenstedt is a noted provider of company information and has a range of German language company directories covering the entire spectrum of German industry. It also produces books on neighbouring countries. Its company information can also be found online. If you are particularly interested in Germany and can cope with the language it is well worth obtaining a complete catalogue of its publications.

### Germany's Top 500 – Frankfurter Allgemeine Zeitung GmbH/The Reference Press/William Snyder

This English-language volume is produced by one of Germany's most respected newspaper publishers. As well as the top manufacturing companies it includes banks and insurance companies. It provides fairly basic but complete information on finances, subsidiaries, activities, major shareholders and directors. There is an interesting introduction on German accounting rules and indexes by industry and by city. If you already have *Dun's Europa* and *Who Owns Whom* it does not add a huge amount to them, but it is interesting to discover who are the major shareholders. It is also available on disk.

*Verzeichnis der Deutschen Stiftungen – Hoppenstedt*

German foundation directory, in German, including contact details, objectives, annual donations, etc. Another source for foundation information is the *Stifterverband für die Deutsche Wissenschaft*. Much German philanthropy is focused on East Germany.

## The press

*Handelsblatt* is the major national business daily, and *Wirtschafts Woche* is a weekly business magazine. The *Frankfurter Allgemeine Zeitung* is a respected national daily containing a business section. It has a sister publication in English named *German Brief* which specialises in the country's economics and politics but includes company profiles. Other major papers include *Der Spiegel* and *Die Zeit*. There is a strong regional press, so if you have a particular interest in Germany look for the local paper as well as the publications of the local chamber of commerce. There are numerous German language business magazines, for example *Capital* and *Forbes von Burda* (the German edition of the US magazine).

## Electronic information

Hosts include *GBI* (which includes a good range of German newspapers and international company information) and *Genios*. *Hoppenstedt* produces a respected company database, as does *Creditreform* (the largest West German credit information agency). *Wer Gehört zu Wem* (who belongs to whom) can provide details of the major shareholders in the larger companies. An alternative is the *DAFNE* company CD-ROM from CD-ROM Verlag und Vertrieb GmbH. If you want someone else to do the research for you *DB-Data* (a subsidiary of Deutsche Bank) will do so for a fee. *Der Spiegel* can be found on the Internet at http://eunet.bda.de/bda/int/spiegel.

# Ireland

The island of Ireland is divided between the Republic of Ireland (Eire, Southern Ireland or simply 'Ireland') whose capital is Dublin, and Northern Ireland (sometimes called Ulster) whose capital is Belfast. The Republic of Ireland left the UK earlier this century, but Northern Ireland remains part of the UK. Although they are officially different countries there is a strong bond between them and some sources will cover both north and south as if they were one.

The number of sources is relatively small as this is a country with a population of just 3.5 million, just under a third of whom live in Dublin. Virtually all sources will be in English, though some addresses will be in Gaelic. Beware when ordering that although the Republic uses pounds (or punts) and pence, Irish currency has a slightly different value from British sterling.

*Ireland: A Directory – Euromonitor*

This is an impressive general reference work on Ireland. It covers government, politics, business, finance, culture, religion and communications. There are details of address, personnel and activities for 2,000 organisations in both the public and private sectors, and an extensive statistical section. Customers in Ireland can buy it together with a diary from the Institute of Public Administration in Dublin.

*Who's Who in Ireland – 'The Influential 1,000' – Hibernian Publishing Co.*

This was last published in 1991 and seems unlikely to be updated. Even so it is a useful publication complete with numerous photographs.

*Aspect Premier Irish Companies – Private Research*

Comprehensive information on 2000 Irish companies as well as financial institutions, banks and building societies. It incorporates a directory of directors, more than half of which include brief biographies. This company also produces *The Irish Stock Market Annual* and a monthly publication which keeps you up to date with recent financial filings at the Companies Registration Office.

*The Irish Funding Handbook – CAFE/Directory of Social Change*

A very thorough book on sources of funding for voluntary and community initiatives in Ireland, north and south. It covers trusts, the EU, the statutory sector and companies, as well as providing general advice on legal issues etc. Since there are so few large companies in Ireland the amount of funding they can provide is limited.

*Funding in the Irish Republic – Directory of Social Change*

A new guide to UK trust and corporate funding sources for the voluntary sector in Ireland including research on the attitudes of UK funders.

## The press

*The Irish Times* is a leading national newspaper which includes Dublin Stock Exchange quotations. It is also available on the Internet at *http://www.ieunet.ie/ ois/irishtimes/*. *Business and Finance* (from Belenos Publications) is a weekly general business magazine. The subscription includes an annual ranking of the top 1000 Irish companies with a more detailed analysis of all listed companies.

# Italy

Although one of the leading economies of Europe, Italy is sharply divided between the affluent, industrialised north and the poor, agricultural south.

*Who's Who in Italy (Sutter's international red series) – Eurospan*

An English language who's who. It also contains surveys of Italy's history, government, diplomatic representation, media, universities, associations, religions, etc., as well as profiles of the major companies.

*Il Taccuino dell'Azionista – Databank SpA*

Detailed information on all companies on the Italian Stock Exchange. Written in Italian, the main focus is financial, but it also includes the names of directors and main shareholders, company history, activities and recent developments. Databank also produces English language services such as company information and reports on specific industries in Italy, though the Italian versions are fuller.

*Annuario Generale Italiano and Annuario Amministrativo Italiano – Guida Monaci*

Directories of the industrial and services sector (including administrative organisations) and of the government, administration and statutory bodies respectively. Written in Italian.

*Calepino dell'Azionista and Le Principali Società Italiane – Mediobanca*

The former is a directory of all Italian listed companies giving financials, directors, activities, major shareholders, etc. The latter is a series of ranking tables for the largest industrial companies, banks, insurance companies, etc. Both are written in Italian and available free of charge.

## The press

Europrospects produces an English language newsletter called *Italian Business Trends*. It covers the main political, macroeconomic, financial and sectoral developments in the country.

### Electronic information

*Cerved* is the online service of the Italian chambers of commerce. As it is so difficult to obtain information from the chambers of commerce themselves this is an immensely useful source. A daily Internet news service in English is provided by the Agenzia Nazionale Stampa Associata. It also provides links to other sites. Called Windows on Italy it can be found at *http://www.mi.cnr.it/ WOI/.*

# Liechtenstein

This is a small, German speaking principality which is notorious for its secrecy. It is not easy to discover much about the people or companies domiciled there, which is a pity as they are likely to be interesting. As this country is so small the information is often parcelled together with Swiss information (e.g. in the Swiss St Gallen telephone directory). Publications which have included Liechtenstein in the past include: *Who is Who in Switzerland*, Kompass titles, *Swiss Export Directory* and *Swiss Financial Yearbook.*

# Norway

*Norges Handels-Kalender – Okonomisk Litteratur*

Written in Norwegian, though in a standard format, this directory gives basic facts for around 120,000 Norwegian companies. They include contact details, name of key director, and activities. This company also produces other business directories, for example on banks, printing companies, and advertising bureaux. The non-Norwegian speaker might prefer its *Norwegian Largest Companies* which is partly in English and provides more information for a smaller range of companies. Alternatively Dun & Bradstreet produces Norwegian language directories which include some credit information.

*Hvem Hva Hvor – Chr. Schibsteds Forlag*

Literally 'Who What Where', this is a small yearbook rather than a who's who. It details the year's events, people who have died during the year, and it has a small biographical section covering important people worldwide. It is written in Norwegian.

# Spain

Spain was a dictatorship until 1975. It remains one of the poorer countries of the EU though industrial investment has been expanding.

*Quien es Quien en España – Editorial Campillo*

Who's who in Spain in Spanish. Standard biographical details, though many entries are not very detailed. Also a sizeable section on the addresses and key personnel of national and local government departments, embassies, and companies.

*Who's Who in Spain (Sutter's International Red Series) – Eurospan*

An English language who's who. It also contains surveys of Spain's history, government, diplomatic representation, media, universities, associations, religions, etc., as well as profiles of the major companies.

*Anuario de Sociedades, Consejeros y Directivos – Dicodi SA*

Details of the top 50,000 companies, written in Spanish, and including board of directors, sales, activities and number of employees. Indexed alphabetically, by province, and by activity, as well as by directors' names. Also ranked by sales and employees. It is also available on CD-ROM. Dun & Bradstreet produces a competitor as well as *Norms and Ratios* for industry comparisons and *Spanish Market Guide* for credit appraisals.

*(Maxwell Espinosa) Shareholders Directory – SPA/The Reference Press/William Snyder*

An English language guide to around 2000 of Spain's top companies and financial institutions. Information includes contact details, names of top management, lawyers, bankers, and sales and profits over four years. Its strength is the details of shareholders.

*Las Fundaciones en la Acción Social – Ministerio de Asuntos Sociales*

This is a Spanish language directory of foundations operating in the field of social action. It is arranged geographically and gives basic details such as address and telephone, name of director, classification of activity and geographical coverage. It is a typical example of a ministry's interest in the foundations in its field. For a more general approach try *Directorio de las fundaciones españolas* from the Centro de Fundaciones.

### The press

A good general paper is *La Vanguardia Españolas*. A more specifically business paper is *Expansión*. Business Spain produces the monthly (though costly) English language journal *Business Spain* and is putting together a series of diskettes on particular industry sectors. It also has a sizeable library on Spanish business.

### Electronic information

Spanish Internet resources can be found at *http://www.uji.es/spain_www.html*.

# Sweden

*Vem är Det – Norstedts Förlag*

This is a Swedish Who's Who. It is written in Swedish, and rather difficult to translate as the language is abbreviated.

*Ekonomijournalisterna Intressanterna – BNL Information*

This provides address and phone number, names and direct numbers of the top management, revenue, largest shareholders, and numbers of employees for 1000 companies. It includes all Swedish stock market companies. For a more extensive range of companies try *Ekonomifakta* from Dun & Bradstreet.

*Swedish Export Directory – Swedish Trade Council*

Written in English (and four other languages), this covers Swedish companies which export to anywhere in the world. The coverage is not complete as only those companies which wish to pay are included. In effect it is an advertising tool, with size and content of entries determined by each company. Each should provide contact details and details of the products or services supplied. It is also possible to look up a product and cross-reference to the producers, and there is an index of trade names where they differ from company names.

*Storföretagen 500 – AffärsForlaget*

Supplement to the weekly magazine *Veckans Affärer*, written in English and Swedish. Tables show the top 500 industrial companies, plus banks and insurance companies. It provides standard company information including parent, directors, sales and profit, and activities. There is also a directory of directors. It includes two PC disks.

*Kulturfonder i Sverige – Norstedts Förlag*

Literally cultural funds in Sweden. Despite its name this Swedish language book includes foundations in fields such as science.

## The press

*Svenska Dagbladet* is a general paper, while *Dagens Industri* specialises in business and finance. Non-Swedish speakers might prefer *Focus Sweden* from Affärsvarlden or *Sweden International* from Erlandsson.

# Switzerland

This is a wealthy country with a strong financial sector. Its main language is German (often with a strong Swiss accent), though there are French and Italian regions and a small number of Romansch speakers. It has a federal system of semi-autonomous cantons.

*Who is Who in Switzerland and Liechtenstein – Orell Füssli*

A standard who's who. Formerly published by Nagel, the 1996 edition is the first from Orell Füssli.

*Verzeichnis der Verwaltungsräte/Répertoire des Administrateurs – Orell Füssli*

Directory of directors in French and German. Straightforward listings of names, addresses and company names rather than personal information. Orell Füssli's other publications include a comprehensive annual directory of all companies in the commercial register named *Schweizerisches Ragionenbuch/Annuaire Suisse du Registre du Commerce*. It is in French, German and Italian. It also publishes a *Who Owns Whom* and books more specific to particular industries.

*Swiss Financial Year Book – Elvetica Edizioni SA*

Sections on the largest companies, banks, insurance companies, etc., including directors, turnover and profit, branches and subsidiaries, and shareholders. Also ranking tables giving top banks, companies, etc., and a directory of directors. Written in English and also available on CD-ROM.

*Handbuch der Öffentlichen und Privaten Kulturförderung in der Schweiz – Orell Füssli*

This is a directory of Swiss foundations which operate in the field of culture. It is confusingly written in a mixture of German, French, Italian and Romansch, as appropriate to each particular foundation. It provides address, telephone and fax, and aims and activities, but unfortunately not names of trustees or much information on the scale of giving. Arranged both alphabetically and by subject area. There are also some foundations to be found in another of Orell Füssli's publications: *Gemeinnützige Institutionen in der Schweiz/Institutions d'Utilité Publique en Suisse*, though these are more likely to be fund-raisers than donors.

## The press

*Neue Zürcher Zeitung* is a general newspaper with a good company section. If you prefer a French paper try *Agefi Switzerland*. English language business magazines include *Bulletin* from Crédit Suisse and *Swiss Business* free from HandelsZeitung Publications. The latter produces lists of Switzerland's top companies.

# 17. Central and Eastern Europe

## Political background

This is a vast geographical area, ranging from Western Europe right across to Asia. The people are very different in language, religion and ethnic background. The major relocations of people which occurred under Soviet authority have only heightened existing tensions by causing resentment against the incomers. The collapse of the Soviet empire inevitably led to some bloody conflicts.

The region has suffered many wars during the course of this century, each resulting in a carving up of the spoils. Borders have moved backwards and forwards, sometimes taking the people with them, but often leaving them stranded in what has become a foreign country. Many areas are still the subject of dispute. Although each modern country has its own political and business characteristics, they are still haunted by the shadows of former systems.

The collapse of the Soviet Union resulted in the adoption of more Western styles of democracy. However transition to the market economy is painful. For many people the old system represented security: jobs, subsidised facilities, pensions. The new system has resulted in widespread unemployment and higher prices so is not universally seen as being better; therefore some areas experienced a backlash as former socialist leaders were voted back into power.

To some of those accustomed to socialism, capitalism represents greedy self-interest and is thus morally wrong. This view is strengthened by the dubious nature of some of those who have become rich under the new regimes. There have been allegations that they succeeded through foul means such as bribery or intimidation. The Mafia is said to be taking an interest. It is therefore very important not to accept businesses or people at face value as you might find your reputation is devalued.

## Business environment

- *State ownership of businesses.* Many countries are rapidly privatising their large enterprises, but some still lack the political consensus or organisational ability to do so. The most successful so far is the DDR, now part of a unified Germany. The Czech Republic and Poland have the majority of their enterprises in private hands, with Hungary and Russia following. As in Western

Europe, some companies are at an intermediate stage, being owned by a combination of the state and private investors.

Privatisation methods vary from country to country. In some countries citizens were given credits or encouraged to invest in their national companies. In others overseas investors were invited to bring outside capital into the country. Eastern Germany is in the unusual position of having been incorporated into another state, which means that the taxpayers of Western Germany have contributed towards its regeneration.

- *Unreliability of accounts.* As the alternative to meeting the targets of the central planners might have been distinctly unpleasant, Soviet factories tended to exaggerate their production levels. Until recently there was no concept of profitability, only of meeting targets. The temptation now might be to understate production figures so as to avoid taxes. This lack of either ability or willingness to achieve accuracy means that any figures that are available should be taken with a pinch of salt.

Western accounting procedures are slowly spreading, but there is no guarantee that managers who are not accustomed to them will be able or willing to produce the right results. It is not uncommon for a publisher to base its figures simply on telephone or postal questionnaires, without taking into account whether the suppliers of this information understand or care about the questions. It will take some years before all companies have the training and motivation to provide totally accurate accounts.

Rather than try to deduce a trend from the figures it might be more useful to ask whether western advisors have been brought in, new management installed, etc.

- *Uncompetitiveness.* The Soviet system meant that the planners rather than the customers and managers determined how the factory operated. Innovation carried penalties for failure but limited rewards for success.

The inflexibility of the plan resulted in either gluts or chronic shortages, which meant it was in a factory's interest to hoard secret stocks of raw materials. It was also common for them to skimp on quality in order to meet their (often unrealistic) production targets. It has been claimed that at one stage factories were destroying machinery in order to meet targets for scrap metal.

It will take some time to entrench a western business mentality and to increase the level of investment to a point where techniques obsolete in the west are no longer used.

251

- *Large monopoly factories.* It was common to locate all of a country's production of a specific item in a single factory. The factory would take in the raw materials, handle all stages of the production process itself and produce a single product. This was simpler for the central plan to deal with, but resulted in an inefficient and inflexible system. Competition and broader product lines are now slowly being introduced.

- *Political and economic uncertainty.* These states are still balancing between capitalism and communism. New governments are experimenting with investment incentives, legal and tax structures, banking and finance, labour regulations, and a whole host of other issues which can have a major effect on corporate structure and performance.

# Sources

Accurate information was not a strong point of the Soviet Union. The move towards democracy and the market economy is slowly improving the situation. Newspapers have more (but not necessarily complete) freedom of speech, and companies are being forced to produce more accurate profit figures in order to attract investment. Biographical works are still often written by academics as only they have the necessary depth of knowledge about the area. The whole area is in such a state of flux that information rapidly becomes out of date and it seems likely that these countries will be in a state of transition for some years to come.

Rather than a centralised Soviet information source, each of the new states now has its own offices. The desire to attract western investment has meant that they are all making an effort to provide more business information and it is often available in English. As the volume of information grows so does its reliability, but it still has flaws. Accounting is relatively primitive and financial information is often difficult to obtain. This means that many directories contain only contact details, activities and number of employees.

As well as sources emerging from the area itself, Western European directories are beginning to include information on the East. These are easier to obtain and are often in English, but do not let their accessibility and standardised format persuade you that the information is entirely representative and reliable. The region's problems are so great even the major publishers find it difficult to collect accurate data. See the general Western Europe section for further directories which cover both sides of the divide.

Official registries are mostly of little use. Until there are sound frameworks of company law and managers are trained in accountancy procedures it would be better to rely on other sources. There are still very few companies listed on their national stockmarkets, some preferring to raise capital on more established stockmarkets, e.g. Hungarian companies might be found listed in Vienna.

There is a steady stream of new information as formerly state-owned enterprises are offered for sale. These are often advertised in the press, possibly with much useful detail. Information on the overall state of the privatisation process can be obtained from a government yearbook or Europa's *World Yearbook*, while sources such as *East European Privatisation News* (available on *FT-Profile*) will provide more specific detail.

There are a growing number of trade associations which might collect industry data. The large western accountancy firms which are moving in as advisors can sometimes provide guides to corporate financial structures. Also look out for government-sponsored advertising supplements in international journals such as *Business Week* or *Forbes*. These do not generally appear in the online version. Alternatively you might obtain trade fair catalogues, for example those of the German 'Messe'. Industry newsletters can be a useful English language source as the region is so important in fields such as oil and gas production.

*Guide to Libraries in Central and Eastern Europe – The British Library*

Contact details for libraries in government departments and 'official' ones with a national role, e.g. patent offices. If you are not able to visit the library then you will often find it is willing to answer telephone or postal enquiries, though language might be a barrier. Services might be free or fee-paying, and they might range from telling you where to look to conducting a substantial search on your behalf. A companion volume to *Guide to Libraries in Western Europe* but with less detail because of the difficulties of compilation.

*Central and East European Information – Gale*

Produced by the London Business School (which also operates an information service – see below). Each country chapter begins with a brief overview of recent events, chambers of commerce, etc., then moves on to list books, databases, etc., their contents, and how to obtain them. Informative and useful.

*Asian & Australasian Companies and European Companies – CBD Research Ltd*

A guide to further sources of information rather than to companies. Relatively small sections of each are devoted to the countries of the former Soviet Union (which are divided roughly 50/50 between Europe and Asia). For each country they provide details of the official registry, stock exchanges, credit reporting services, company directories, electronic sources, newspapers and periodicals, etc. These books date particularly rapidly and the space devoted to this area is not great but they are still useful.

## Current European Directories – CBD Research Ltd

Similar to *European Companies* (above), but restricted to directories. It covers a much wider range of subjects, including many directories for specific industries and associations which publish lists of members.

## CIS-Middle Europe Information Service – London Business School

As this region is quite difficult to research you might prefer to pay someone else to do it for you. LBS has one such service. It has the necessary databases, books and contacts to enable it to provide reports on companies, products, legislation, country profiles, etc. Other academic institutions might also be able to help.

## Who's Who in Russia and the CIS Republics – Henry Holt

A more recent who's who than the following, which is an important consideration given the rapid pace of change in the region.

## Who's Who in Russia and the New States – IB Tauris & Co Ltd

Part one provides a state by state round up of ministries, parliamentary buildings, the state committees and other national bodies, and the holders of the most important offices. Part two provides almost 7000 biographical entries on leading figures in political, economic, cultural, social and military positions. Most entries provide addresses and telephone numbers as well as career history, publications, honours and awards. It is edited by two experts on the former Soviet Union, Leonard Geron and Alex Pravda.

## Longman Biographical Directory of Decision-Makers in Russia & The Successor States – Cartermill

This is primarily a who's who of individuals in politics or government, though it also extends to the worlds of business, the military, the media, religion and culture. Its entries are very full, often running to several pages of text. It is invaluable if you are looking for an independent and informative biography of a political figure. Entries are indexed by state and by topic area (e.g. dissidents, media, etc.). It is edited by Dr Martin McCauley, a leading Russian specialist at the University of London. The *Russia and the Successor States* bulletins below provide useful updates.

## The Biographical Dictionary of the Former Soviet Union – Bowker-Saur, part of Reed Elsevier

Yet another set of portraits of the top figures in the region. A sister volume is *Who's Who in Russia Today*.

*Vniioeng's Who's Who – Arguments and Facts International*

A directory of the leading oil and gas executives in the former USSR. Includes family details, career, etc.

*Directory of the Russian Parliament and Government – East Consult/DW Thorpe*

One of a series of directories guiding you to the contact details for hundreds of top officials. Cartermill also produces political directories for the countries of the former Soviet Union.

*Russia 1996 (etc.) – The Reference Press*

This lists Russian firms by industry as well as explaining the historical, political, social and economic background to doing business in Russia.

*Cracking Eastern Europe – The Reference Press*

The economic and political background to doing business in the various countries. Useful information includes etiquette and key business contacts and resources. It is more of a guide for those wishing to set up in business than a source for company information.

*Directory of East European Businesses – The Reference Press*

The top manufacturing and engineering companies are listed alphabetically for each country. Information is not very extensive but includes address, phone/fax/telex number, contact name, type of business, and possibly sales or profit figures, though these are not so reliable in this part of the world.

*MZM World Business Directory – MZM Publications*

This would be better titled Business Directory of the ex-Socialist World. It covers 33 countries, mostly in Eastern Europe, but also others such as China, Mongolia, Vietnam and North Korea. It is written in English. As usual Dun & Bradstreet produces a more extensive, though more expensive competitor covering the Central Europe area only. Alternatives are available from Gale, Hoppenstedt, and Graham & Whiteside. There are also indigenous directories, e.g. Immarcon's *Russian General Register*, though there is no guarantee that they are any more accurate.

*Inform Katalog – VP International*

Czech and Slovak business directories, covering 20,000 and 7000 companies respectively. You can look them up alphabetically or by industry and find basic details such as address and names of senior executives.

### The Ross Register of Siberian Industry – Norman Ross Publishing Inc

Available on paper or diskette, this is compiled in Novosibirsk in English. For each factory, mine or other enterprise it provides name, address, telephone and fax, name of one director, lists of major products, and scale of operations. It also describes the geographic and industrial characteristics of each region and lists the languages spoken there.

More narrowly based publications such as this may have a better chance of obtaining more representative and accurate coverage. The new national governments are themselves taking an interest in publishing English language directories so as to encourage investment, e.g. *Lithuanian Companies and Organisations* (Lithuanian Information Institute) and *Latvian Export Directory* (Latvian Development Agency). There are also directories specific to certain industries, e.g. oil and gas. Embassies should be able to provide information on the latest publications.

### International Guide to Funders Interested in Central and Eastern Europe – European Foundation Centre

A directory of funding sources for Central and Eastern Europe, the Newly Independent States and the Baltic States. It contains only around 75 entries many of which are American and many have interests elsewhere; however it is well laid out and thorough.

### The press

Norman Ross Publishing produces microfilm versions of many Eastern European newspapers, but unfortunately they are not indexed. Apart from a few English language papers like *The Prague Post* and *The Baltic Observer* most require knowledge of the local language. Ask the appropriate embassy whether a local English publication exists, or try an online database such as *Textline*.

The tremendous investment potential of the region has spawned numerous journals and information services produced in the West. An example is the monthly *Eastern Europe Monitor* from Business Monitor International. It covers the countries of Eastern Europe and the former Soviet Union, reporting on government, the economy, finance and the business environment. The same publisher also produces annual in-depth reports on specific countries. The focus is on the overall picture rather than individual companies.

Similarly, *The Economist* produces the monthly *Business Central Europe*. This provides coverage of political and economic developments in Central Europe as well as profiles of companies engaged in international and intra-regional trade. It is backed by the reputation of *The Economist* and a strong network of local contributors. An alternative is the quarterly *Country Reports* series from *The Economist Intelligence Unit.*

Cartermill produces *Russia and the Successor States.* By the same editor as the *Longman Biographical Directory,* this is a news briefing service with six bulletins a year. It contains political commentary, features on key individuals and a chronological summary of developments.

## Electronic information

Database producers have rushed eagerly into this new area, resulting in the strange situation that business information is often available online that cannot be found from any other source. However there might be no way of checking that the figures are accurate short of asking the companies yourself. *Genios* and *GBI* are useful hosts, though check whether you can cope with the level of German. *GBI* contains SovInfoLink's *Who's Who in the Soviet Union* database. *Data-Star* (Knight-Ridder) and *Cerved* are also taking an interest in the area. Press databases of interest include *APA* (Austrian Press Agency – again German might be a problem) and *Textline.*

Free English language news services are available over the Internet. For *Central Europe Today* send the message 'subscribe' to *cet-online-request@eunet.cz.* Archives are available at *http://www.eunet.cz/.* Alternatively try OMRI's daily digest for the former Soviet Union and Central Europe: send the message subscribe OMRI-L firstname lastname (i.e. your name) to *listserv@ubvm.cc. buffalo.edu.* Archives are at *http://www.omri.cz/OMRI.html. Monitor* and *Prism* are daily and weekly newsletters covering the post-Soviet states: sub Jamestown-l to *listserv@peach.ease.lsoft.com.* For news and companies in the St Petersburg region try *http://www.spb.su.sppress/.*

# 18. Asia-Pacific

This area is rapidly growing in economic importance, and the expansion of trade and investment opportunities inevitably led to the expansion of published business information. Many sources are fairly recent and not quite as satisfactory in terms of coverage or detail as those in the more established economic power-houses. However there are growing numbers of companies quoted on stock markets which means a higher level of publicly available information.

Apart from well known success stories like Japan, Hong Kong, South Korea and Taiwan one area which is rapidly growing in economic power is ASEAN. This is not a misspelling of Asian, but rather an informal regional grouping known as The Association of South East Asia Nations. At its heart are Indonesia, Malaysia, the Philippines, Singapore, Thailand and Brunei. Vietnam recently joined and neighbours such as Myanmar (Burma) are becoming more closely involved. India and China which for long have been relatively poor are such large countries that their economic development should have a significant impact on the rest of the world.

Huge swathes of this region have been under colonial influence. The British presence was felt in countries such as Australia, New Zealand, India, Hong Kong, Singapore and Malaysia. As a consequence English is widely spoken and continues to be popular as an international trading language. In some countries there are so many native tongues that the best way of communicating has been to adopt English as a universal second language. The high level of education found in some of these countries also helps the spread of English, especially among younger people.

The populations of many of these countries are ethnically diverse. Ethnic Chinese are particularly widespread and successful. There are populations in countries such as Taiwan, Hong Kong, Singapore, Malaysia, Thailand, Indonesia and the Philippines. They carried with them their strong sense of family and regional loyalty, which means cross-national affiliations with people originally from the same area or family. However be careful about exploiting these international networks. Many countries have experienced ethnic tensions and instability in the past few decades and it might be politically unwise to focus on a particular ethnic group. The Chinese are in a particularly difficult situation because they are often more successful and wealthy than their neighbours.

The Asia-Pacific region is in some ways quite inward looking, e.g. the large overseas Chinese community is particularly interested in aid and investment for China, while Japan and Australia wish to be involved in the rapid growth of their neighbours. This is hardly surprising considering the size and potential for economic growth which exists in the region. In much of Asia philanthropy tends to be the domain of individuals rather than companies (though a cheque may come from company funds) partly because businesses tend to be family-owned; however the reverse is true in Japan.

However the scars of war and occupation are still there. Economic pressures are forcing nations to co-operate, but on a personal level they do not necessarily forgive the events of the past. There are also tensions between communist and capitalist countries as extremes exist side by side. The situation is improving as parts of China open up to foreign trade, though relations with some neighbours are still tense.

Part of the reason for the stability from which some of these countries benefit is the strength of the ruling political party; however the party should not be seen as homogeneous. Where a single party remains in power for a considerable time and the opposition is weak it is likely that personalities within the ruling party are quite important. Divisions and power bases might appear within the party rather than between parties.

It is important to understand the culture of these countries. People of Chinese or Japanese origin tend to look for sincerity and a long term relationship, being wary of brash Westerners who want to make a quick killing. Rather than hoping to arrange a meeting at the last minute you need to ensure that a third party of sufficient status introduces you. These people in effect stake their reputation on your good behaviour. This means that constant networking is vital. It is also important to have good contacts in order to gain information as this is often only passed on personally. It is thus vital that you research people carefully as a mistake can cause serious damage to your social standing and business success. If you do not know anyone your embassy might be able to help.

You must also research the networks that underlie the business world. There are large groupings of corporations known as *keiretsu* in Japan, *chaebols* in Korea and, more recently, *jituan* in China. Once you build up a relationship with one member you should be careful not to antagonise them by dealing with a member of a competing group.

In some more traditional countries (for example Japan) it is difficult for a woman to be taken as seriously as a man. It might be the case that women normally stop work when they marry, hence making it difficult for them to reach positions of power. Status is very important and if a woman is assumed to be a secretary then it would be inappropriate to take much notice of her. It might also make the men feel uncomfortable if a woman were to be invited to an all-male gathering, especially if heavy drinking is involved. Although these attitudes might not be tolerated in your own country, it is no use trying to ignore them when dealing with a region where they are the norm. At the least you should be aware of the problem, and acknowledge that in some cases a male contact will have more success simply because he is male.

**Names**

Names can cause endless problems in foreign cultures. Below are some examples of typical problems you might encounter with two of the more numerous populations in the region.

Some of the peoples of this area (notably the Chinese) traditionally place the family name (or surname) before the given names. In response to the confusion that this causes to westerners they sometimes transpose their names. Unfortunately that leaves the westerners even more confused as they do not know which pattern they are following. It can therefore be very difficult to know what to call someone, and it is often best to check both ways round when searching a directory. Directories will normally attempt to index under the family name, but there is no guarantee that the compilers have got it right. When searching an electronic database use a connector which means the words could be in any order, e.g. in Knight-Ridder's *Dialog*: Lee(2n)Kuan(2n)Yew.

The matter is further complicated by the practice, common in Hong Kong, of having both Chinese given names and a western one as well. Similarly, a Chinese person living in Thailand might have both a Thai name and a Chinese name, using them interchangeably as the situation requires. Translating from oriental characters to western script can also create problems as unless you know the language well you might not be able to tell whether two similar names are actually versions of the same one. Thus, if a search of an electronic database produces very little try several alternatives or search only for two names rather than all three.

The Chinese generally have two given names, one of which might denote the generation and be shared by brothers and male cousins. This is not a standard 'surname' because there will be a new one for the next generation. To add to the confusion, a Chinese woman often keeps her own family name after marriage.

Indians have a variety of approaches towards names. They might have a standard family name which passes from generation to generation, though they do not necessarily choose to use it. They might have only a given name followed by 'son of x' or 'daughter of y' where x and y are the given names of their fathers. Alternatively they might simply place their father's initial before their own given name and leave it at that. Whether a man uses his given name or his family name it is correct to place 'Mr' before it. Married women drop their father's name and take their husband's given name. Thus they become 'Mrs z' where z is the given name of their husband. Sikhs tend to follow the same pattern but with the addition of a further given name: males use the name 'Singh' as a second given name and females 'Kaur'. Of course, they can if they wish forget this totally and adopt a western pattern.

## General sources

*Asian & Australasian Companies – CBD Research Ltd*

A guide to further sources of information rather than to companies. It has a particularly broad coverage of 69 countries ranging from Western Samoa to Saudi Arabia. For each it provides details of the official registry, stock exchanges, credit reporting services, company directories, electronic sources, newspapers and periodicals, etc. Although some of the details are a little out of date it is still a very valuable source.

*Asian Markets: A Guide to Company and Industry Information Sources – Washington Researchers*

Sources of business information for some of the most important Asian nations. Written from a US perspective but including international sources.

*The Asia & Japan Business Information Sourcebook – John Wiley*

A country by country list of sources for East Asia and South East Asia. Some are a little out of date and the vast majority are books rather than electronic sources, however generally a very useful reference particularly for sources from the region itself.

*ASEAN Who's Who – Kasuya Publishing*

A three-volume English language who's who covering Brunei, Indonesia, Malaysia, the Philippines, Singapore and Thailand. Some entries are fuller than others and many are accompanied by photographs. This publication has the advantage of being produced locally and includes a useful introduction to the region. Besides the biographies it provides detailed descriptions of ASEAN and its member states, information on political leaders, useful addresses, titles and honours, and an index of companies. Late entries occasionally throw the alphabeticisation out of order, but a very useful set.

261

## Who's Who of the Asian Pacific Rim – Barons Who's Who

Countries covered are: China, Hong Kong, Indonesia, Japan, Malaysia, The Philippines, Singapore, South Korea, Taiwan, and Thailand. An attempt has been made to include as full a list as possible of top executives of major firms in the region. There are also representatives from the fields of government, the civil service, journalism, medicine and education, but it is primarily a directory for business users. Where people did not submit their own biographies these have been compiled by Barons staff. The result is over 3500 biographies, concentrating on business career and contact details, but generally including other information such as date of birth, education, and honours, and even the occasional photograph. There is also an index by type of business, which includes country codes. You can thus easily pick out, for example, all listed developers in Hong Kong.

## Who's Who in Australasia and the Far East – International Biographical Centre

This contains 5500 biographies covering 32 countries and territories, but is heavily biassed towards Australia. Although no charge is made for inclusion, IBC encourages its biographees to buy the book in which they feature. There are no indexes to this book.

## Who's Who in Asian and Australasian Politics – Bowker-Saur, part of Reed Elsevier

Over 3000 biographies covering the Pacific Basin and Indian sub-continent. Includes an index by country. Unfortunately not updated annually.

## Asian Company Handbook – Toyo Keizai

A small English language paperback covering selected companies on the stock exchanges of Hong Kong, the Republic of Korea, Malaysia, Singapore, Taiwan, Thailand, Indonesia and China. A page per company including four years' financials, activities, recent events, a couple of directors, etc. Not as informative as Toyo Keizai's Japanese Handbook, probably because less information is available in these markets, however it is still a useful basic reference book.

## Asia Pacific Handbook – Extel Financial Ltd

A large, informative paperback giving contact details, three years' financials, several directors, activities, and major shareholders for 1300 companies. It covers Malaysia, Singapore, Thailand, Japan, Hong Kong, Australia and Korea. It also includes lists of the top companies in the region, in each country, and in various industries. Extel also produces 'cards' for some of these countries. These are an alternative to building up a library of corporate annual reports and press cuttings for the country.

Dun & Bradstreet and Riddell Information Services also produce a range of directories for Australia, ASEAN and neighbouring countries, some of which are well indexed, e.g. by directors. It might be worth contacting regional offices for their booklists as they might contain more titles than your local office's list. This is because they act as agents for other local publishers. Graham & Whiteside also produces a clearly laid out company directory which is strong on directors' and executives' names and also gives shareholders, basic finances, etc.

*MZM World Business Directory – MZM Publications*

This would be better titled Business Directory of the ex-Socialist World. It covers 33 countries, mostly in Eastern Europe, but also some in Asia such as China, Mongolia, Vietnam and North Korea. It is written in English.

*The Asian Bank Directory – Euromoney*

Contact details and names of directors but little more. An alternative is *Major Financial Institutions of the Far East & Australasia* from Graham & Whiteside. This is a new directory covering the major banks of the region including foreign banks based there, investment companies, and insurance and reinsurance companies. It gives contact details, names of directors and senior executives, branches and subsidiaries, finances, principal shareholders, etc.

*Asia Yearbook – Review Publishing Co Ltd*

A comprehensive country by country overview of economic and political developments over the past year. Also overviews of industries, trade, etc. It covers 36 countries, including parts of the former Soviet Union. This publisher also produces numerous other publications on Asia, for example the *All-Asia Travel Guide* and *Review 200: Asia's Leading Companies Survey Report.*

The latter takes leading companies in each country plus multinationals operating in the region and ranks them in numerous ways. It is unusual in basing its rankings on questionnaires about issues like leadership, quality, vision, etc., filled in by randomly selected subscribers to business magazines. For a more straightforward ranking of the top companies in various countries try *The Times 1000* (Times newspapers/Reference Press).

*Country Business Guide Series – The Reference Press*

This is a relatively cheap series of books providing overviews of the economic and business environment in specific countries: China, Hong Kong, Japan, Korea, The Philippines, Singapore, and Taiwan. They include financial institutions, industry reviews, trade fairs, etiquette, translations of business terms, etc.

### Cracking the Pacific Rim – The Reference Press

Country profiles include key business contacts and resources, etiquette, a brief history, etc. However it focuses on the financial background to doing business there.

### Emerging Civil Society in the Asia Pacific Community – Institute of Southeast Asian Studies

An overview of the pattern of NGO activity in the Far East. It describes the current patterns of philanthropy in each country in comparison with countries such as the US, and explains the political and economic constraints under which NGOs operate. It also looks at the nature of Japanese and US involvement in the region. Included are lists of some of the major foundations. An alternative is *Evolving Patterns of Asia-Pacific Philanthropy* (Yonsei University Institute of East and West Studies).

### Asiaweek 1000 and Financial 500 – Asiaweek Ltd

These are on disk listings of Asia's top 1000 companies and 500 largest banks and insurance companies respectively. They are produced by the publisher of *Asiaweek* magazine. They provide figures for sales, assets, employees, etc., and names and contact details of CEOs in a downloadable format for mailing lists.

### Asian Customs and Manners – Meadowbrook

It is essential to read some sort of guide to Asian practices and beliefs before trying to deal with the people. This book includes etiquette, body language, key phrases, etc. An alternative is *When Business East Meets Business West: The Guide to Practice and Protocol in the Pacific Rim* (John Wiley).

### The press

Many publications cover this region. One of the best known is the weekly *Far Eastern Economic Review* (Review Publishing Co Ltd). It provides authoritative articles on political and economic developments in Asia, plus more indepth pieces on industries, companies and personalities. An index can be purchased separately or it can be found online, e.g. on *Dow Jones*.

An alternative is the more expensive monthly *South East Asia Monitor* (Business Monitor International). This provides news, data and analysis on the countries of South East Asia. It reports on government, the economy, finance and the business environment. The same publisher also produces annual in-depth reports on specific countries. The focus is on the overall picture rather than individual companies.

For a stronger business slant try *Asia Inc* or *Asian Business* (Far East Trade Press). *The Asian Wall Street Journal* (Dow Jones) is also quite highly regarded for business information.

Fund-raisers might be interested in the Australian publication *Fundraising Australasia*.

## Electronic sources

Apart from the *Asiaweek* company disks (above) there are numerous online sources. Knight-Ridder's *Dialog*, for example, has good press coverage through files 728, 748 and 726, and company information is available in file 758. Alternatively you might try the onesearches Asianews and Asiaco. *FT-Profile* also has Asian coverage, especially of Japan (Nikkei). This is part of a general trend for hosts to take an increasing interest in the region. Major English-language newspapers to look out for are *Asian Wall Street Journal* (online on DataTimes and Dow Jones) and *South China Morning Post*. *Euromoney* occasionally produces articles on Asia's most powerful families which read rather like a rich list.

An Internet news service is available from AsiaInfo Services. The headlines and a few highlights are free. Send the message: sub headline firstname lastname (i.e. your name) to *listserv@asiainfo.com*. The full daily news is for subscribers only. A list of useful sites in the Far East can be found through Asia Online at *http://www.asia-Online.com/* or the Committee on East Asian Libraries at *http://darkwing.uoregon.edu/~felsing/ceal/welcome.html*. An Asian Business Directory covering Thailand, Singapore, Indonesia and Malaysia can be found at *http://www.asiatrade.com/*. Alternatively there is Asia Trade at *http://www.colossus.net/asiadir*.

# Australia

*Who's Who in Australia – Information Australia*

A comprehensive, long-established work, including details on the honours system and the governments and courts of the states. This publisher also produces *Who's Who in Business in Australia*. This should not be confused with Dun & Bradstreet's *Business Who's Who of Australia* which cross-references the directors but focuses more on their companies. D&B also produces *The Government Who's Who of Australia* which lists names, responsibilities and contact details. For a more historical view try *Monash Biographical Dictionary of 20th Century Australia* from DW Thorpe.

## The Business Who's Who Australian Rankings – Riddell Information Services

Rankings of the top companies in each state. Riddell's produces several corporate directories, so if you are interested in Australasia it might be worth obtaining the full list.

## Shareholder – Australian Financial Review Books

This is a sister publication of *The Australian Financial Review*. It provides investment information on the top 500 Australian companies, including forecasts for the major stock market sectors and a report on the performance of each company. It gives major shareholders, recent events, five years of financials, etc., is revised twice a year, yet is relatively cheap.

## Australian Stock Exchange Yearbook – Australian Stock Exchange/The Reference Press/William Snyder

Profiles of all companies listed on the Australian Stock Exchange. It has a companion volume, *All Ordinaries Index Companies Handbook*, which profiles the 314 companies on the ASE All Ordinaries Index plus the 39 top 300 companies that are not in the Index. This gives comprehensive information including history, operations, recent events, five years of finances, and directors.

## Australian Public Companies Guide – Information Australia

Information includes financials, shareholders and a directory of directors. This publisher also produces other company and biographical reference books.

## Australian Directory of Philanthropy – DW Thorpe

This is published in association with the Australian Association of Philanthropy, which aims to make it the definitive source of information about trusts and foundations in this country. It still has a little way to go to bring it up to US or UK standards. A slim paperback giving contact details, purpose, priorities and limitations. Organisations are also indexed by fields of interest. Unfortunately it does not necessarily give the full list of trustees and it does not always say how much money is available. This can be supplemented with Information Australia's *Guide to Government Assistance to Businesses and Nonprofit Organisations*.

## The press

*The Australian Financial Review* is a leading financial newspaper. *Business Review Weekly* publishes an annual rich list (also available via the *Textline* online database which can be accessed via several hosts). Australia is a huge country with many regional papers.

Fund-raisers might be interested in *Philanthropy* (Australian Association of Philanthropy). This is a magazine for trustees and fund-raisers considering issues such as how to apply for funds, trends in giving, etc. Also case studies of successful applications. The Association also holds workshops for grant-seekers.

# China

There is comparatively little written on China apart from guides to investing there. Western-style who's whos and company directories do not fit well with a communist structure, but as China seeks foreign investment the amount of information is rapidly increasing. Figures are not necessarily totally reliable, particularly for newly listed companies, as this form of accounting is new to them and the company might not have existed in the same form beforehand. China now has stock exchanges and many joint ventures with foreign investors, and several companies have listed in Hong Kong. It has demarcated particular areas for economic progress, so the overall degree of modernisation varies widely. The southern coastal cities are particularly wealthy and outward-looking, while agricultural areas remain very poor. The reabsorption of Hong Kong has long been anticipated by local businessmen, many of whom have built up strong links with the mainland.

Beware of confusing the People's Republic of China (what we normally know as 'China') with the Republic of China (Taiwan – sometimes described as Taiwan ROC). Earlier this century Taiwan became home to Chinese refugees and the two competing Chinas have never overcome their enmity. Taiwan is still not formally recognised by many countries, though trade continues regardless.

Because of the desire for foreign investment you might be able to obtain company and market information from government bodies such as the *China Council of International Commerce*. You can also obtain information from departments closer to home such as Manchester Business School's China Research Unit. Hong Kong is also a good source of English language information on China, though it might now become less independent.

*China: Guide to Investment and Financial Information Sources – Effective Technology Marketing Ltd*

A report covering online, CD-ROM and Internet sources as well as journals, market surveys, directories, and other publications.

*Who's Who in the People's Republic of China – KG Saur, part of Reed Elsevier*

Unfortunately not updated annually, but nonetheless of great value as there are so few alternatives. Over 4000 profiles, many with photos.

*Directory of Chinese Officials and Organizations – National Technical Information Service*

A CIA-produced guide to who does what in the Party, judiciary, ministries, etc. It is not a biographical work, but useful for finding names and titles of officials. Useful so long as it is updated regularly.

*Directory of Manufacturing Companies – Dun & Bradstreet*

Details of 17,000 leading companies. Information is basic but includes contact details, the name of the chief executive, number of employees and some financial information. An alternative is Kompass China (Reed Information Services). D&B's Hong Kong office also sells a few non-D&B books e.g. *Guangdong Directory of Industry and Commerce*. For slightly more company information try Edinburgh Financial Publishing's *Guide to the Companies of Hong Kong and China.*

A larger alternative, covering 30,000 companies and 1500 foreign business agents with offices in China is *Register of Chinese Business* from 3W International Digital Publishing Corp. It is arranged by industry and gives telephone number, senior executive, owner (normally the state), products, assets, etc. Not as informative as Western directories, but good by Chinese standards.

*The China Phone Book & Business Directory – The China Phone Book Company*

Addresses and telephone numbers for Chinese companies, arranged by both industry and region. It also contains details of major trade fairs and exhibitions, major contracts signed in the last six months, and an advertising section.

*China Fax & Telex Directory – The China Phone Book Company*

Names and numbers (but unfortunately not addresses) indexed by industries, by companies and numerically.

*Almanac of China's Foreign Economic Relations and Trade – The China Phone Book Company*

Unless you want a detailed overview of overseas trade, statistics and regulations the majority of this book is of little use. It does have occasional areas of interest, such as a (chronological) listing of boardroom changes and a listing of China's 500 largest import and export enterprises, but these might not be sufficient to justify buying it.

*China Securities Handbook – The China Phone Book Company*

This book provides much more editorial comment than the others. There are articles on the stock exchanges and business topics, forthcoming share issues, listings of stockbrokers and banks, and full page profiles of listed companies.

*Dealing with the Chinese – Warner Books*

A guide to etiquette and how to conduct business with the Chinese.

## The press

*Business China* (The Economist Intelligence Unit) is a fortnightly overview of political, economic and legal trends. It also has some case studies of businesses operating in China. The EIU can also provide further information such as a country report and a guide to operating a business in China.

*China Trade Report* (Review Publishing Company) provides monthly overviews and predictions for various industries. Also tables for China's top foreign trade corporations, major exhibitions in China, major awards of contracts, etc.

*China Business Review* gives an American slant, focusing on specific industries and giving details of contracts awarded as well as book reviews.

## Electronic information

China is usually to be found in an Asian or international file, for example *Reedbase Kompass* includes a substantial number of companies. A local supplier of company information is *Wanfang Data Corporation*. The Hong Kong-based *South China Morning Post* is available online, e.g. on Knight-Ridder's *Dialog*. Alternatively there is an English language version of *China Daily* which gives the government view and has a weekly business supplement. There is a growing number of Internet sites, for example *China News Digest* contains both back issues and links to other useful pages: *http://www.cnd.org*. Also of use for business information sources is the Institute of High Energy Physics at *http://www.ihep.ac.cn/china.html*. *China Net* is at *http://www.cnd.org*.

# Hong Kong

From 1 July 1997 the main part of Hong Kong reintegrates with China. The future is uncertain, but it seems likely that it will retain an independent identity and its own publications.

*Hong Kong: A Complete Guide to Business Information Sources – Effective Technology Marketing Ltd*

A report written by an expert on business information, Lawrence Tagg. It includes online, CD-ROM and Internet sources as well as journals, market surveys, directories, and other publications.

*Who's Who in Hong Kong – Manager Trade Publishing.*

Last published in 1988 by Kevin Sinclair and Asianet Information Services Ltd. If you can obtain a copy of the old edition it might still be of some use. The entries are quite informative and most are accompanied by photographs. There is also an index by profession. Unfortunately the new owner shows no sign of producing another edition.

*Company Handbook – Hong Kong – Corporate International Ltd*

A small paperback full of useful information on nearly 500 companies listed on the Hong Kong stock exchange. Financials, comments on history and recent performance, major shareholders, and a couple of directors' names.

For a broader range try Edinburgh Financial Publishing's *Guide to the Companies of Hong Kong and China*. *Directory of Hong Kong Industries* (Hong Kong Productivity Council) lists over 5000 firms, arranged by product and cross-indexed by name, but with only one director. Fuller listings of directors are given in the paperback *Federation of Hong Kong Industries: Members' Directory* (Federation of Hong Kong Industries).

*Affiliates of Hong Kong Enterprises in Asia-Pacific – Dun & Bradstreet*

There is much cross-investment in the region particularly between the Chinese-speaking enclaves. This publication enables you to track them. D&B also produces a range of other useful directories covering Hong Kong and its overseas links. Obtain its latest brochure for fuller details.

*Directory of Charitable and Trust Funds – Hong Kong Government Social Welfare Dept*

A small but useful directory. Philanthropy in this region tends to be the province of wealthy individuals rather than organisations, though there are exceptions such as the Hong Kong Jockey Club. It is not well documented, though large gifts are often well publicised in the press.

**The press**

The *South China Morning Post* is a major newspaper, also available online, e.g. on *Dialog* (Knight-Ridder). The Federation of Hong Kong Industries produces the monthly *Hong Kong Industrialist*. *Hong Kong Tattler* is useful for the social world. So far Hong Kong's press has been relatively free in comparison with some other parts of Asia, though this might now change.

# India

*India Who's Who – Infa Publications*

An established English language reference book, though prone to repeated delays in publication dates. The 5000 entries are divided into business, humanities, science, etc., so check the index in the back for the person's name. Confusingly it has three series of page numbers, so take particular notice of 'a' and 'b' after the number. It is also interspersed with general information on the government, the states, top companies, etc.

*Hindustan Year-Book and Who's Who – MC Sarkar & Sons*

Again, a long-established English language book. It contains very little biographical information, but as a yearbook for Hindustan and India as a whole it is quite useful. The quality of the binding is not of Western standards, but neither is the price.

*Indian Companies Handbook – Euromoney*

Compiled in association with *Capital Market*, the foremost investment fortnightly in India. For the top 300 companies by market capitalisation it provides financial and contact details. Also less detailed information on a further 200 companies. Basic information on many more companies can be found in Dun & Bradstreet's *Key Business Directory of India*.

**The press**

An Indian business magazine named *E-Square* occasionally publishes rich lists. *Business India* is a respected weekly magazine.

# Japan

Unfortunately many Japanese publications are available in Japanese only. Because of the difficulty of translating Japanese characters and the strength of the Yen you might like to look at resources in your own country.

Japanese embassies and trade organisations are normally good sources of information, for example JETRO (the Japan External Trade Relations Organisation) in cities such as London and New York has a business library and produces directories. It can probably recommend specialist Japanese book shops (examples in London are: The Japan Centre, Tel +44 (0) 171 439 8035; Books Nippon, Tel +44 (0) 171 248 4956; OCS Books, Tel +44 (0) 181 992 6335). Alternatively, you could try an information service such as that run by the British Library's Science Reference and Information Service (SRIS). Its Japanese Information Service (Tel +44 (0) 171 323 7924) will search the major online databases for you.

Investors in Japanese companies are often trade contacts such as suppliers who are interested in growth rather than profit. Companies form informal groups which cross-invest. In the US this pattern only tends to occur where companies are in common ownership, and cross-shareholdings are cancelled out in the accounts. In Japan it might appear less formal than outright ownership, but these linkages are very strong and you should always be aware of which group you are dealing with so that your other business dealings do not offend them.

Japan is a very formal society, so those unfamiliar with it should be particularly careful to learn the key points of etiquette before visiting. You must, for example, know how to show appropriate respect to a business card, how to obtain a useful introduction, and how to build and maintain a laborious but long-term relationship. There are numerous guides available, e.g. *Japanese Etiquette Today: A Guide to Business and Social Customs* by James M Vardaman Jr and Michiko Sasaki Vardaman (Charles E Tuttle). Alternatively, try *Japanese Business Etiquette* by Diana Rowland (Warner Books).

One peculiarity of the Japanese is their fondness for comic strips. Do not entirely discount cartoon style business books: they might appear light-hearted, but can still contain useful information.

*Japanese Resources: A Guide to Information on Japanese Business and Grantmaking Activities- Taft*

A useful starting point for those not familiar with Japanese research.

*Information Bulletin – Public Information & Cultural Affairs Bureau/Japan Times*

A yearbook full of brief English articles on agriculture, education, business, etc., as well as social matters such as female equality and the aging society. Interesting for its perspective on Japanese society rather than business information. Alternatives are *Japan – Profile of a Nation* (Kodansha International) or for straightforward facts *Japan Almanac* (Asahi Shimbun).

*Who's Who in Japan – Asia Press*

Although very expensive this book is light on detail with most entries running to just three or four lines. This possibly reflects the tendency of the Japanese to stay with the same employer long-term, which at least means that it does not date quite so rapidly. (This aspect of Japanese culture is now changing as the prolonged economic recession has shaken confidence and weakened the paternalistic 'jobs for life' ethos.)

Even so, if you have a serious interest in Japan it is difficult to do without this book. It features prominent figures from the fields of government, commerce and industry, medicine, journalism, education, and the arts. There is a marked predominance of men as this is still a relatively traditional society. Entries give name, current position, date of birth, where educated, career (minimal), honours, spouse's name, hobbies (frequently golf), home address and telephone number. It also indexes its biographies according to occupation, though the categories are possibly too broad to be of much use.

There is also a directory of institutions, government agencies, companies, universities, non-profit foundations, libraries and museums. This last section enables you to find, for example, the names, addresses, telephone numbers and sizes of companies involved in automobile sales or in construction.

If this publisher proves difficult to contact try a specialist Japanese book shop. You can also obtain a *Who's Who in Japan* from KG Saur (part of Reed) and a *Japan Society Directory* from Japan Press Ltd in Tokyo.

*Who's Who in Japanese Government – International Cultural Association*

The official guide to Japan's government. It includes organisational charts as well as detailed descriptions of the ministries.

*Japan Company Handbook – Toyo Keizai*

This claims to be the most comprehensive publication on Japanese corporations available in the English language. It appears in two small paperback volumes per quarter, which are also available separately. The first volume covers all corporations in First Section markets (Tokyo, Osaka, Nagoya), while the second covers the Second Section, OTC and local markets as well as over 200 unlisted firms.

Information includes five years' financials, activities, outlook, share price movements, major shareholders and foreign owners, and a couple of directors. It is arranged by industry. Be careful of the indexes as each volume also contains the index to the other.

Toyo Keizai also has other publications covering Japan and neighbouring countries (e.g. *Japanese Overseas Investment*) and provides an online service.

More expensive alternatives are Edinburgh Financial Publishing's *Guide to the Companies of Japan* and Diamond Lead's *Diamond's Japan Business Directory*. The latter includes brand and trade names and provides thorough two-page company profiles.

## *Industrial Groupings in Japan – Dodwell Marketing Consultants*

An immensely useful guide to affiliations amongst Japanese businesses. It lists the companies in each group, their degree of affiliation, major shareholders, etc. These links are of great importance in Japanese business so it is vital that you research them.

## *Access Nippon – Access Nippon Inc/William Snyder/The Reference Press*

How to live in and do business with Japan. Articles on the Japanese economy, specific industries, how to start up a business there (e.g. names of market research agencies), living in Japan (hotels, banking, holidays, etc.) and a directory of the largest companies. It includes industrial associations and major trade shows. A light-weight starter volume for Japanese research.

## *Japanese Addresses in the UK – Insight Japan*

This booklet, published in association with the Anglo-Japanese Economic Institute, lists the UK offices of Japanese companies together with their addresses and telephone numbers. They are divided up by business sector, but indexed at the back. You might wish to supplement this with *Japan Contact* (Brennan Publications), a newsletter about Japanese investment and involvement in the UK and Ireland. Brennan also produces a directory of Japanese companies and institutions in the UK and Ireland which is similar to but more expensive than Insight Japan's. Ask Japanese embassies for equivalents in other countries.

## Foundation Library Center of Japan

This gathers information on foundations that award grants, prizes or scholarships and provides information to the public. If you cannot visit its library it will reply to English language enquiries, though slowly and possibly including Japanese photocopies unless you specify that you do not understand the language.

It publishes a bimonthly journal (*Josei Zaidan*) and two directories of grant-making foundations and organizations in Japan, unfortunately all written in Japanese. Taft distributes the English language version of its book *Inside Japanese Support*. The US Foundation Center also sells publications on the subject and occasionally so does the Directory of Social Change. Another source is *Directory of Non-governmental Organizations in Japan Active in International Cooperation* from the Japanese NGO Center for International Cooperation.

Japanese foundations must decide which area of philanthropy they wish to support (e.g. education) and then register with the appropriate ministry. This means they tend to be rather narrower in their aims than US or UK ones. They are also more heavily influenced by the government, some being run by people who view themselves as government employees.

There is a fairly high proportion of large foundations linked with major companies, particularly as foundations cannot register for tax exemption unless their funds are over a certain size. Thus, although smaller civic groups do exist they can be difficult to track down. They might deliberately avoid registering to retain independence from the government.

The pattern and motivation for giving is different from that in the West. Personal philanthropy is not practised on a very large scale, but large companies feel bound to support their country. However you must be very careful to build a relationship slowly and carefully. A straightforward approach to the top person is likely to be considered vulgar and crass.

### The press

*Tokyo Business Today* from Toyo Keizai claims to be Japan's leading English language business and finance monthly. It combines overviews of the Japanese economy with in-depth reports on business, industry, politics and culture. The leading financial newspaper is *Nihon Keizai Shimbun ('Nikkei')* which occasionally publishes listings of Japan's top companies or highest taxpayers. It has sister publications such as the English language *Japan Economic Journal*. A less business-oriented alternative is *Japan Times*, a daily English language paper which takes an interest in Asia and the rest of the world and has an index.

### Electronic information

Most major international online services will include some access to the Japanese press in English. You can also go to the databases direct, for example through *Nikkei Telecom* or *Teikoku Databank*. The latter is particularly strong on Japanese companies and is also available via other hosts, e.g. Knight-Ridder.

# Korea (South)

*Korea Annual – Yonhap News Agency*

A yearbook covering politics, sport, social life, etc. It also includes a short who's who of the business world and the names of top government officials.

*Korean Business Directory – The Korea Chamber of Commerce and Industry*

A paperback listing of brief facts such as name of senior executive, capital, number of employees, activities. Companies are listed alphabetically, though indexed by industry.

*Korea Business and Industry Yearbook – InfoServ*

A much more detailed set of company profiles including financials. Also a great deal of analysis, for example on the *chaebols*, i.e. the huge conglomerates which dominate Korean business.

## The press

*Business Korea* provides monthly analyses of the business environment and industries.

# Malaysia

English is quite widely spoken in the more developed areas of Malaysia. The following sources are all in English.

*New Malaysian Who's Who – Kasuya Publishing*

These two volumes contain entries of varying lengths, but many are full and accompanied by pictures. There is also a very useful introductory section on the country, its royal families (who take it in turn to be overall 'king'), doing business in Malaysia, political parties, the states, titles and the honours system, etc.

*Key Business Directory of Malaysia – Dun & Bradstreet*

Basic factual information on 2500 of the largest companies. Lists of the top companies in Malaysia from different perspectives can be found in *The Times 1000* (Times newspapers/Reference Press) and *Review 200: Asia's Leading Companies Survey Report* (Review Publishing Co Ltd).

*Guide to the Companies of Singapore and Malaysia – Edinburgh Financial Publishing Ltd*

A standard company directory. An alternative is *Times Business Directory of Malaysia* (Times Trade Directories). This profiles both public and private companies giving the key two or three directors, business activities, etc., though no financials. *Corporate Handbook – Malaysia* (Thomson Information) covers listed companies only but provides financial and share price information plus a textual description, though again not the full list of directors.

*Information Malaysia Yearbook – Berita Publishing*

General information about the country.

## The Press

*The New Straits Times* is a major daily. Also of interest is the business magazine *Malaysian Business* (Berita). Although publishers in Malaysia might be linked with those in other countries, government restrictions might prevent sister companies from supplying the Malaysian press or even providing information regarding it. *The Star* is available over the Internet: *http://www.jaring.my/-star.*

# New Zealand

*Who's Who in New Zealand – Reed Elsevier plc*

A straightforward who's who with a good list of abbreviations. As with many major publishers, Reed is so huge that it might not know of this book's existence. If so mention that it comes from a subsidiary named Octopus Publishing Group (NZ) Ltd of 39 Rawene Road, Auckland.

*Marketing Guide to New Zealand Businesses – Dun & Bradstreet*

The 3000 largest businesses by turnover. Basic facts including contact details, a business description, finances, chief executive.

*A Directory of Philanthropic Trusts in New Zealand – New Zealand Council for Educational Research*

There is also a database produced by the Funding Information Service which is made available free of charge within New Zealand through Department of Internal Affairs Link Centres. The Directory contains some, but not all, of the information on this database.

### The press

Besides business coverage, *The National Business Review* publishes a New Zealand rich list.

# Singapore

Although Singapore and Malaysia are linked geographically and historically, they are very different in culture. Singapore's majority population is Chinese, and English is spoken almost universally. Singapore's growth has been such that it is now considered a developed country. Its employment levels are so high and its attractiveness to foreign firms is so great that it hosts large numbers of expats.

This is a small country, but if you want more information on business sources a report is available from Effective Technology Marketing Ltd. Times Books is a major publisher and bookshop in Singapore. It can supply books covering Singapore and the rest of the region.

*Leaders of Singapore – Resource Press Pte Ltd*

A large-scale book containing lengthy interviews with Singapore's major figures or, in the case of those now dead, their proud sons. Singapore has undergone a major transformation since the war and these are the politicians, business leaders, university founders, etc., who helped it happen. Even those who are dead are likely to be held in great reverence by their families as the founders of their fortunes, so this is useful background reading on the present day wealthy. Written by an academic and containing a historical introduction to the country.

*Singapore Government Directory – SNP Corpn Ltd*

A guide to the ministries and departments of the government. It explains the function of each, listing key officers and their telephone numbers. Published every six months.

*Guide to the Companies of Singapore and Malaysia – Edinburgh Financial Publishing Ltd*

A paperback company directory. An alternative is Thomson Information's *Corporate Handbook – Singapore*, another paperback which comes out twice a year and covers listed companies only. This is geared towards investors, providing financials, a breakdown by segment, ratios, share prices, shareholders, etc., as well as a textual description, though not the full list of directors.

As usual Dun & Bradstreet has a directory for this country, this one including a directory of directors. Alternatively *Times Business Directory of Singapore* (Times Trade Directories) cross-indexes by both personal names and products and also covers the government. It profiles both public and private companies giving the key two or three directors, business activities, etc., though no financials.

Lists of the top companies in Singapore from different perspectives can be found in *The Times 1000* (Times newspapers/Reference Press) and *Review 200: Asia's Leading Companies Survey Report* (Review Publishing Co Ltd).

*Emerging Civil Society in the Asia Pacific Community – Institute of Southeast Asian Studies*

An interesting chapter explaining the constraints on NGOs operating in Singapore and describing some of the major philanthropic foundations.

## The press

The Singaporean press is not very varied. The major newspaper – *The Straits Times* – is costly to obtain overseas, partly because it is very bulky. An alternative is *The Business Times*.

## Electronic sources

TCS (Television Corporation of Singapore) has produced a multimedia package on specific Singaporean entrepreneurs based on a television series. The Singapore government has set up a series of Internet pages on living and working in the country. *Singapore Infomap* gives information on business, government and culture and can be found at *http://www.sg*. The National Computer Board has a useful page giving links to various business and other sites at *http://www.ncb.gov.sg/index.html*. There are also various business directories, such as *Asia Business* at *http://www.asia-directory.com/-bruno*.

# Thailand

*The MFC Investment Handbook – The Mutual Fund Public Co Ltd/Reference Press/William Snyder*

A small paperback covering the companies listed on the Stock Exchange of Thailand (including major shareholders and directors' names). It includes a round-up of the past year's events in the Thai economy and the stock exchange, and the outlook for the coming year. The entries are organised by industry. A companion volume, *The Handbook of Mutual Funds*, covers unit trusts in more detail. As usual, basic information on a wider range of companies can be found through Dun & Bradstreet: *Key Business Directory of Indonesia & Thailand*.

## The press

*The Bangkok Post* is a lively daily which produces a weekly international edition. Also of interest is the monthly *Business Review* (Nation Publishing Group).

# Vietnam

*Vietnam Business Directory – The Chamber of Commerce and Industry of Vietnam in Singapore/The Reference Press*

A basic guide listing companies by city within industry groupings. There is also information on foreign organisations within Vietnam, and a profile of the economy, government, geography, etc.

## The press

The London-based *Vietnam Investment Review* provides a weekly overview of economic and business developments. An Internet source is VietGATE at *http://www.saigon.com*.

# 19. The United States

The information available here is unparalleled. It is also one part of the world where local prospect research manuals are already available. *Where the Money Is* (BioGuide Press) is clear, thorough and well worth obtaining if you intend to devote a lot of time to the US. CASE's *Prospect Research: A How-to Guide* is a rather older and less cohesive collection of articles.

While in other countries it is a struggle to find any information, in the US it is more a case of how to choose between all the alternatives. The Foundation Center and Taft publications are particularly useful starting points. It is also useful to have more general reference books such as *The Universal Almanac* or *The National Directory of Addresses and Telephone Numbers*, both of which are available from the Reference Press. However in such a large and wealthy country with so many prospects and so many sources it is impossible to list the ones which will be most useful to everyone.

Sources which cover the entire country can be useful for finding the biggest prospects; however the specialist American researcher will want to look for prospects which might not be ranked at national level but are still very significant, especially in their localities. Each city or state has its own character and regulations, and probably a range of sources devoted specifically to it. Local libraries should be able to suggest resources specifically designed for their own area.

Screening is big business in the US, taking information from the census, registrations of yachts or cars, household expenditure records, etc., depending on state regulations. There are many products available, for example POW&R. Advertisements in the fund-raising press will provide names. Which you choose depends on your own requirements in areas such as price, geographical coverage, information required, and ethical standards.

Another source which is possibly used more in the US than elsewhere is the public library. This is partly due to the fact that the US generates so many local reference sources that even the largest libraries could not hope to cover the whole country in such depth. Directory enquiries will give you the number of the one where your prospect lives. Over the phone they might read out an entry in a directory or agree (for a fee) to post you newspaper clippings. If it is a small place or your prospect is important the librarian might even be able to provide information himself, though it is just possible that in a small community news of your interest might reach the prospect. As usual, politeness and open-ended questions can often elicit unexpected results.

## People

In order to find a person's wealth you might start with the national lists such as those published by *Forbes* and *Fortune* magazines. Another source is Taft's *Guide to Private Fortunes* and its sister volumes. If the person does not appear in these then move to the local level. Many regional magazines produce occasional rich lists, e.g. *Texas Monthly*, *Chicago Magazine* and *Boston Magazine*. If you do not know where the list appears try asking a local library.

If the prospect is a company director look for details of his stock holdings and possibly remuneration in *Quantus* or *CDA/Spectrum*. If he is a lawyer try the *Am Law 100* list or *The National Law Journal*'s supplement on what lawyers earn.

If he does not appear in the rich lists you might use a publication such as *The Official Guide to American Incomes* or *American Salaries & Wages Survey* (Gale) to match up your prospect's characteristics with a typical income and expenditure pattern for similar people. Similarly, you could check the *National Zip Code Directory* (Claritas) which will give demographic information for each postal code.

Alternatively in some states you can gain access to records of car, yacht or aircraft ownership. You can look at plat books which detail real estate holdings (at title and trust companies) and check property maps for large land-owners. You can also visit the tax assessor's office for property assessments (be sure you check what date it was done). Records of the major donors to political parties might also be of interest.

Information on people can also be gleaned from company reports. Proxies give details such as age, directorships in other public companies and details of compensation for the top officers. In the last proxy before retirement there will also be a statement of retirement benefits, which can be substantial. The 'insiders' who have to provide information on their holdings range from 10% owners (or 5% if a takeover is likely), to directors, policy making officers, and holders of founder's stock. Through their filings it might be possible to detect gifts of stock, though these might sometimes be untraceable until the recipient sells them.

There is so much information available in the US that the problem is increasingly not how you find it, but rather whether you ought to find it. One particularly sore point is the social security number. Many databases use this to identify people, thus making it easier and cheaper to obtain all sorts of information if you routinely record it too.

Wills are another source of personal information. Again each state's procedures vary, but you might need to know details such as name, address and date of death. If a will exists it is likely to be in the county where the person died or had his main residence. It will be lodged with an official such as the Registrar of Wills or the County Probate Court and a copy will be sent to you for a fee.

Sources for unknown addresses and telephone numbers are official registers (voters, vehicle registrations, etc.) the US Postal Service National Change of Address database, telecom directories, and even credit agencies (TRW, Equifax, TransUnion, etc.). There are numerous ready-made databases which have already accumulated information from several sources. Some will do batch updates of large numbers of records or sell you a subscription to a CD-ROM while others will allow you online access. You could, for example, use Pro-Cd's *Prophone-Select*.

### *Prospect Researcher's Guide to Biographical Research Collections – Taft*

Although it is not updated every year, this is still a valuable resource for finding specialised sources. It tells you how to contact libraries, what services they offer, etc., vastly expanding the number of sources available to you. Taft has many other interesting publications, e.g. *Power Funding, FRI Prospect Research Resource Directory*, and *The American Prospector*.

### *Guide to Private Fortunes (3 vols) – Taft*

These books are specifically designed for fund-raisers, and are effectively basic, ready-made research reports. Each volume provides very full profiles of 1000 to 1250 of what are judged to be some of the wealthiest and most philanthropically inclined people in the US. They also include several overseas millionaires who do business in the US. Most are believed to have a minimum net worth of $25m and an established history of charitable giving. Information includes birthplace, family and education, contact address, wealth, career and philanthropic activities. They also provide brief historical essays on prominent philanthropic families such as the Rockefellers. They are extensively indexed by the following criteria: place of birth, state/country of residence, college/university, company, charitable affiliation, links with philanthropic foundations (private, corporate or community), and club affiliations. The volumes are cumulative, each claiming to cover the same range of wealth. Taft has too many useful publications to list here so ask for its catalogue.

### *The Rich Register and The Junior Rich Register – The Rich Register*

Founded by a former *Forbes* rich list compiler, these books are ideal for fund-raisers. They list over 2,200 Americans with net worths from $25m upwards. Each entry includes a business address and phone number (plus a residential one where available), a wealth estimate, source of wealth, alma mater, and a brief biography. To ensure that the books are totally up to date each is individually printed from the database only after receiving an order. Also available are *Mini Rich Registers* for specific states and diskette versions which can be merged with your own database.

## Who's Who In America – Marquis, part of Reed Elsevier

This is the pre-eminent US who's who. It is a three volume set covering more than 80,000 leading and influential Americans. The third volume indexes the entries by geographic location and occupation. It has a tendency to select people who are of worth to the community (educators, lawyers, hospice directors, etc.) rather than those who are merely wealthy or members of the establishment. This can be rather irritating to prospect researchers. It also includes some non-US people, notably Canadians and Mexicans.

If you want a still wider coverage of the US you might prefer to obtain its sister publications, e.g. *Who's Who in the West* (though the complete set would be rather expensive). There is also a *Who was Who in America* series going back to 1607.

There are Marquis who's whos for subjects as diverse as nursing, entertainment, religion, science and engineering, with a bias towards Americans. If you have access to the full range of Marquis who's whos there is also an overall index, available in book form or online through *Dialog* (Knight-Ridder) file 234. Smaller publishers produce city who's whos, e.g. if you are interested in Texan cities try RL Polk. These city directories can be quite informative, e.g. occupation, spouse's name and possibly children's names. Local libraries can help you find these.

## The Social Register – Social Register Association

A list of the names, addresses and telephone numbers of members of prominent families, the clubs to which they belong, colleges attended, and (in the summer edition) a list of yachts and their owners. Some cities publish their own registers (e.g. Washington DC is published by Thomas J Murray), but this is the national one. Social registers can provide useful information on family ties as they might group together members of the same family even if they are at different addresses. They are also useful sources of home addresses, but tend to protect their entrants' confidentiality by restricting their circulation.

## Lives in Trust: The Fortunes of Dynastic Families in Late Twentieth-Century America – Westview Press

This is more of an academic study of patterns within these families. They include the controllers of some of America's major philanthropic trusts. The book is slightly old, but good for obtaining an overview of the subject.

*Who's Who in American Politics – RR Bowker, part of Reed Elsevier*

Biographies of politicians plus lists of the Cabinet, US Courts of Appeals Judgeships, state representatives, etc. If you are more interested in contact details for post holders than in biographies the Yellow Books from Leadership Directories might be more useful.

*Who's Who in American Law – Reed Elsevier*

More than 27,800 biographies of leading attorneys, judges, educators, etc. Indexed by field of practice or interest.

*The Official ABMS Directory of Board Certified Medical Specialists – Marquis, part of Reed Elsevier*

Professional and biographical information on specialist physicians. As with lawyers, these are likely to be wealthy people.

*Reference Book of Corporate Managements – Dun & Bradstreet*

US business directories often contain better indexes than their foreign counterparts. However this one excels. Its four large volumes contain information on the top executives at over 12,000 leading companies including birth year, marital status, colleges attended, degrees earned, military service, current and former positions, etc. You can search by name, by company name, geographically or by business classification. Its advantage is its scope, including many executives who would not appear elsewhere.

*African-American Business Leaders – Greenwood Publishing Group*

A small but useful biographical dictionary of 123 African-American business leaders, many of them historical figures but some from the present day.

*Outstanding Women in Business and Outstanding Women in Government – Oryx Press/Eurospan*

Biographies of US women past and present from a broad range of social and ethnic backgrounds.

*Quantus – PC Research Services*

Details of US shareholdings, listed under the names of the officers and directors of 1500 publicly traded companies. It has the advantage of analysing shares according to whether they are held in the person's own interest or on behalf of someone else, or whether they are options to buy. It also lists shares held by foundations or charitable institutions which are of interest because they might indicate a philanthropic donation. Also a small amount of biographical information (such as alma mater) and remuneration where available. It is also indexed by company.

### The local courthouse

The type of information available varies between different states or even counties, and it can be time-consuming to search these records (though they are increasingly being made available through electronic sources). Your ethical code might debar you from using some of these sources. Non-US researchers might be astonished at what is available as many countries consider some of these documents to be too personal to be made available to the public. They are free and can yield useful information, particularly on wealth or for prospects who are not covered by published sources. The following are some examples of the information you might find.

Marriage records can tell you the spouse's name and a woman's maiden name. Probate gives information on inherited assets and names and addresses of heirs, and you might also find an inventory of the estate including business interests. Financing statements show details of loans such as value and any security that was offered. Property records or voter registration records can provide a home address. Property records might include details of the size and value of the house for taxation purposes, though the assessed value is not necessarily a very fair reflection of the market value. Mortgage, lien or sale documents might give a better value, as well as showing how much is borrowed against the property. Company records are also very useful (remember to check for trading names – 'doing business as' – as well as the prospect's own name). There are also litigation records of various types, e.g. divorces, if you are happy to make use of them.

### The press

There are too many publications to list here, but look out for society magazines such as *Town and Country*. Waltman Associates has produced an index to this particular title. A few other magazines provide their own index, but if you have access to them online there is no need for one. Due to the size of the US there are very many local papers which might be relevant. There are also journals devoted to specific ethnic groups, e.g. *Hispanic Business* which produces lists such as the largest Hispanic-owned businesses. Similarly *Irish America* produces a rich list of Irish Americans.

## Business

For information on public companies you might start with the annual report sent to shareholders. Official filings with the Securities and Exchange Commission (SEC) are also useful. These filings include: 10-Ks (similar to the annual report); 20-Fs (the equivalent of 10-Ks filed by non-US and non-Canadian companies); 10-Qs (quarterly reports); 8-Ks (exceptional events); and proxy statements (notification of dates and agendas of shareholder meetings).

Much of this information is available online, notably through *Disclosure* databases available on hosts such as Knight-Ridder's *Dialog* (files 541-4), *CompuServe*, and *Dow Jones*. *Disclosure* also produces a CD-ROM version called *Compact D/SEC*. Libraries sometimes maintain a collection of annual reports and proxies, or you can ask companies to send them to you. Alternatively you can contact the relevant state government office and ask for the Secretary of State's office (corporate annual reports and stock disclosure laws) or the Boards of Registration for professionals. A more recent source is the Edgar database on the Internet. This can be found at *http://town.hall.org/edgar/edgar.html*. There is a related listserv to which you can subscribe via *edgar-interest-request@town.hall.org*. Edgar's data is raw ASCII providing problems with formatting, field tagging, etc., so you might still find yourself using a product such as *Disclosure's EdgarPlus*.

There is no uniform system of company registration: states have their own laws and registries, and there is no guarantee that you will be able to see the records of an unlisted company. This is one reason why SEC filings are so useful. However private companies can be a problem. Dun & Bradstreet covers them though not in a great deal of detail. It might be necessary to look for probate and inventory records at the courthouse to work out who owns what and what it is worth (though if the death was not recent these might be out of date).

Lists of top companies in the New York area can be found in *Crain's New York Business*. Lists of top companies in 50 business sectors can be found in *The National Book of Lists* from the Reference Press. Alternatively Gale's *Business Rankings Annual* gives an even wider range of 'top ten' business lists for the US.

The US is Dun & Bradstreet's home territory so it provides a range of directories, including private companies, specific industries, credit information, industry norms and ratios, etc. Its *Reference Book of Corporate Management* even includes an index of university attendance. In comparison Hoover books are popular for providing quite detailed information on a relatively small number of the largest companies at a low price.

*How to Find Information About Companies – Washington Researchers Ltd*

Sources of company information with descriptions and contact details. Part 1 is organised by source, part 2 covers how to research each aspect of a company, and part 3 deals with the most difficult companies such as private companies, subsidiaries and foreign firms. These books are part of a series of similar publications. If you do not wish to spend so much you might prefer the source guides available from the Reference Press such as *Business Information Sources* or *Who Knows What.*

### American Companies – CBD Research Ltd

A guide to sources of information rather than to companies. It covers 50 countries in North, South and Central America plus the Caribbean. For each it provides details of the official registry, stock exchanges, credit reporting services, company directories, electronic sources, newspapers and periodicals, etc. It is more a list of sources than a description of how to use them. Alternatively Gale produces an *Encyclopaedia of Business Information Sources* for the US, arranged alphabetically and by subject.

### Walker's Corporate Directory of US Public Companies – Walker's Western Research/Macmillan

10,000 leading companies are profiled, giving five years of sales figures, directors, officers and subsidiaries. Well indexed by location, activity, related companies, and directors. For a much wider range of companies (135,000) you might prefer *Ward's Business Directory of US Private and Public Companies* from Gale.

### Hoover's Handbook of American Business – The Reference Press

This is a very popular, cheap and informative source of information on the largest US public and private companies. It also includes the top 'growth companies' and lists of the top performers in various categories. It is very user-friendly and contains more text than most business sources, though the number of companies is limited to 750. Interesting features include key competitors, overview of operations, lists of products, and names of executives.

### Hoover's Guide to Private Companies – The Reference Press

Profiles of the 500 largest privately owned enterprises in the US. Similar to *Hoover's Handbook of American Business.* It includes not only the majority of the companies in the *Forbes 400* list, but also cooperatives, joint ventures, large universities and hospitals, investment companies, governmental organisations, research institutes and foundations. It also makes a point of including the largest private black, Hispanic and female-owned enterprises.

### Hoover's Handbook of Emerging Companies – The Reference Press

250 US companies are profiled. These companies can move up or down very

rapidly, so the list alters considerably between editions. It includes both well known names and those with potential. An alternative (and available from the same supplier) is Moody's *The Inc 100 Handbook* which covers the finances, officers, contact details, etc., of America's fastest growing small public companies as identified by *Inc* magazine. These are worth tracking as the owners are likely to become very wealthy overnight.

### Hoover's Company and Industry Database on CD-ROM – *The Reference Press*

An amalgamation of Hoover's American Business, World Business, Emerging Companies, and Private Companies. These are supplemented by information from *US Industrial Outlook*, plus extra unprinted information. As well as company profiles it includes various comparative tables.

### Hoover's MasterList of Major US Companies – *The Reference Press*

Less information but more companies than the other Hoover guides. It includes every public company traded on the New York, AMEX and NASDAQ Exchanges plus 500 major private enterprises, some of the fastest growing companies, and some foreign-owned companies. The information is much more basic: contact details, names of key officers only, sales, number of employees, and type of products.

### The Texas 500 and The Bay Area 500 – *The Reference Press*

Focuses on the top companies in Texas and the San Francisco Area respectively. Over 50 in-depth profiles, the rest rather shorter. Includes both the largest names and growth companies. Also a useful overview of the area and its most important industries plus lists of top accountancy firms, banks, etc. Indexes by city and by industry.

### Corporate Yellow Book – *Leadership Directories Inc*

This provides lists of directors, officers and management at the largest public and private US firms. It gives their titles and direct dial numbers plus a small amount of information on what the company does. Its index is useful for finding a list of a person's corporate affiliations. Other 'Yellow Books' provide similar lists of people in politics, finance, associations, news media and the law. They are also available as CD-ROMs from Chadwyck-Healey.

### Directory of Directors in the City of New York and Tri-State Area – *Directory of Directors Co Inc*

For each of 3000 companies, partnerships and foundations this provides address, telephone and fax, activities and a list of directors. It includes some major companies from outside the area that have directors who live within it.

There is also a separate list of 15,000 people giving residential address (unless requested otherwise) and directorships (including non-profits). A geographical index lists the companies by state.

*Connections Files – Waltman Associates*

A set of directories of directors for various cities, e.g. Dallas, Houston, Denver, Atlanta. People are listed alphabetically with their primary affiliation (business, non-profit, civic, etc.). Also indexed by organisations, plus a who's who of business leaders, and top law firms, accountants, etc. Similar information is available from DDH Enterprises Inc: *The Relational Directory* series covers cities like Chicago, Detroit and St Louis.

*CDA/Spectrum Insider Holdings – CDA Investment Technologies Inc*

Details of shareholdings, listed by company. Taken from filings with the Securities and Exchange Commission (SEC) of the holdings of officers, directors and 10% principal stockholders ('insiders'). CDA also has various similar products. See also *Quantus* for listings by individual. If you use the online version (*Dialog* file 540) it is possible to search *Spectrum* by individual too.

*The Am Law 100 – The American Lawyer*

This is a supplement to the *American Lawyer* magazine. It provides a listing of the top 100 US law firms by gross revenue. Also listings of profits per partner, revenue per lawyer, profitability, compensation per partner and pro bono work. This could be supplemented by *The Insider's Guide to Law Firms* from the Reference Press which provides rankings, in-depth profiles and inside accounts of major law firms in a cheap and easy to use publication. For a complete list of American law firms and lawyers there is the 24-volume *Martindale-Hubbell Law Directory* from Reed Elsevier. This is also available online via the *Lexis/Nexis* service and on CD-ROM.

*The Directory of Management Consultants in the USA – AP Information Services*

Profiles of over 1600 consultancy firms giving a range of useful information including principals and key consultants and turnover. Indexed by specialisation, industry and location. Dun & Bradstreet also provides a *Consultants Directory*, as does Gale.

## The press

*The Wall Street Journal* has a sound reputation for financial journalism. There is a wide range of business magazines, *Forbes* and *Fortune* being popular. They include articles on industries, companies and executives, as well as listings of top companies and wealthiest people.

# Foundations and philanthropy

## The Foundation Center

Fund-raising is such big business in America that the Foundation Center produces books to suit every taste and purpose. There are directories of corporate giving, individual/foundation giving, giving to a specific type of charity (e.g. the environment), a directory which covers a large number of foundations in minimal detail, and others which cover a small number of foundations in greater detail. As well as information on the funders there are also books which focus on who received what.

Many US foundations will be irrelevant to overseas fund-raisers as they have restrictions on foreign gifts. If this is your situation then the best book to obtain would probably be *The Guide to Funding for International and Foreign Programs*. This gives addresses, finances, categories of gift, key officials, lists of sample gifts, and a range of indexes. Overseas purchasers should beware of the high postage and packing costs imposed by this organisation (20% of the price of the books).

If you are close enough you can visit one of the Center's information centers; there are numerous co-operating collections around the US. You can also ring for information if you become a member. Alternatively you could contact the relevant state's Attorney General's Office, the IRS (Internal Revenue Service), or the charity itself. There are also electronic products such as Orca Knowledge Systems' *Sources of Foundations* which enables you to search by key word. Foundation directories are also available via some of the major hosts, e.g. Knight-Ridder's *Dialog* and *CompuServe*.

The tax forms which private foundations must file each year with the IRS are called 990PFs (public charities file 990s). 990PFs contain information on finances, activities, a complete listing of grants, staff salaries, application guidelines, etc. The appropriate IRS Center will send you a copy of all or part of it for a modest fee though this might take four to six weeks. Locating the foundation is made easier if you know its EIN (employee identification number).

## Taft

Taft too provides a wide range of sources for the prospect researcher. The *Prospector's Choice* database contains 8000 profiles of top private foundations, corporate foundations and corporate direct giving programs, complete with biographical information on their officers and directors and listings of their more recent grants. It is well indexed, e.g. by officer/director name, and allows you to build up your own prospect lists on the basis of location, type of grant, etc. It is available on CD-ROM or diskettes and you have the choice of buying specific groups of states separately. There are many more useful products so ask for the catalogue. Overseas researchers might be particularly interested in *Directory of International Corporate Giving in America and Abroad.*

*Directory of Grants in the Humanities – Oryx Press/Eurospan*

Others in this series cover grants for higher education, research grants, and how to apply for grants.

*Directory of Directors in the City of New York and Tri-State Area – Directory of Directors Co Inc*

Unlike similar directories in other countries, this one includes non-profits amongst the companies. It is therefore possible to find boards of trustees and check a person's non-profit affiliations.

*National Directory of College and University Trustees – Waltman Associates*

Alphabetical list of people giving college or university and residence. Also addresses for all colleges and universities. It covers some 2000 four-year institutions in the US and Canada. Its importance lies in the likelihood that a trustee is also a donor.

*National Directory of Corporate Public Affairs – The Reference Press*

As well as listing over 13,500 public relations and public affairs professionals in over 1800 corporations this book provides key facts and figures on philanthropic and political action funding.

*Philanthropic Digest – American Prospect Research Association*

Monthly listing of US gifts and grants from corporations, foundations, individuals, etc., including bequests. It includes an annual supplement called *Million Dollar Gifts and Grants*. Historical information dating back to 1976 can also be obtained.

*US Foundation Support in Europe – Directory of Social Change*

Profiles of around 150 US foundations that have given support to European organisations, most of which are in the UK.

*Chronicle of Philanthropy and Chronicle of Higher Education*

These two journals provide news, reviews, information, job adverts, etc., for fund-raisers and those in higher education. They are very US-oriented. As American higher education establishments are heavily involved in fund-raising there is some overlap between the two. Although they are published by the same company, it insists on keeping payments and correspondence regarding the two publications entirely separate. Other newsletters on philanthropy can be obtained from Taft, the Council on Foundations, or CD Publications. There are also *Fund Raising Management* and the NSFRE's *Advancing Philanthropy*.

## Electronic information

There are very many US online suppliers, of which the following are only a sample.

*Dialog* (Knight-Ridder Information) is not only popular within the US; its American focus, link with the Europe-oriented *Data-Star*, and international availability make it a useful source for foreigners researching the US. Its hundreds of databases include numerous regional and national newspapers (which can be searched as a group) and business databases. The latter include: Dun & Bradstreet products (e.g. file 519 provides profiles of directors of private companies); annual reports and SEC filings (files 541-4); CDA/Spectrum (540); and Investext analysts' reports (545). There are also who's whos (234, 236, 287 – nb: they might provide only limited biographical information, or else merely tell you where to look); and foundations (26, 27, 85) as well as international information.

*America Online* is another popular service within the US, including a personal interest range of databases. It can be contacted on 1800 827 6364. *DataTimes* is widely used for its coverage of the US press and company information and is also available via other hosts, e.g. *Dow Jones*. The latter is particularly strong on US business. *Lexis/Nexis* is also useful, carrying files such as the *Martindale-Hubbell Law Directory* as well as the full text of the major US press.

An Internet discussion list favoured by business librarians is *buslib-l*. Send the message: subscribe buslib-l firstname lastname (i.e. your own name) to *listserv@idbsu.idbsu.edu*. Some journals are available on the Internet, e.g. DowVision (Wall Street Journal) at *http://dowvision.wais.net/*.

## Membership and training organisations

### APRA (Association of Professional Researchers for Advancement)

This US-based organisation is increasingly looking overseas for members, notably in Canada. As well as producing a newsletter it holds an annual conference at a different location in the US each year. Although this conference is costly it is well worth attending as it is an excellent way of learning the techniques of prospect research in America. APRA also publishes useful information on philanthropic gifts.

## CASE (Council for Advancement and Support of Education)

For fund-raisers in the field of education. It originated in the US and is still very much US-centred, but it recently opened a European office in London and claims members in 25 countries around the world. It holds conferences and training courses, publishes a newsletter, books and membership directory, and provides fund-raising information and services.

## NSFRE (National Society of Fund Raising Executives)

Membership body for fund-raisers.

# 20. Canada

Canada inevitably has close economic ties with its neighbour, the USA. Its main language is English, but there is a sizeable minority which speaks French as its mother tongue. French-speaking Quebec feels itself to be so different that it has even threatened to separate from the rest of Canada. When contacting the Quebec area you should therefore be prepared for a conversation in French. When buying books from Canada check what the price is without the local sales tax as you might not have to pay it, though the postage might outweigh that benefit. Also be aware that Canadian dollars are not the same as US dollars.

Some useful books on wealthy families have been written by Peter C Newman (e.g. *The Canadian Establishment* and *The Aquisitors*). Another interesting book is *Controlling Interest: Who Owns Canada* by Diane Francis.

*American Companies – CBD Research Ltd*

A guide to further sources of information rather than to companies. It covers 50 countries in North, South and Central America plus the Caribbean. For each it provides details of the official registry, stock exchanges, credit reporting services, company directories, electronic sources, newspapers and periodicals, etc.

*Canadian Who's Who – University of Toronto Press*

There are two who's whos for Canada, with confusingly similar sounding names. This is much larger than *Who's Who in Canada*, but it does not contain photos. If you are very interested in Canada it might be worth acquiring its index (which dates back to 1898) together with microfiche copies of old editions, which are available from the same publisher. Even from the earliest editions biographees were chosen on merit alone rather than being charged for inclusion, and if they do not wish to provide an entry there is no obligation to do so. This is a respected publisher with a wide range of titles including *Canadian Books in Print* and *Dictionary of Canadian Biography*.

*Who's Who in Canada – Gage Distribution Company or International Press Publications*

This is much smaller than the other who's who, but it has the advantage of containing photos and a cross-reference section for companies and government officials.

*Who's Who in Canadian Business – Canadian Business Media Ltd*

This publisher also produces *Who's Who of Canadian Women* and business magazines.

*The Canadian Address Book – International Press Publications*

As its name suggests, this book provides otherwise difficult to obtain addresses for more than 2000 important Canadians (some of whom live overseas). It covers the worlds of sport, entertainment, literature, business, politics, art, education, etc.

*Canadian Almanac & Directory – Canadian Almanac & Directory Publishing Co Ltd – Toronto/Gale – USA/Europa – UK.*

A long-established and thorough almanack giving standard coverage of Canada's geography, history, government, economy, sport, current events, etc., as well as general world information. The same publisher also produces *The Register of Canadian Honours* and *Associations Canada*.

*The Blue Book of Canadian Business – Canadian Newspaper Services/ International Press Publications*

This claims to be the most comprehensive directory available on Canada's leading business enterprises. It provides impressive textual profiles of top public, private and government-owned Canadian companies including names of principal officers and directors and some executive profiles. Also company rankings by sales, assets, net income, advertising expenditures and stock trading, including a reprint of *Canadian Business* magazine's ranking of top companies.

*Canada Company Handbook – International Press Publications, Reference Press, or William Snyder*

Data on over 1500 Canadian public and private companies compiled by Canada's leading financial newspaper, *The Globe and Mail.* They include all current and former Toronto Stock Exchange 300 companies. Information includes rankings, brief descriptions, contact details and executives' names. Dun & Bradstreet also provides a range of Canadian directories.

*Directory of Directors – International Press Publications*

This provides the names, business and residential addresses, degrees and colleges, and corporate affiliations of over 16,000 officers and directors of Canadian corporations. Also organised by company name. IPP also distributes *Who's Who in Canadian Business* (Trans-Canada Press) and *Best in the Business* as well as many more Canadian and international directories which are too numerous to list here. Ask for the full catalogue.

*The Directory of Corporate Giving in Canada – Rainforest Publications*

Policy statements on donations for the largest Canadian companies. Rainforest also publishes other books useful to fund-raisers.

*Canadian Directory to Foundations – The Canadian Centre for Philanthropy*

A comprehensive guide to the major foundations in Canada plus 50 US foundations with a history of giving to Canada. It is indexed by foundations, fields of interest, geographical location, recipient organisation and individuals. It is thus possible to see what similar organisations to your own have received.

The Centre is also able to do a search of its database for foundations that would serve your particular purpose. It publishes a newspaper for fund-raisers called *Front and Centre* and can send you a bibliography on resources for fund-raisers. Another source is *The Directory of Private Foundations* from Rainforest Publications. Alternatively International Press Publications can supply a smaller directory of foundations including an index by region entitled *Canadian Book of Charities*.

*Charitable Donations Database – Statistics Canada*

Organised by postal area, this database permits you to see the number of tax-filers, charitable donors, average donation, average age of donors, median income of donors, etc. You can choose to buy particular areas, for example the major cities.

**The press**

Canada's leading financial newspaper is *The Globe and Mail*. *Canadian Business* magazine produces an annual ranking of the top companies (which is reprinted in *The Blue Book of Canadian Business*) and occasional salary surveys. *The Financial Post* is also a good source of surveys as well as producing useful directories. *Canadian Business* and its sister publication, *Profit*, are produced by Canadian Business Media Ltd. For fund-raisers there are *Canadian FundRaiser* (a newsletter from Hilborn) and the Canadian Centre for Philanthropy's *Front and Centre*.

**Electronic information**

*Infoglobe* and *Infomart* are sources of online information on Canada, as are some of the big US hosts. There are also CD-ROMs such as *Canadian Business and Current Affairs* and *The Canadian News Disc*, as well as *Disclosure's Compact D/Canada* for corporate records. A useful Internet site can be found at *gopher://gord.asdo.uwo.ca/*.

# 21. The Rest of the World

## Latin America

Information on Central and Southern America is quite hard to come by, which is unfortunate as some of these countries have substantial numbers of millionaires. See the break-downs in the *Forbes* and *Fortune* international rich lists for an indication of just how important these countries are. Prospects are likely to come from this ultra-rich class as there is a relatively small middle class and the poor are extremely poor.

The region's stock markets are generally much less developed than in North America, Europe or the Far East. Mexico, being close to the US, has one of the largest stock markets in the area and some of the best corporate information. Because of the weakness of their own markets companies that want to raise money often look overseas; thus corporate information might be gleaned from sources such as US SEC filings or Eurobond prospectuses. Internal information is weak. Information on private companies is particularly difficult to obtain, though Argentina makes an attempt to collect it. As in other regions, the results of public companies can be found in the official publications of their stock markets as well as in official registries (which may be decentralised). However the accuracy or timeliness of corporate filings cannot always be relied upon. You should also be conscious of the need to take inflation into account.

Political and economic volatility is a factor in this region. Changes in government and the level of inflation can be dramatic. Most of the region is primarily Spanish-speaking, though a notable exception is Brazil whose main language is Portuguese. The people are culturally diverse (e.g. Peru recently had a president of Japanese origin), and English speakers are not uncommon.

*American Companies – CBD Research Ltd*

A guide to further sources of information rather than to companies. It covers 50 countries in North, South and Central America plus the Caribbean. For each it provides details of the official registry, stock exchanges, credit reporting services, company directories, electronic sources, newspapers and periodicals, etc.

*Latin American Markets: A Guide to Company and Industry Information Sources – Washington Researchers*

Sources of business information on every country in Central and South America and the Caribbean. Written from a US perspective but including international sources. For a more specific focus on Chilean business sources there is a report available from Effective Technology Marketing Ltd.

*Country Business Guide Series – Argentina and Mexico – Reference Press*

Overviews of the economic and business environment of each country.

*Who's Who in Latin America – Norman Ross Publishing Inc*

Biographies of more than 2000 prominent individuals in 35 countries, including the Caribbean. It covers most spheres, including government, politics, banking and industry. It is compiled from multilingual questionnaires completed by the biographees themselves with gaps filled in where possible from secondary sources. Although slim it is a useful acquisition.

*Biographical Dictionary of Latin American and Caribbean Political Leaders – Greenwood Publishing Group*

Somewhat out of date by now but it might still be of interest.

*Who's Who in Mexico Today – Westview Press*

A small book and infrequently published, but it might prove useful if you are particularly interested in this country. This publisher produces various academic books on Latin America.

*Hoover's MasterList of Major Latin American Companies – The Reference Press or William Snyder*

Mini-profiles of the top 1250 public and private companies in 20 Latin American countries. Information is basic: contact details, key officers, industry descriptions, sales and employment data. A wider range of companies can be found in Dun & Bradstreet's directories. Graham & Whiteside also produces a clearly laid out directory.

*Latin American Handbook – Moody's*

A useful overview of the major companies in the region giving finances, executive officers, nature of business, etc. Also country profiles.

*Company Handbooks – Mexico, Brazil, Venezuela, Argentina – Reference Press or William Snyder*

This series provides profiles of each country's major companies and investment funds. They also describe the economy, trade situation, accounting principles, investment advisors, etc.

*Trade Directory of Mexico – The Reference Press*

Over 4200 Mexican companies involved in foreign trade are listed. Also a profile of Mexico and its states and listings of over 2000 organisations supporting foreign trade such as consultants and transportation companies.

*Latin American Companies Handbook – Euromoney*

How the region's top listed companies are performing. Contact details and figures for investors. Euromoney also produces country profiles, again designed for investors.

### Foundations

*The Mexican Center on Philanthropy* can help for what is possibly one of the more accessible countries in Latin America. Even there philanthropy cannot compare with the US. There are occasional directories for other countries, e.g. *Primera guia Uruguaya de Fundaciones 1995s* (Universidad Catolica Del Uruguay, Montevideo) which contains information on 75 foundations in Spanish. Generally it might be more profitable to approach wealthy people as there are so many worthy causes within these countries and so few sources.

*Latin America Monitor – Business Monitor International*

It reports on government, the economy, finance and the business environment in each of several specific countries. The focus is on the overall picture rather than individual companies.

*Latin American Newsletters – Lettres (UK) Ltd*

A range of services on specific countries and the region as a whole, for example *Latin American Weekly Report*. Primarily political summaries with occasional information on business.

## The Middle East

Royal families are particularly prominent in this region, especially those which control the oil. The forms of democracy which exist in these countries are influenced by Islam and by traditional hierarchical structures. This should be considered when deciding what sort of contacts would be appropriate.

Although it is sometimes assumed that women are subordinate in this region, in some countries philanthropy is considered to fall within the domain of the wife; you should therefore not automatically neglect her when arranging meetings. It is best to seek advice on whether or not it would be considered appropriate to meet her as well.

Corporate information is difficult to obtain in many countries of the region. Israel and Jordan are improving, but elsewhere it can be a problem. Where there is massive personal wealth investment can be kept private.

Muslim communities in both the Arabic world and elsewhere, e.g. Malaysia, tend to share common features in their names, though spellings vary. There are often words for 'son of' (e.g. *bin* or *ibn*), or 'daughter of' (*binti*). Increasingly people have the opportunity to go on pilgrimages, which they commemorate by adding a word to their name (often abbreviated to *hj*). Because the name Mohammed is so common it may be abbreviated to *Mohd* or even *Md*.

## Asian & Australasian Companies – CBD Research Ltd

A guide to further sources of information rather than to companies. It has a particularly broad coverage of 69 countries ranging from Western Samoa to Saudi Arabia. For each it provides details of the official registry, stock exchanges, credit reporting services, company directories, electronic sources, newspapers and periodicals, etc. Although the space devoted to the Middle East is relatively brief and some of the details are a little out of date it is still a very valuable source. A report on business sources specifically for Israel is available from Effective Technology Marketing Ltd.

## The Middle East & North Africa – Europa

Details of the historical, political, business and geographical backgrounds of each country in the region. Also contact details for regional and national organisations. These are particularly important in a region where relatively little is published in English. There are various alternatives, for example Kogan Page's *The Middle East Review*.

## Who's Who in the Arab World – KG Saur, part of Reed Elsevier

Over 6000 biographies plus a regional survey and geographical directory. It covers the 19 Arab League countries including foreign residents. A smaller sister volume is *Who's Who in Lebanon*.

### Jewish who's whos

It is difficult to separate Israeli from Jewish directories. Jewish people are often seen as an interesting group because they have a strong sense of identity, include some very wealthy people, and take a strong interest in certain projects.

Who's whos can be disappointing because they are likely to focus heavily on Israel and the US rather than being truly international. The most prominent people are likely to have declined to send in an entry and as with any smaller publisher it is possible that the last edition is now quite old.

One example is *Who's Who in Israel & Jewish Personalities Abroad* from the publisher of the same name. *Who's Who in World Jewry* is a much larger book (though a little old) and is available from the publisher of the same name or from Bowker-Saur (part of Reed). Kuperard can supply books such as *Jewish Profiles* and *Ethical Wills: A Modern Jewish Treasury*. A useful adjunct is *The Jerusalem Post* which is available on CD-ROM, or *Link*, an Israeli business magazine.

*Major Companies of the Arab World – Graham & Whiteside*

A long-established directory providing a useful listing of directors and senior executives as well as contact details, parent and some subsidiaries, bankers, principal shareholders, and a little financial information.

*Major Financial Institutions of the Arab World – Graham & Whiteside*

A new directory covering the major banks of the region including foreign banks based there, investment companies, and insurance and reinsurance companies. It gives contact details, names of directors and senior executives, branches and subsidiaries, finances, principal shareholders, etc.

*Asia-Pacific/Africa-Middle East Petroleum Directory – Penwell Directories*

A country by country listing of companies involved in exploration, marketing, refining, etc., in the Middle East and Asia. It includes narrative overviews of the industry as well as company profiles complete with lists of executives. Indexed by company and geographically.

*Arab British Companies Directory – London Chamber of Commerce and Industry*

Chambers of Commerce are good sources of information on links between your country and a specific region. Occasionally they consider information on their members to be confidential, but as in this case they sometimes produce directories. Saudi Arabian embassies might also be willing to send you free newsletters or magazines covering events in their country.

*Middle East Monitor – Business Monitor International*

It reports on government, the economy, finance and the business environment. The same publisher also produces annual in-depth reports on specific countries. The focus is on the overall picture rather than individual companies.

## Electronic information

As it can be so difficult to find information in this region you are likely to rely quite heavily on the press. One useful database is Reuter's *Textline* (on several hosts, including Knight-Ridder's *Dialog*). Hosts often carry a limited range of specific newspaper databases: *Dialog* and *Dow Jones* are relatively good, while *Lexis/Nexis* also has a few.

There are also sources on the Internet, though as always you should be aware they might be politically biassed and they might have disappeared the second time you look for them. The Saudi Embassy in the US has created a site at *http://imedl.saudi.net*. For news on Iran go to *http://www.maple.net/iranet*. High-tech Egyptian companies can be found at *http://162.121.10.41/tdp/doc/main.htm*.

# Africa

Although there is a great deal of poverty in Africa, those with money are often exceptionally comfortable. South Africa is both wealthy and well served by reference books. Several directories, especially those published in South Africa itself, cover 'Southern Africa' which is a region dominated by but not exclusively consisting of the country known as 'South Africa'. The information available on South Africa is generally very good, and Zimbabwe is also not bad; however coverage of the rest of Africa is patchy. Where who's whos do exist they might be ethnically, politically or economically exclusive.

As imperial ties weaken even those who were born and educated in Europe are increasingly likely to think of an African country as home. This means they are more likely to give their money and attention to projects within Africa, unless they can be persuaded that other countries can provide services (e.g. educational scholarships) which are of benefit to their home country and cannot be obtained there. There is so much need within the continent that it is difficult for non-African causes to have much success.

Until recently the fact that South Africa was looked upon with disapproval meant that it was often boycotted by international publishers. It is now staging a come-back, and its considerable wealth ensures that it is not likely to be overlooked. However it is taking a while for non-South African publishers to restore links.

### *Africa Who's Who, Africa Today, and Makers of Modern Africa – Africa Books Ltd*

Otherwise known as the *Know Africa* series, these comprehensive volumes cover living people, the continent, and dead people respectively. *Africa Today* provides a country by country survey of history, politics, geography, economics, population, government, etc. *Africa Who's Who* attempts to cover eminent personalities from all walks of life, and though some countries inevitably dominate it manages a reasonable spread. The third volume is slightly smaller and probably of less interest to the prospect researcher.

### The Africa Book Centre (London)

This is an example of a bookshop which specialises in African books. It can obtain books such as *Who's Who in Africa, New African Yearbook,* and *Who's*

*Who in Zimbabwe*. They are mostly relatively cheap. This bookshop has an academic bent, but can obtain a variety of directories on request.

*The African Business Handbook – The Reference Press*

A guide for those wishing to invest in Africa. Overviews of individual countries and information on the institutions that facilitate trade between Africa and the US. Its value is not in information on individual companies but as a source of background information and further leads.

*Who's Who of Southern Africa – Who's Who of Southern Africa*

A large, informative publication complete with numerous photographs. Several of the entrants have also provided information on the company they work for (activities, telephone number, etc.). Most of the entrants are white, probably due to the economic dominance of this group. The majority of entries are South African, but there is also some information on Botswana, Lesotho, Malawi, Mauritius, Namibia, Swaziland and Zimbabwe. In addition there are country guides, lists of politicians and diplomats, a guide to forms of address, and details of universities.

*Direct Access to Key People in Southern Africa – Who's Who of Southern Africa*

Basic contact details (names, addresses, telephone numbers) for politicians, officials of government departments, diplomats, offices of agencies and councils, etc. It is primarily South African, but also covers Botswana, Lesotho, Malawi, Namibia, Swaziland and Zimbabwe.

*Who's Who in South African Politics – Hans Zell, part of Reed Elsevier*

Detailed biographical essays on the top 130 people in current politics, accompanied by photos.

*The Donor Community in South Africa: A Directory – Institute for International Education*

*Who's Who in Nigeria – Newswatch Communications Ltd*

The cheapness of this book is probably more a reflection on the quality of the materials than the information. It is a sizeable, thorough who's who, and it is unfortunate that it has not progressed beyond its first edition.

*Major Companies of Africa South of the Sahara – Graham & Whiteside*

The largest 3000 companies in the region. An impressive attempt to cover a great many countries, though information is not always possible to obtain in every case. About a third of the companies covered are in South Africa.

## McGregor's Who Owns Whom – Juta Subscription Services

This is far more than a who owns whom. It is a summary of the annual reports of every company listed on the Johannesburg, Namibian, Botswanan and Zimbabwean Stock Exchanges. It also gives a two-year history of shareholders holding above 1% of the ordinary shares of the company and the author's assessment of who the ultimate controlling shareholder is. This last is no small achievement as many of these companies turn out to be members of the same huge family with multiple cross-shareholdings. 'Family trees' in the front of the book help explain this. There are also indexes of shareholders, directors, subsidiaries and associate companies, and investments. Also a list of companies by sectors.

## Fundraising Forum – Downes, Murray International

This newsletter provides brief articles on fund-raising, some summarising other sources. Downes, Murray is actually part of an international fund-raising consultancy. For further information on grant-makers there is a relatively new organisation named *SAGA* (Southern Africa Grantmakers Association) which aims to make information about its members more widely available.

## Help Yourself – Help Yourself

A guide to fund-raising in Southern Africa. This covers the whole spectrum of fund-raising. It also has useful information on over 300 trusts and foundations in South Africa, North America and Europe, plus addresses for South Africa's top companies.

## The press

*Newswatch* is a weekly magazine focusing on Nigerian politics and business. A more general view of Africa can be obtained from the bi-monthly *Africa Today*. They share the same London distributor (see under Newswatch). The Johannesburg-based *Financial Mail* occasionally produces a rich list for South Africa.

## Electronic sources

Related to *McGregor's Who Owns Whom* is *McGregor's Online Information* which claims to be the definitive database on corporate southern Africa. Alternatively you can obtain information and overviews of companies on the Johannesburg Stock Exchange through the Internet at *http://www.africa.com/*. A list of South African web sites is available at *http://www.is.co.za/www-za/www-za-map.html*.

Apart from southern Africa, information can be very difficult to obtain. There are a few press databases, particularly Reuter's *Textline* (on several hosts, including Knight-Ridder's *Dialog*). As well as *Dialog*, *Dow Jones* and *Lexis/Nexis* carry a few specific journals and briefing services.

## SAIF (Southern Africa Institute of Fundraising)

This is a membership organisation for fund-raisers operating in South Africa and the neighbouring countries. It holds a biannual convention to which international speakers are invited. It is leading the way for groups in other African countries.

# 22. Addresses

All telephone and fax numbers are given in their international form. As countries use different international codes the convention is to place '+' in front of the number to signify that you add the appropriate code (e.g. within the UK you would dial 00 for an international number, so to obtain the US number +1 202 333 3499 you would actually dial 00 1 202 333 3499.) The first group of numbers after the '+' is the country code (1 is for North America). The next group is the town or region code, where one exists (202 is for Washington).

If you are dialling from within the country you should ignore the national code. In some countries you should insert a '0' in front of the number. Thus the UK number +44 (0) 1865 278111 would become 01865 278111 when dialled from within the UK.

**3W International Digital Publishing Corp**
300 Atrium Way, Suite 252, Mt Laurel, NJ 08054, USA.
Tel +1 609 273 9588. Fax +1 609 231 0518.

**AAFRC Trust for Philanthropy**
25 West 43rd Street, New York, NY 10036, USA.
Tel +1 212 354 5799.

**Abercorn Hill Associates**
74 Crewys Road, London NW2 2AD, UK.
Tel +44 (0) 171 624 6340.

**Access Nippon Inc**
604 Samariya Bldg, 1-17-1 Sugamo, Toshima-ku, Tokyo 170, Japan.
Tel +81 3 5395 4800. Fax +81 3 5395 4803.

**AffärsForlaget**
Box 3188, S-103 63 Stockholm, Sweden.
Tel +46 8 736 56 00. Fax +46 8 789 88 42.

**Affärsvarlden**
S-106 12 Stockholm, Sweden.
Tel +46 8 796 65 00. Fax +46 8 20 21 57.

UK distributor: Eagle (Business) Publishing Ltd, PO Box 6090, London SW19 1XQ, UK. Fax +44 (0) 181 544 1292.

**Africa Book Centre Ltd**
38 King Street, Covent Garden, London WC2E 8JT, UK.
Tel +44 (0) 171 240 6649. Fax +44 (0) 171 497 0309.

**Africa Books Ltd**
3 Galena Road, Hammersmith, London W6 0LT, UK.
Tel +44 (0) 181 746 3646. Fax +44 (0) 181 741 4890.

**Akateeminen Kirjakauppa**
PO Box 128, Fin-00101, Helsinki, Finland.
Tel +358 0 121 41. Fax +358 0 121 4249.

**The American Lawyer**
600 Third Avenue, New York, NY 10016, USA.
Tel +1 212 973 2800. Fax +1 212 972 6258.

**America Online**
8619 South Westwood Center Drive, Vienna, Virginia 22182, USA.
Tel +1 703 448 8700.

**AP Information Services**
Roman House, 296 Golders Green Road, London NW11 9PZ, UK.
Tel +44 (0) 181 455 4550. Fax +44 (0) 181 455 6381.

**APRA (Association of Professional Researchers for Advancement)**
414 Plaza Drive, Suite 209, Westmont, IL 60559-1265, USA.
Tel +1 708 655 0177. Fax +1 708 655 0391. Email: apra@adminsys.com.

**Arguments and Facts International**
PO Box 35, Hastings, East Sussex TN34 2UX, UK.
Tel +44 (0) 1424 442741. Fax +44 (0) 1424 442913.

**The Arts Council of England**
Information Department, 14 Great Peter Street, London SW1P 3NQ, UK.
Tel +44 (0) 171 973 6531. Fax +44 (0) 171 973 6590.

**Asahi Shimbun**
5-3-2, Tsukiji, Chuo-ku, Tokyo 104-11, Japan.
Tel +81 3 3545 0131.

**Asia Inc**
31/F Citicorp Centre, 18 Whitfield Road, Causeway Bay, Hong Kong.
Tel +852 2508 3388.

**Asia Press Co Ltd**
4th floor, Dowa Building, (Kyodo PR), 2-22 Ginza 7-chome, Chuo-Ku, Tokyo 104, Japan.
Tel: +81 3 3571 5171. Fax: +81 3 3574 1005.

**Asian Observer Publications**
47 Beattyville Gardens, Barkingside, Ilford, Essex IG6 1JW, UK.
Tel +44 (0) 181 550 3745. Fax +44 (0) 181 551 0990.

**Asiaweek Ltd**
34/F Citicorp Centre, 18 Whitfield Road, Causeway Bay, Hong Kong.
Tel +852 2512 5678. Fax +852 2512 9775.

**Aslib (The Association for Information Management)**
Information House, 20-24 Old Street, London EC1V 9AP, UK.
Tel +44 (0) 171 253 4488. Fax +44 (0) 171 430 0514.
Email: *aslib@aslib.co.uk*, WWW: *http://www.aslib.co.uk/*

**Assecuranz Compass**
Avenue Moliere 256, 1060 Brussels, Belgium.
Tel +32 2 345 1983. Fax +32 2 343 1668.

**Australian Association of Philanthropy Inc**
4th Floor, 20 Queen Street, Melbourne, Victoria 3000, Australia.
Tel +61 3 9614 1491. Fax +61 3 9621 1492.

**Australian Financial Review Books**
PO Box N542, Grosvenor Place, NSW 2000, Australia.
Tel +61 2 241 5385.

**Bangkok Post**
Tel +66 2 240 3700. Fax +66 2 240 3790.

**Barons Who's Who**
412 N. Coast Hwy, B-110, Laguna Beach, CA 92651, US.
Tel +1 714 497 8615. Fax +1 714 786 8918.

**Belenos Publications Ltd**
50 Fitzwilliam Square, Dublin 2, Republic of Ireland.
Tel +353 1 676 4587. Fax +353 1 661 9781.

**Berita Publishing**
31 Jalan Riong, 59100 Kuala Lumpur, Malaysia.
Tel +60 3 282 3131. Fax +60 3 282 4280.

**BiblioData**
PO Box 61, Needham Heights, MA 02194, USA.
Tel +1 617 444 1154. Fax +1 617 449 4584.

**BioGuide Press**
PO Box 16072-B, Alexandria, VA 22302, USA.
Tel +1 703 820 9045.

**A&C Black (Publishers) Ltd**
Howard Road, Eaton Socon, Huntingdon, Cambs PE19 3EZ, UK.
Tel +44 (0) 1480 212666. Fax +44 (0) 1480 405014.

US: St Martin's Press, Scholarly & Reference Books Division, 257 Park
Avenue South, 18th floor, New York, NY 10010, USA.
Tel +1 212 726 0200. Fax +1 212 777 6359.

**The Blewbury Press**
Pound House, Church Road, Blewbury, Oxon OX11 9PY, UK.
Tel +44 (0) 1235 850110. Fax +44 (0) 1420 478664.

**BNL Information AB**
Stora Nygatan 45, Box 2208, 103 15 Stockholm, Sweden.
Tel +46 8 24 54 25. Fax +46 8 10 34 75.

**A/S Forlaget Børsen**
Børsens Boger, Møntergade 19, DK-1140 København K, Denmark.
Tel +45 33 32 01 02. Fax +45 33 93 54 22.

**Bottin SA**
4 rue André Boulle, 94000 Créteil, France.
Tel +33 49 81 53 53. Fax +33 42 07 78 79.

**Brainstorm Publishing Ltd**
4 Post Office Walk, Fore Street, Hertford, Herts SG14 1DL, UK.
Tel +44 (0) 1992 501177. Fax +44 (0) 1992 500387.

**Brennan Publications**
148 Birchover Way, Allestree, Derby DE22 2RW, UK.
Tel/fax +44 (0) 1332 551884.

**The British Library Science Reference and Information Service (SRIS)**
Turpin Distribution, Blackhorse Road, Letchworth, Herts SG6 1HN, UK.
Tel +44 (0) 1462 672555 (British Library section). Fax +44 (0) 1462
480947.

Further information: SRIS,
Tel +44 (0) 171 323 7472. Fax +44 (0) 171 323 7947.

### Burke's Peerage

Premier House, Hinton Road, Bournemouth BH1 2EF, UK.
Tel +44 (0) 1202 299277. Fax +44 (0) 1202 291505.

### Business India

Tel +91 22 204 2253. Fax +91 22 204 1974.

### Business Korea Co Ltd

CPO Box 8819, Seoul 100-688, South Korea.
Tel +82 2 234 4010. Fax +82 2 253 4040.

### Business Monitor International

56-60 St John Street, London EC1M 4DT, UK.
Tel +44 (0) 171 608 3646. Fax +44 (0) 171 608 3620.

### Business Spain

5 Newton Road, Wimbledon, London, SW19 3PJ, UK.
Tel +44 (0) 181 540 8520. Fax +44 (0) 181 542 9185.

### BusinessWeek International

PO Box 647, Hightstown, NJ 08520-0647, USA.

Europe: McGraw-Hill House, Shoppenhangers Road, Maidenhead,
Berkshire SL6 2QL, UK.
Tel +44 (0) 1628 23431.

### CAFE (Creative Activity for Everyone)

The City Arts Centre, 23-25 Moss Street, Dublin 2, Republic of Ireland.
Tel +353 1 677 0330. Fax +353 1 671 3268.

### Canadian Business Media Ltd

777 Bay Street, 5th Floor, Toronto, Ontario M5W 1A7.
Tel +1 416 596 5100.

### The Canadian Centre for Philanthropy

1329 Bay Street, 2nd Floor, Toronto, Ontario M5R 2CP, Canada.
Tel +1 416 515 0764. Fax +1 416 515 0773.

### Canadian Newspaper Services International Ltd

65 Overlea Blvd, Suite 207, Toronto, Ontario M4H 1P1, Canada.

**Carrick Media**
2-7 Galt House, 31 Bank Street, Irvine, Scotland KA12 0LL, UK.
Tel/fax +44 (0) 1294 311322.

**Cartermill Publishing (part of Pearson)**
UK: Maple House, 149 Tottenham Court Road, London W1P 9LL, UK.
Tel +44 (0) 171 896 2424. Fax +44 (0) 171 896 2449.

US: Stockton Press, 49 West 24th Street, New York, NY 10010-3206, USA.
Tel +1 212 627 5757. Fax +1 212 627 9256.

Asia: Asia Pacific Business and Professional, Cornwall House, 2nd Floor,
Taikoo Place, Quarry Bay, Hong Kong.
Tel +852 2811 8168. Fax +852 2856 9578.

**CASE (Council for Advancement and Support of Education)**
Suite 400, 11 Dupont Circle, Washington, DC 20036-1261, USA.
Tel +1 202 328 5900. Fax +1 202 387 4973.

CASE Europe, Third Floor, 23 Neal Street, London WC2H 9PU, UK.
Tel +44 (0) 171 240 8017. Fax +44 (0) 171 240 8071. Email
cboswell@eurocase.demon.co.uk.

**CBD Research Ltd**
Chancery House, 15 Wickham Road, Beckenham, Kent BR3 2JS, UK.
Tel +44 (0) 181 650 7745. Fax +44 (0) 181 650 0768.

**CDA Investment Technologies Inc**
1355 Piccard Drive, Rockville, MD 20850, USA. Fax +1 301 590 1365.

**CD-ROM Verlag und Vertrieb GmbH**
Merkurhaus Am Hauptbahnhof 12, W-6000 Frankfurt-am-Main, Germany.
Tel +49 69 27 100 258. Fax +49 69 27 100 210.

**Cedar Tree House**
7-9 Church Hill, Loughton, Essex IG10 1QP, UK.
Tel/fax: +44 (0) 181 508 8856.

**Centro de Fundaciones**
Don Ramón de la Cruz 36, 2°, 28001 Madrid, Spain.

**Cerved SpA**
Via Aristide Staderini 93, 00155 Roma, Italy.
Tel +39 6 22 59 11. Fax +39 6 22 59 12 55.

## Chambers & Partners Publishing
74 Long Lane, London EC1A 9ET, UK.
Tel +44 (0) 171 606 2266.

## Chapter One Group Ltd
Green Lane, Tewkesbury, Gloucestershire GL20 8EZ.
Tel +44 (0) 1684 850040. Fax +44 (0) 1684 850113.

## Charities Aid Foundation
Kings Hill, West Malling, Kent ME19 4TA, UK.
Tel +44 (0) 1732 520000.

## The Charity Commission
St Alban's House, 57-60 Haymarket, London SW1Y 4QX, UK.
Tel: +44 (0) 171 210 4405/4533/4477.

Graeme House, Derby Square, Liverpool L2 7SB, UK.
Tel: +44 (0) 151 227 3191.

Woodfield House, Tangier, Taunton, Somerset TA1 4BL, UK.
Tel: +44 (0) 1823 345000/345030.

## Charterhouse Business Publications
PO Box 66, Wokingham, Berkshire RG11 4RQ, UK.
Tel +44 (0) 1734 772770. Fax +44 (0) 1734 774522.

## China Business Review
1818 North Street NW, Suite 500, Washington DC 20036-5559, USA.
Tel +1 202 775 0340. Fax +1 202 775 2476.

## The China Phone Book Co Ltd
See Review Publishing Co Ltd.

## CHM Consultants Ltd
6 Stoneleigh Crescent, Ewell, Surrey KT19 0RP, UK.
Tel/fax +44 (0) 181 393 3885.

## Chronicle of Higher Education
PO Box 1955, Marion, Ohio 43305-1955, USA.

## Chronicle of Philanthropy
PO Box 1989, Marion, Ohio 43305-1989, USA.

## Chr. Schibsteds Forlag A/S
Postboks 1178 Sentrum, 0107 Oslo, Norway.
Tel +47 22 86 30 00. Fax +47 22 42 54 92.

**City Press**
Seatrade House, 42-48 North Station Road, Colchester CO1 1RB, UK.
Tel +44 (0) 1206 45121. Fax +44 (0) 1206 45190.

**Community Affairs Briefing**
14 Soho Square, London W1V 5FB, UK.
Tel +44 (0) 171 287 6676. Fax +44 (0) 171 287 8139.

**CompuServe**
5000 Arlington Centre Blvd, PO Box 20212, Columbus, Ohio 43220, USA.

1 Redcliff Street, PO Box 676, Bristol BS99 1YN, UK.
Tel +44 (0) 117 976 0681.

**Computers & Geotechnics**
27 Henrefoilan Drive, Sketty, Swansea SA2 7NG, UK.
Tel +44 (0) 1792 208373.

**Corporate International Ltd**
9/F Shun Ho Tower, 30 Ice House Street, Central, Hong Kong. Fax: +852 2845 7271.

**Crédit Suisse**
PO Box 590, CH-8021 Zürich, Switzerland.
Tel +41 1 249 2121. Fax +41 1 249 2978.

**Croner Publications Ltd**
PO Box 291, Croner House, London Road, Kingston-upon-Thames, Surrey KT2 6SX, UK.
Tel +44 (0) 181 547 3333. Fax +44 (0) 181 547 2638.

**Council on Foundations**
1828 L Street NW, Washington DC 20036, USA.
Tel +1 202 466 6512.

**Danish Foreign Trade Information Office**
Hellerupvej 78, DK-2900 Hellerup, Denmark.
Tel +45 31 611 611. Fax +45 31 611 169.

**Danish Ministry of Foreign Affairs**
Asiatisk Plads 2, DK-1448 København K, Denmark.
Tel +45 33 92 00 00. Fax +45 33 54 05 33.

**Databank SpA**
Via dei Piatti 11, I-20123 Milano, Italy.
Tel +39 2 80 95 56. Fax +39 2 80 56 495.

**DB-Data Informations-Service**
Postfach 10 06 11, D-60006 Frankfurt am Main, Germany.
Tel +49 69 71007 460. Fax +49 69 71007 322.

**DDH Enterprises Inc**
3930 North Pine Grove Street, Suite 1111, Chicago, IL 60613-3359.
Tel +1 312 880 0089.

**Debrett's Peerage Ltd**
73/77 Britannia Road, PO Box 357, London SW6 2JY, UK.
Tel +44 (0) 171 736 6524. Fax +44 (0) 171 731 7768.

**Devon Publishing**
2700 Virginia Avenue, NW, Washington, DC 20037, USA.
Tel +1 202 337 5179.

**Diamond Lead Co**
4-2, Kasumigaseki 1-chome, Chiyoda-ku, Tokyo 100, Japan.
Tel +81 3 3504 6791. Fax +81 3 3504 6798.

**Dicodi SA**
Doctor Castelo, 10, 4º, E-28009 Madrid, Spain.
Tel +34 1 573 70 02. Fax +34 1 504 01 34.

**Directory of Directors Co Inc**
PO Box 462, Southport, CT 06490-0462, USA.
Tel/fax +1 203 255 8525.

**The Directory of Social Change**
24 Stephenson Way, London NW1 2DP, UK.
Tel +44 (0) 171 209 5151. Fax +44 (0) 171 209 5049.

**Disclosure**
5161 River Road, Bethesda, MD 20816, USA.
Tel +1 301 961 2789. Fax +1 301 718 2343.

26-31 Whiskin Street, London EC1R 0BP, UK.
Tel +44 (0) 171 278 8277. Fax +44 (0) 171 278 3898.

**Dod's Parliamentary Companion**
(Not to be confused with DPR Publishing whose books look similar.)
PO Box 3700, Westminster, London SW1E 5NP, UK.
Tel +44 (0) 171 828 7256. Fax +44 (0) 171 828 7269.

**Dodwell Marketing Consultants**
CPO Box 297, Tokyo 100-91, Japan.
Tel +81 3 211 4451.

**Donors Magazine**
CVSS, Compton Martin, Bristol BS18 6JP, UK.
Tel +44 (0) 1761 221810. Fax +44 (0) 1761 221910.

**Dow Jones Business Information Services**
PO Box 300, Princeton, NJ 08543-0300.
Tel +1 609 520 4000.

10 Fleet Place, London EC4M 7RB, UK.
Tel +44 (0) 171 832 9690. Fax +44 (0) 171 832 9861.

**Downes, Murray International**
4th floor, 641 Ridge Road, Durban, 4001, South Africa.
Tel +27 31 2073755. Fax +27 31 296643.

**DPR Publishing Ltd**
(Originally linked with Dod's Parliamentary Companion, but now a separate
company.)

33 John Street, London WC1N 2AT, UK.
Tel +44 (0) 171 753 7762. Fax +44 (0) 171 753 7763.

**Dudley Jenkins List Broking Ltd**
2A Southwark Bridge Office Village, Thrale Street, London SE1 9JG, UK.
Tel +44 (0) 171 407 4753. Fax +44 (0) 171 407 6294.

**Dun & Bradstreet Ltd**
Three Sylvan Way, Parsippany, NJ 07054-3896, USA.
Tel +1 800 526 0651.

Holmers Farm Way, High Wycombe, Bucks HP12 4UL, UK.
Tel +44 (0) 1494 422000. Fax +44 (0) 1494 422260.

Dun & Bradstreet (HK) Ltd, 12/F, K Wah Centre, 191 Java Road, North
Point, Hong Kong.
Tel +852 2516 1350. Fax +852 2562 6147.

**The Economist and Economist Intelligence Unit**
PO Box 14, Harold Hill, Romford RM3 8EQ, UK.
Tel +44 (0) 1708 381555. Fax +44 (0) 1708 381211.

111 West 57th Street, New York, NY 10019, USA.
Tel +1 212 541 5730. Fax +1 212 541 9378.

25/F Dah Sing Financial Centre, 108 Gloucester Road, Wanchai, Hong Kong.
Tel +852 2585 3888. Fax +852 2802 7638.

### Edinburgh Financial Publishing Ltd

14/F 75-77 Wyndham Street, Central, Hong Kong.
Tel +852 2869 8969. Fax +852 2804 6492.

### Editions Apogée

4 Bd Gaëtan Hervé, 35200 Rennes, France.
Tel +33 99 32 45 95. Fax +33 99 32 45 98.

### Editions Delta

55 rue Scailquin, B-1030 Bruxelles, Belgium.
Tel +32 2 217 55 55. Fax +32 2 217 93 93.

### Editions Jacques Lafitte

38 rue de Constantinople, 75008 Paris, France.
Tel +33 1 45 22 05 05. Fax +33 1 45 22 51 08.

### Editions Jean-François Doumic

5 rue Papillon, F-75009 Paris, France.
Tel +33 1 42 46 58 10. Fax +33 1 40 22 07 18.

### Editorial Campillo SL

Azalea 521, Soto de la Moraleja, 28109 Alcobendas (Madrid), Spain.
Tel +34 1 650 48 82. Fax +34 1 650 86 15.

### Effective Technology Marketing Ltd

Enterprise House, PO Box 171, Grimsby DN35 OTP, UK.
Tel/fax +44 (0) 1472 699027.

### ELC
ELC International, 109 Uxbridge Road, Ealing, London W5 5TL, UK.
Tel +44 (0) 181 566 2288. Fax +44 (0) 181 566 4931.

### Elvetica Edizioni SA
PO Box 134, CH-6834 Morbio, Switzerland.
Tel +41 91 435056. Fax +41 91 437605.

### Erlandsson Ltd
Reprovägen 6, S-183 64 Täby, Sweden.
Tel +46 8 630 10 60. Fax +46 8 756 57 40.

**Euromoney Publications**
Nestor House, Playhouse Yard, London EC4V 5EX, UK.
Tel +44 (0) 171 779 8999. Fax +44 (0) 171 779 8400.

**Euromonitor plc**
60-61 Britton St, London EC1M 5NA.
Tel +44 (0) 171 251 1105. Fax +44 (0) 171 251 0985.

111 West Washington Street, Suite 920, Chicago, Illinois 60602, USA.
Tel +1 312 541 8024. Fax +1 312 541 1567.

**Europa Publications**
18 Bedford Square, London WC1B 3JN, UK.
Tel +44 (0) 171 580 8236. Fax +44 (0) 171 636 1664.

**European Foundation Centre**
51 rue de la Concorde, B-1050 Brussels, Belgium.
Tel +32 2 512 8938. Fax +32 2 512 3265.

**L'Européenne de Données**
164 rue d'Aguesseau, F-92100 Boulogne-Billancourt, France.
Tel +33 1 46 05 29 29. Fax +33 1 46 05 42 55.

**Europrospects Ltd**
38 Mount Pleasant, London WC1X 0AP, UK.
Tel +44 (0) 171 833 5621. Fax +44 (0) 171 278 4707.

**The Eurospan Group**
3 Henrietta Street, Covent Garden, London WC2E 8LU, UK.
Tel +44 (0) 171 240 0856. Fax +44 (0) 171 379 0609.

**Extel Financial Ltd (part of the Financial Times group)**
Fitzroy House, 13-17 Epworth Street, London EC2A 4DL, UK.
Tel +44 (0) 171 825 8000. Fax +44 (0) 171 251 2725.

Asia-Pacific: ExTel Financial Ltd, Suite 3603A, 36/F One Exchange Square,
8 Connaught Place, Central, Hong Kong.
Tel +852 2524 3226. Fax +852 2596 0946.

US: ExTel Financial Inc, One Norwalk West, 40 Richards Avenue, Norwalk,
Connecticut CT 06854, USA.
Tel +1 203 857 7400. Fax +1 203 957 7444.

**Far East Trade Press Ltd**
Block C, 10/F, Seaview Estate, 2-8 Watson Road, North Point, Hong Kong.
Tel +852 2566 8381. Fax +852 2508 0197.

US distributor: World Publications Service, 19 Union Avenue, Suite 202, Rutherford, New Jersey 07070, US.
Tel +1 201 531 0760. Fax +1 201 531 0827.

### Federation of Hong Kong Industries
4th Floor, Hankow Centre, 5-15 Hankow Road, Tsimshatsui, Kowloon, Hong Kong.
Tel +852 2723 0818. Fax +852 2721 3494.

### Financial Times Annual Reports Service (UK)
Westmead House, 123 Westmead Road, Sutton, Surrey SM1 4RZ, UK.
Tel +44 (0) 181 770 0770. Fax +44 (0) 181 770 3822.

### Fondation de France
40 avenue Hoche, F-75008 Paris, France.
Tel +33 16 44 21 31 00. Fax +33 16 44 21 31 01.

### Forbes
Forbes Inc, 60 Fifth Avenue, New York, NY 10011, USA.
PO Box 10051, Des Moines, IA 50340-0051, USA.

### Fortune
Time & Life Building, Rockefeller Center, New York, NY 10020, USA. Fax +1 212 765 2699.

Europe: Time & Life Building, Ottho Heldringstraat 5, 1066 AZ Amsterdam, The Netherlands.
Tel +31 20 510 4911. Fax +31 20 617 5077.

### The Foundation Center
Sales Dept, 79 Fifth Avenue, New York 10003-3076, USA.
Tel +1 212 620 4230. Fax +1 212 807 3677. http://fdncenter.org/.

### Foundation Library Center of Japan
YKB Shinjuku-gyoen Building 5F, 1-3-8 Shinjuku, Shinjuku-ku, Tokyo 160, Japan.
Tel +81 3 3350 1857. Fax +81 3 3350 1858.

### Fourth Estate Ltd
289 Westbourne Grove, London W11 2QA, UK.
Tel +44 (0) 171 727 8993. Fax +44 (0) 171 792 3176.

US: Trafalgar Square Publishers, Box 257, Howe Hill Road, North Pomfret, Vermont 05053, USA.
Tel +1 802 457 1911. Fax +1 802 457 1913.

### Frankfurter Allgemeine Zeitung GmbH
Information Services, D-60267 Frankfurt am Main, Germany.
Tel +49 69 7591 2219. Fax +49 69 7591 2178.

US distributor for papers: European Business Publications Inc, PO Box 891, Darien, Connecticut 06820, USA.
Tel +1 203 656 2701. Fax +1 203 655 8332.

### FT-Profile
Fitzroy House, 13-17 Epworth Street, London EC2A 4DL, UK.
Tel +44 (0) 171 825 8000. Fax +44 (0) 171 825 7999.

### FunderFinder Ltd
65 Raglan Road, Leeds LS2 9DZ, UK.
Tel +44 (0) 113 243 3008. Fax +44 (0) 113 243 2966.

### Funding Digest
4 The Terrace, Ovingham, Northumberland NE42 6AJ, UK.
Tel +44 (0) 1661 832296.

### Fundraising Australasia
PO Box 458, Lutwyche, Qld 4030, Australia.
Tel +61 7 857 8668. Fax +61 7 857 8288.

### Fund Raising Management
224 Seventh Street, Garden City, NY 11530-5771, USA.
Tel +1 516 746 6700. Fax +1 516 294 8141.

### Gage Distribution Company
164 Commander Bld, Agincourt, Ontario, M1S 3C7, Canada.
Tel +1 416 293 8141. Fax +1 416 293 0846.

### Gale Research Inc (see also Taft)
835 Penobscot Bldg, 645 Griswold St, Detroit, MI 48226-4094, USA.
Tel +1 313 961 2242. Fax +1 313 961 6083.

UK distributor: Gale Research International, PO Box 699, Cheriton House, North Way, Andover SP10 5YE, UK.
Tel +44 (0) 1264 342962. Fax +44 (0) 1264 342763.

### GBI (Gesellschaft für betriebswirtschaftliche Information mbH / German Business Information)
Freischützstrasse 96, 81927 München, Germany.
Tel +49 89 957 0064. Fax +49 89 957 4229.

### Genios Wirtschaftsdatenbanken
Grosse Eschenheimerstrasse 16-18, W-6000 Frankfurt-am-Main 1, Germany.
Tel +49 69 92 01 91 04. Fax +49 69 29 56 27.

### Graham & Whiteside
Tuition House, 5-6 Francis Grove, London SW19 4DT, UK.
Tel +44 (0) 181 947 1011. Fax +44 (0) 181 947 1163.

### Graphic Arts Center Publishing Co
PO Box 10306, Portland, OR 97210, USA.
Tel +1 503 226 2402. Fax +1 503 226 1410.

### Greenwood Publishing Group
3 Henrietta Street, Covent Garden, London WC2E 8LU, UK.
Tel +44 (0) 171 240 0856. Fax +44 (0) 171 379 0609.

### Groupe Expansion Magazines SA
Le Ponant, 25 rue Leblanc, F-75842 Paris Cedex 15, France.
Tel +33 1 40 60 40 60. Fax +33 1 40 60 41 22.

### Groupe Juris Service
12 quai André Lassagne, 69001 Lyon, France.
Tel +33 78 27 00 38. Fax +33 78 28 93 83.

### Guida Monaci SpA
I-00189 Roma, Via Vitorchiano 107-109, Italy.
Tel +39 6 333 1333. Fax +39 6 333 5555.

### HandelsZeitung Publications
Seestrasse 37, CH-8027 Zürich, Switzerland.
Tel +41 1 288 3546. Fax +41 1 288 3577.

### Hansib Publishing
Third Floor, Tower House, 141-149 Fonthill Road, London N4 3HF, UK.
Tel +44 (0) 171 281 1191. Fax +44 (0) 171 263 9656.

### HarperCollins Publishers
Westerhill Road, Bishopbriggs, Glasgow G64 2QT, UK.
Tel +44 (0) 141 772 2281.

10 E 53rd Street, New York, NY 10022, USA.
Tel +1 212 207 7000. Fax +1 212 207 7617.

### Otto Harrassowitz
Taunusstrasse 5, PO Box 2929, 65019 Wiesbaden, Germany.
Tel +49 611 530 0. Fax +49 611 530 560.

**Help Yourself**
Box 50676, Waterfront, 8002, South Africa.

**Hemmington Scott Publishing Ltd**
City Innovation Centre, 26-31 Whiskin Street, London EC1R OBP, UK.
Tel +44 (0) 171 278 7769. Fax +44 (0) 171 278 9808.

**Hibernian Publishing Co Ltd**
22 Crofton Road, Dun Laoghaire, Co. Dublin, Republic of Ireland.
Tel +353 1 2808 415. Fax +353 1 2808 309.

**Hilborn Group**
109 Vanderhoof Avenue, Suite 205, Toronto, Ontario M4G 2H7, Canada.
Tel +1 416 696 8816. Fax +1 416 424 3016.

**Hispanic Business**
HB Inc, 360 South Hope Avenue #300C, Santa Barbara, CA 93105-4017, USA
Tel +1 805 682 5843.

**Hollis Directories Ltd**
Harlequin House, 7 High Street, Teddington, Middlesex TW11 8EY, UK.
Tel +44 (0) 181 977 7711. Fax +44 (0) 181 977 1133.

**Henry Holt and Co Inc**
115 West 18th Street, New York, NY 10011, USA.
Tel +1 212 886 9200. Fax +1 212 633 0748.

**Hong Kong Government Social Welfare Dept**
Office of the Director, 8/F Wu Chung House, 197-221 Queen's Road East,
Wanchai, Hong Kong.
Tel +852 2892 5290. Fax +852 2838 0757.

**Hong Kong Productivity Council**
Management and Industrial Consultancy Division, HKNC Building, 78 Tat
Chee Avenue, Kowloon, Hong Kong.

**Hong Kong Tattler**
1811 Hong Kong Plaza, 188 Connaught Road West, Hong Kong.

**Verlag Hoppenstedt & Co**
Havelstrasse 9, D-64295 Darmstadt, Germany.
Tel +49 6151 380 0. Fax +49 6151 380 360.

**ICFM (Institute of Charity Fundraising Managers)**
Market Towers, 1 Nine Elms Lane, London SW8 5NQ, UK.
Tel +44 (0) 171 627 3436. Fax +44 (0) 171 627 3508.

## IDS (Incomes Data Services Ltd)
193 St John Street, London EC1V 4LS, UK.
Tel +44 (0) 171 250 3434. Fax +44 (0) 171 608 0949.

## IIS (Institute of Information Scientists)
44-45 Museum Street, London WC1A 1LY, UK.
Tel +44 (0) 171 831 8003. Fax +44 (0) 171 430 1270.

## Infa Publications
Jeevan Deep, Parliament Street, New Delhi-110001, India.
Tel +91 11 343330/31/32. Fax +91 11 3746788.

## Information Australia Group Pty Ltd
45 Flinders Lane, Melbourne 3000, Australia.
Tel +61 3 654 2800. Fax +61 3 650 5261.

## Informed Business Services
41-47 Old Street, London EC1V 9HX, UK.
Tel +44 (0) 171 490 2811. Fax +44 (0) 171 490 4068.

## InfoServ
PO Box 923, Yongdungpo-gu, Seoul 150-609, South Korea.
Tel +82 2 785 0909. Fax +82 2 785 5340.

## Ingerstedt Publishing
rue Gabrielle 13, B-1180 Bruxelles, Belgium.
Tel +32 2 346 3976. Fax +32 2 344 1704.

## Inland Revenue, Claims (Scotland)
Trinity Park House, South Trinity Road, Edinburgh EH5 3SD, UK.
Tel +44 (0) 131 551 8127.

## Insight Japan
19 Hugh Street, London SW1V 1QJ, UK.
Tel (Anglo-Japanese Economic Institute) +44 (0) 171 637 7872.

## Institute for International Education
809 UN Plaza, New York, NY 10017-3580, USA.

## Institute of Southeast Asian Studies
Heng Mui Keng Terrace, Pasir Panjang, Singapore 119596.
Tel +65 778 0955. Fax +65 775 6259.

## Intercontinental Book Publishing Co
10 rue du Mont Dore, 75017 Paris, France.
Tel +33 1 43 87 04 93.

**International Biographical Centre**
Melrose Press Ltd, 3 Regal Lane, Soham, Ely, Cambridgeshire CB7 5BA.
Tel: +44 (0) 1353 721091. Fax: +44 (0) 1353 721839.

**International Business Development**
181 avenue Charles de Gaulle, F-92200 Neuilly-sur-Seine, France.
Tel +33 1 46 37 93 93. Fax +33 1 46 37 06 51.

**International Cultural Association**
30-9, Sakuragaoka-cho, Shibuya-ku, Tokyo 150, Japan.
Tel +81 3 3463 4633. Fax +81 3 3463 4675.

**The International Fund Raising Group**
295 Kennington Road, London SE11 4QE, UK.
Tel +44 (0) 171 587 0287. Fax +44 (0) 171 582 4335.

**International Philanthropy**
24 Concord Street, Fairfield, CT 06430, USA.
Tel +1 203 319 1011. Fax +1 203 319 1012.

**International Press Publications Inc**
90 Nolan Court, Suite 21, Markham (Toronto), Ontario L3R 4L9, Canada.
Tel +1 905 946 9588. Fax +1 905 946 9590.

**Irish America**
PO Box 209, Pearl River, New York, NY 10965, USA.
Tel +1 212 725 2993.

**Peter Isaacson Publications Pty Ltd**
46-50 Porter Street, Prahran, Victoria 3181, Australia.
Tel +61 3 245 7777. Fax +61 3 245 7605.

**Japanese NGO Center for International Cooperation**
5F, Saito Bldg, 2-9-1 Kanda Nishiki-Cho, Chiyoda-ku, Tokyo 101, Japan.
Tel +81 3 3294-5370. Fax +81 3 3294 5398.

**JETRO (The Japanese External Trade Organisation)**
Leconfield House, Curzon Street, London W1, UK.
Tel +44 (0) 171 493 7226.

This has offices and business libraries in various locations, e.g. New York,
Tel +1 212 997 0400.

**Japan Times**
The Japan Times Circulation Dept, 5-4, Shibaura 4-chome, Minato-ku,
Tokyo 108. Fax +81 3 3452 1298.

**Jordan & Sons Ltd**
21 St Thomas Street, Bristol BS1 6JS, UK.
Tel +44 (0) 117 923 0600. Fax +44 (0) 117 923 0063.

**Juta Subscription Services**
PO Box 14373, Kenwyn 7790, South Africa.
Tel +27 21 797 5101. Fax +27 21 762 7424.

**Kasuya Publishing Sdn Bhd**
Suite 5.54-5.56, 5th floor, Wisma Central (Box #322), 147 Jalan Ampang,
50450 Kuala Lumpur, Malaysia.
Tel +60 3 2622080. Fax +60 3 2621885.

**Kauppakaari-yhtymä Oy**
Uudenmaankatu 4-6 A, FIN-00120 Helsinki, Finland.
Tel +358 0 647 101. Fax +358 0 611 230.

**Knight-Ridder Information Inc**
2440 El Camino Real, Mountain View, CA 94040, USA.
Tel +1 415 254 7000. Fax +1 415 254 7070.

Knight-Ridder Information Ltd, Haymarket House, 1 Oxendon Street,
London SW1Y 4EE, UK.
Tel +44 (0) 171 930 5503. Fax +44 (0) 171 930 2581.

**Kogan Page**
120 Pentonville Road, London N1 9BR, UK.
Tel +44 (0) 171 278 0433. Fax +44 (0) 171 837 6348.

**Kompass – see Reed Information Services Ltd**

**The Korea Chamber of Commerce and Industry**
CPO Box 25, Seoul 100, South Korea.
Tel +82 2 316 3114. Fax +82 2 757 9475.

**Kraks Forlag AS**
Virumgårdsvej 21, DK-2830 Virum, Denmark.
Tel +45 45 83 45 83. Fax +45 45 83 10 11.

**Kuperard (London) Ltd**
No 9 Hampstead West, 224 Iverson Road, West Hampstead, London NW6
2HL, UK. Tel +44 (0) 171 372 4722. Fax +44 (0) 171 372 4599.

**The Law Society**
Directories Dept, Law Society House, 50 Chancery Lane, London WC2A
1SX, UK. Tel +44 (0) 171 242 1222. Fax +44 (0) 171 831 0869.

**Mr Alastair Layzell**
c/o Colonial American, PO Box 341, Jersey, Channel Islands.
Tel +44 (0) 1534 43678. Fax +44 (0) 1534 46613.

**Leadership Directories Inc**
2nd Floor, 104 Fifth Avenue, New York, NY 10011, USA.
Tel +1 212 627 4140. Fax +1 212 645 0931.

**Learned Information (Europe) Ltd**
Woodside, Hinksey Hill, Oxford OX1 5AU, UK.
Tel +44 (0) 1865 730275. Fax +44 (0) 1865 736354.

**Legalease**

28-33 Cato Street, London W1H 5HS, UK.
Tel +44 (0) 171 396 9292. Fax +44 (0) 171 396 9300.

**Lettres (UK) Ltd.**

61 Old Street, London EC1V 9HX, UK.
Tel +44 (0) 171 251 0012. Fax +44 (0) 171 253 8193.

**Lexis/Nexis**

International House, 1 St Katherine's Way, London E1 9UN, UK.
Tel +44 (0) 171 369 1300.

**The Library Association**

7 Ridgmount Street, London WC1E 7BR, UK.
Tel +44 (0) 171 636 7543. Fax +44 (0) 171 436 7218.

**Link**

PO Box 57500, Tel Aviv, 61574, Israel.
Tel +972 3 5624949. Fax +972 3 5628512.

**London Business School**

CIS-Middle Europe Information Service, Sussex Place, Regent's Park,
London NW1 4SA, UK.
Tel +44 (0) 171 706 6870. Fax +44 (0) 171 402 8979.

**London Chamber of Commerce and Industry**

33 Queen Street, London EC4R 1AP, UK.
Tel +44 (0) 171 248 4444. Fax +44 (0) 171 489 0391.

**Macmillan Press Ltd**
Houndmills, Basingstoke, Hampshire RG21 2XS, UK.
Tel +44 (0) 1256 29242 or 1256 817245. Fax +44 (0) 1256 842084.

**MAID**
MAID plc, The Communications Building, 48 Leicester Square, London
WC2H 7DB, UK.
Tel +44 (0) 171 930 6900. Fax +44 (0) 171 930 6006.

Market Analysis & Information Database Inc, 655 Madison Avenue, 12th
Floor, New York, NY 10022, USA.
Tel +1 212 750 6900. Fax +1 212 750 0660.

**Manager Trade Publishing Ltd**
7/F Ka Nin Wah Commercial Building, 423-425 Hennessy Road, Wanchai,
Hong Kong.
Tel +852 2838 3181. Fax +852 2573 2362.

**Meadowbrook Inc**

18318 Minnetonka Blvd, Deephaven, MN 55391, USA.
Tel +1 612 473 5400. Fax +1 612 475 0736.

**Mediobanca**

Via Filodrammatici 10, 20121 Milano, Italy.
Tel +39 2 882 91. Fax +39 2 882 93 67.

**Mercury Business Intelligence**

1 Riverbank Way, Great West Road, Brentford, Middlesex TW8 9RS, UK.
Tel +44 (0) 181 914 2337.

**Mexican Center on Philanthropy**

Campos Eliseos #400 piso 10, Col Polanco, Mexico DF.
Tel +525 280 8462. Fax +525 280 2851.

**Miller Freeman Information Services Ltd**

Riverbank House, Angel Lane, Tonbridge, Kent TN9 1SE, UK.
Tel +44 (0) 1732 362666. Fax +44 (0) 1732 367301.

**Ministerio de Asuntos Sociales**
Centro de Publicaciones, José Abascal 39, 28003 Madrid, Spain.
Tel +34 91 347 70 00. Fax +34 91 571 22 75.

## Minitel

InTelmatique SA, 175 rue de Chevaleret, F-75013 Paris, France.
Tel +33 1 40 77 68 40. Fax +33 1 45 82 21 16.

## Mitre House Publishing Ltd

The Clifton Centre, 110 Clifton Street, London EC2A 4HD, UK.
Tel +44 (0) 171 729 6644.

## Moody's

5250 77 Center Drive, Charlotte, North Carolina 28217, USA.
Tel +1 704 559 6997. Fax +1 704 559 7905. Also distributed through Dun
& Bradstreet, qv.

## Thomas J Murray

10335 Kensington Parkway, Kensington, Md 20895, USA.
Tel +1 301 949 7544.

## The Mutual Fund Public Co Ltd

30-32 Floors, Lake Rajada Building, 193-195 Ratchadaphisek Road,
Khlong-Toey, Bangkok 10110, Thailand.
Tel +66 2 661 9000 99. Fax +66 2 661 9106.

## MZM Publications Co

PO Box 465, PL 81-705 Sopot 5, Poland.
Tel/fax +48 58 513706.

## Nation Publishing Group Co Ltd

44 Moo 10 Bangna-Trat Road, KM 4.5 Bangna, Prakanong, Bangkok
10260, Thailand.
Tel +66 2 317 0420. Fax +66 2 317 1384.

## The National Gardens Scheme Charitable Trust

Hatchlands Park, East Clandon, Guildford, Surrey GU4 7RT, UK.
Tel +44 (0) 1483 211535. Fax +44 (0) 1483 211537.

## National Society of Fund Raising Executives (NSFRE)

1101 King Street, Suite 700, Alexandria, VA 22314-2967, USA.
Tel +1 703 684 0410. Fax +1 703 684 0540.

## National Technical Information Service

5285 Port Royal Road, Springfield, VA 22161, USA.
Tel +1 703 487 4650. Fax +1 703 487 4009.

## NCVO Publications (National Council for Voluntary Organisations)

Regents Wharf, All Saints Street, London N1 9RL, UK.
Tel +44 (0) 171 713 6161.

## Marion Nelson

35 West 90th Street, New York, NY 10024, USA.
Tel +1 212 580 4819. Fax +1 212 362 9855.

## New Prestel Ltd

Knightsbridge House, 197 Knightsbridge, London SW7 1RB, UK.
Tel +44 (0) 171 591 9008. Fax +44 (0) 171 591 9001.

## Newswatch Communications Ltd

3 Billings Way, PMB 21499, Ikeja, Lagos, Nigeria. Fax +234 1 4960 950.

UK distributor (magazines only): Africa Today, Premier House, 313 Kilburn Lane, London W9 3EG, UK.
Tel +44 (0) 181 960 2242.

## New Zealand Council for Educational Research

PO Box 3237, Wellington 6000, New Zealand.
Tel +64 4 384 7939. Fax +64 4 384 7933.

## Norstedts Förlag AB

Box 2052, 103 12 Stockholm, Sweden.
Tel +46 8 789 30 00. Fax +46 8 796 49 05.

## Northern Ireland Voluntary Trust

22 Mount Charles, Belfast BT7 1NZ, UK.
Tel +44 (0) 1232 245927.

## Nyt Nordisk Forlag, Arnold Busck A/S

Købmagergade 49, 1150 København K, Denmark.
Tel +45 33 11 11 03. Fax +45 33 93 44 90.

## Okonomisk Literatur A/S

Lorenvn, Postboks 315, Okern, N-0511 Oslo, Norway.
Tel +47 22 42 60 89. Fax +47 22 42 00 42.

**Orca Knowledge Systems**
POB 280, San Anselmo, CA 94979, USA.
Tel +1 415 461 4912. Fax +1 415 461 6603.

**Orell Füssli Verlag**
Dietzingerstrasse 3, Postfach, CH-8036 Zürich, Switzerland.
Tel +41 1 466 74 26. Fax +41 1 466 74 12.

**Oryx Press**
4041 North Central at Indian School Road, Phoenix 85012-3397, USA.
Tel +1 602 265 2651. Fax +1 602 265 6250.

**Otava Kustannus Oy.**
Uudenmaankatu 8-12, Helsinki, Finland.

**Oxford Analytica**
5 Alfred Street, Oxford OX1 4EH, UK.
Tel: +44 (0) 1865 261600. Fax +44 (0) 1865 242018.

**Oy Novomedia Ltd**
Vapaalantie 2A, SF-01650 Vantaa, Finland.
Tel +358 0 840 144. Fax +358 0 840 110.

**Parliamentary Profile Services Ltd**
2 Queen Anne's Gate Buildings, Dartmouth Street, London SW1H 9BP, UK.
Tel +44 (0) 171 222 5884. Fax +44 (0) 171 222 5889.

**PC Research Services**
9492 Peninsula Drive, Traverse City, MI 49686, USA.
Tel +1 616 941 9880.

**Penwell Directories**
Box 21278, Tulsa, OK 74121, USA.
Tel +1 918 835 3161. Fax +1 918 932 9319.

**Pitman Publishing**
128 Long Acre, London WC2E 9BR, UK.
Tel +44 (0) 171 379 7383. Fax +44 (0) 171 240 5771.

**POW&R Inc**
1215 Cameron Street, Alexandria, VA 22314, USA.
Tel +1 703 549 1122. Fax +1 703 549 5915.

**Private Research Ltd**
7-8 Mount Street Crescent, Dublin 2, Republic of Ireland.
Tel +353 1 676 0774. Fax +353 1 676 0773.

## Questel

Le Capitole, 55 avenue des Champs Pierreux, F-92012 Nanterre Cedex, France.
Tel +33 1 46 14 55 55. Fax +33 1 46 14 55 11.

## Rainforest Publications

404-2010 Barclay Street, Vancouver, British Columbia V6G 1L5, Canada.
Tel +1 604 684 7729.

## Reed Elsevier plc

RR Bowker/Martindale-Hubbell, 121 Chanlon Road, New Providence,
New Jersey 07974, USA.
Tel +1 908 464 6800. Fax +1 908 464 3553.

Bowker-Saur, Maypole House, Maypole Road, East Grinstead, West Sussex,
RH19 1HH, UK.
Tel +44 (0) 1342 330100. Fax +44 (0) 1342 330198.

Reed Information Services, Windsor Court, East Grinstead House, East
Grinstead, West Sussex RH19 1XA, UK.
Tel +44 (0) 1342 335872. Fax +44 (0) 1342 335948.

Reed Elsevier is an international publishing giant. Its biographical directories are
published under several names including Marquis and Bowker-Saur, but the
major division is between these and Reed Information which is responsible for
company directories such as *Kompass* and *Directory of Directors*.

## The Reference Press Inc

6448 Highway 290 East, Suite E-104, Austin, Texas 78723-9965, USA.
Tel +1 512 454 7778. Fax +1 512 454 9401.

UK distributor: William Snyder, qv.

Some publications are also available online, e.g. on CompuServe, America
Online and Lexis/Nexis.

## Researchers In Fundraising Network

Barbara Mostyn, R&D Appeals, Barnardo's, Tanners Lane, Ilford, Essex IG6
1QG, UK. Tel +44 (0) 181 550 8822.

Christopher Carnie, The Factary, The Coach House, 2 Upper York Street, St
Paul's, Bristol BS2 8QN, UK.
Tel +44 (0) 117 924 0663. Fax +44 (0) 117 944 6262.

**Review Publishing Co Ltd**
24th Floor, Citicorp Centre, 18 Whitfield Road, Hong Kong.
Tel +852 2508 4448. Fax +852 2503 1526.

**The Rich Register**
7520 Stonecliff Drive, Austin, Texas 78731, USA.
Tel +1 512 477 8871.

**Riddell Information Services**
Level 1, King's Row, 215-243 Coronation Drive, Milton, Qld 4064,
Australia.
Tel +61 7 360 0633. (Also available through Dun & Bradstreet)

**Norman Ross Publishing Inc**
330 West 58th Street, New York, NY 10019, USA.
Tel +1 212 765 8200. Fax +1 212 765 2393.

**SAIF (Southern Africa Institute of Fundraising)**
PO Box 31836, Bloemfontein 2017, South Africa.
Tel/fax +27 11 444 6297.

**MC Sarkar & Sons Private Ltd**
14 Bankim Chatterjee Street, Calcutta-700073, India.
Tel +91 33 31 2490.

**Schmidt Römhild**
Mengstr. 16, 23552 Lübeck, Germany.
Tel +49 451 70 31 01. Fax +49 451 70 31 2 53.

**SCVO (Scottish Council for Voluntary Organisations)**
18/19 Claremont Crescent, Edinburgh EH7 4QD, UK.
Tel +44 (0) 131 556 3882. Fax +44 (0) 131 556 0279.

**Smee & Ford Ltd**
2nd Floor, St George's House, 195/203 Waterloo Road, London SE1 8UX,
UK.
Tel +44 (0) 171 928 4050.

**SNP Corpn Ltd**
97 Ubi Ave 4, Singapore 408754.
Tel +65 741 2500. Fax +65 744 4096.

**William Snyder Publishing Associates**
5 Five Mile Drive, Oxford OX2 8HT, UK.
Tel/fax +44 (0) 1865 513186.

**Social Register Association**
381 Park Avenue South, New York, NY 10016, USA.
Tel +1 212 685 2634.

**Société du Bottin Mondain**
15 place de la Madeleine, 75008 Paris, France.
Tel +33 44 51 13 13. Fax +33 42 66 69 01.

**SPA**
Guzman el Bueno 21, 28015 Madrid, Spain.
Tel +34 1 544 1300. Fax +34 1 544 1778.

**Startel Oy**
Uudenmaankatu 16-20, SF-00120 Helsinki, Finland.
Tel +358 0 122 33 11.

**The Stationery Office (previously HMSO Publications Centre)**
PO Box 276, London SW8 5DT, UK.
Tel +44 (0) 171 873 9090.

**Statistics Canada**
120 Parkdale Avenue, Ottawa, Ontario K1A 9Z9, Canada.
Tel +1 613 973 6586. Fax +1 613 973 7475.

**Stifterverband für die Deutsche Wissenschaft**
Barkhovenallee 1, D-45239 Essen, Germany.
Tel +49 201 8401 0. Fax +49 201 8401 301.

**Suomen Asiakastieto Oy**
Pl 592, SF-20101 Turku, Finland.
Tel +358 21 516 514. Fax +358 21 518 065.

**Swedish Trade Council**
UK: 73 Welbeck Street, London W1M 8AN, UK.
Tel +44 (0) 171 935 9601. Fax +44 (0) 171 935 4130.

US: 599 Lexington Avenue, 42nd floor, New York, NY 10022, USA.
Tel +1 212 486 8699. Fax +1 212 486 8799.

**Swiss Office for Trade Promotion**
Stampfenbachstrasse 85, CH-8035 Zürich, Switzerland.

**Taft**

835 Penobscot Building, 645 Griswold Street, Detroit, MI 48226, USA.
Tel +1 313 961 2242 (US toll free 1 800 877 TAFT). Fax +1 313 961 6083.

UK distributor: Gale Research International Ltd, PO Box 699, Cheriton House, North Way, Andover, Hants SP10 5YE, UK.
Tel +44 (0) 1264 342962. Fax +44 (0) 1264 334158.

It might take a little persistence to convince GRI that some of the Taft titles exist. There may also be discrepancies in the prices charged by GRI and Taft.

## IB Tauris & Co Ltd

45 Bloomsbury Square, London WC1A 2HY, UK.
Tel +44 (0) 171 916 1069. Fax +44 (0) 171 916 1068.

## Teikoku Databank

Teikoku Databank America Inc, 750 Lexington Avenue, 28th floor, New York, NY 10022, USA.
Tel +1 212 486 2637. Fax +1 212 486 2638.

## TFPL Ltd

17-18 Britton Street, London EC1M 5NQ, UK.
Tel +44 (0) 171 251 5522. Fax +44 (0) 171 490 4984.

US: TFPL Publishing, 1301 Twentieth St NW #702, Washington DC 20036, USA.
Tel +1 202 296 6009. Fax +1 202 296 6343.

## Third Sector

4 Assam Street, London E1 7QS, UK.
Tel +44 (0) 171 247 0066. Fax +44 (0) 171 247 6868.

## Thomson Information

30 Prinsep Street, #04-01 LKN Prinsep House, Singapore 188647.
Tel +65 332 7989. Fax +65 332 7970.

## DW Thorpe (distributor for Reed Elsevier)

18 Salmon Street, Port Melbourne, Victoria 3207, Australia.
Tel +61 3 245 7370. Fax +61 3 245 7395.

## Times Trade Directories Pte Ltd

Times Centre, 1 New Industrial Road, Singapore 536196.
Tel +65 284 8844. Fax +65 285 0161.
(Times Bookshops: same Telephone number but fax +65 382 2571.)

**Toyo Keizai Inc**
1-2-1 Nihonbashi Hongoku-cho, Chuo-ku, Tokyo 103, Japan.
Tel +81 3 3246 5655. Fax +81 3 3241 5543.

Toyo Keizai America Inc, 380 Lexington Avenue, 45th floor, New York, NY 10168, USA.
Tel +1 212 949 6737. Fax +1 212 949 6648.

**Charles E Tuttle**
2-6 Suido 1-chome, Bunkyo-ku, Tokyo, Japan, or Rutland, Vermont, USA.

**TNT Newsfast International**
280 Coward Street, PO Box 351, Mascot, NSW 2020, Australia.
Tel +61 2 317 7717. Fax +61 2 669 3152.

**University of Toronto Press**
5201 Dufferin Street, Downsview, Ontario M3H 5T8, Canada.
Tel +1 416 667 7791. Fax +1 416 667 7832.

UK: Trevor Brown Associates, 114-115 Tottenham Court Road, Midford Place, London W1P 0BY, UK.
Tel +44 (0) 171 388 8500. Fax +44 (0) 171 388 5950.

**Vietnam Investment Review**
Tel +44 (0) 171 823 2888. Fax +44 (0) 171 235 5475.

**VNU Business Publications**
32-34 Broadwick Street, London W1E 2AD, UK.
Tel +44 (0) 171 316 9000. Fax +44 (0) 171 316 9612.

**VP International**
Red Hill House, Hope Street, Chester CH4 8BU, UK.
Tel +44 (0) 1244 681619. Fax +44 (0) 1244 681617.

**Walker's Western Research**
1650 Borel Place, #130, San Mateo, CA 94402, USA.
Tel +1 415 341 1110. Fax +1 415 341 2351.

**Waltman Associates**
1111 Third Avenue South, Suite 144, Minneapolis, MN 55404, USA.
Tel +1 612 338 0772. Fax +1 612 688 6970.

**Warner Books**
1271 Avenue of the Americas, New York, NY 10020, USA.
Tel +1 212 522 7200. Fax +1 212 522 7991.

**Washington Researchers Ltd**
PO Box 19005, 20th St Station, Washington, DC 20036-9005, USA.
Tel +1 202 333 3499. Fax +1 202 625 0656.

**Waterlow Legal Publishing**
Paulton House, 8 Shepherdess Walk, London N1 7LB, UK.
Tel +44 (0) 171 490 0049. Fax +44 (0) 171 253 1308.

**Westview Press**
5500 Central Avenue, Boulder, Colorado 80301-2877, USA.
Tel +1 303 444 3541. Fax +1 303 449 3356.

**Who is Who, Verlag für Prominentenenzyklopädien AG**
Storchengasse 1, 1150 Wien, Austria.
Tel +43 1 894 98 31. Fax +43 1 894 98 20.

CH-6304 Zug, Alpenstrasse 16, Postfach 4703, Switzerland.
Tel +41 42 22 12 46.

**Who's Who Edition GmbH**
Stürmerweg 7, D-82211 Herrsching, Germany.
Tel +49 81 52 10 61. Fax +49 81 52 10 93.

UK distributors: William Snyder and Cedar Tree House, qqv.

**Who's Who in Israel & Jewish Personalities Abroad Publications Ltd**
55 Reines Street,
Tel-Aviv 64587, PO Box 11245, Israel.
Tel +972 3 233040.

**Who's Who in World Jewry Inc**
Enterprise Press Inc, 627 Greenwich Street, New York, New York 10014,
USA.
Tel +1 212 741 2111.

**Who's Who of Southern Africa (Pty) Ltd**
PO Box 81284, Parkhurst, 2120, South Africa.
Tel +27 11 880 2406. Fax +27 11 880 2366.

**John Wiley & Sons**
605 Third Avenue, New York, NY 10158-0012, USA.
Tel +1 212 850 6000. Fax +1 212 850 6088.

**Women in Fundraising Development**
42 Middleton Drive, Pinner, Middlesex HA5 2PG, UK.
Tel +44 (0) 181 868 0207.

**World Fundraising Council**
1101 King Street, Suite 700, Alexandria, VA 22314, USA.
Tel +1 703 684 0410.

**Yonhap News Agency**
PO Box 1039, Kwanghwamun, Seoul 150-602, South Korea.
Tel +82 2 390 3114. Fax +82 2 738 0820.

**Yonsei University Institute of East and West Studies**
134 Shinchon-Dong, Seodaemoon-Gu, Seoul 120-749, Korea.
Tel +82 2 361 3506. Fax +82 2 363 9027.

**York Probate Registry**
Duncombe Place, York YO1 2EA, UK.
Tel +44 (0) 1904 624210.

# Index

non-grant-making, 156
statutory disclosure, 219-20
unspecified legacies to, 223

China
electronic information, 269
information concerning, 267-69
press in, 269

Client
business interests, investigating, 5

Clubs
rich and famous, of, 84

Companies
business interests in target and own country, with, 180-1
Companies House, information from, 211-3
foreign, information on, 178-81
Western Europe, in, 229

Companies House
information from, 211-3

Company financial statements
collecting, 58

Company information
annual reports, 125-6
basic resources, 124-9
credit, need for, 127
databases, on, 127-8
government registries, from, 124-5
investment, desire for, 125-7
obscure private companies, on, 129-30
secondary sources, 127-9
stock market reactions, 129
United Kingdom, in, 211-8
United States, in, 285-9
Western Europe, in, 229-37

Company reports
activities, 135-6
appendices, 142
company history, 134

updating information on, 58-60
Denmark
information concerning, 237-8

Electronic information
Africa, on, 304
Asia-Pacific region, in, 265
Canada, in, 296
change, keeping up with, 64
China, on, 269
European Union, in, 237
foreign countries, on, 197-9
France, in, 240-1
Germany, in, 243
Middle East, in, 301-2
quantity and range of, 18
Singapore, in, 278-9
Spain, in, 247
United Kingdom, in, 224
United States, in, 292
Employees
job change, information taken on, 46
Ethics
effect of actions, considering, 37
freedom of information laws, 38
restrictions, reasons for employing, 36-9
sensitive information, exclusion of, 38-9
sources of information, in using, 41-2
staff, binding, 47
standards, applying, 36-7
European Union
electronic information in, 237
European Information Centres, 237
evolution of, 235-6
publications on, 236-7